About the Author

Marie D. Jones is the author of over a dozen nonfiction books on cutting-edge science, the paranormal, conspiracies, ancient knowledge, and unknown mysteries, including Visible Ink Press' *Celebrity Ghosts and Notorious Hauntings*; *Demons, the Devil, and Fallen Angels*; and *The Disaster Survival Guide: How to Prepare for and Survive Floods, Fires, Earthquakes and More,* as well as books by other publishers: *PSIence: How New Discoveries in Quantum Physics and New Science May Explain the Existence of Paranormal Phenomena*; *The Grid: Exploring the Hidden Infrastructure of Reality*; *Supervolcano: The Catastrophic Event That Changed the Course of Human History*; and *The Déjà Vu Enigma.* She has contributed to *New Dawn Magazine, FATE, Paranoia Magazine, Paranormal Underground* and other periodicals. Jones has been interviewed on over a thousand radio shows worldwide, including *Coast-to-Coast AM,* and has appeared on History Channel's *Ancient Aliens and Nostradamus Effect.* She makes her home in San Marcos, California, and is the mom of one brilliant son, Max.

EARTH MAGIC

YOUR COMPLETE GUIDE TO NATURAL SPELLS, POTIONS, PLANTS, HERBS, WITCHCRAFT, AND MORE

EARTH MAGIC

YOUR COMPLETE GUIDE TO NATURAL SPELLS, POTIONS, PLANTS, HERBS, WITCHCRAFT, AND MORE

MARIE D. JONES

VISIBLE INK PRESS

Detroit

EARTH
MAGIC

Visible Ink Press®
43311 Joy Rd., #414
Canton, MI 48187-2075

Visible Ink Press is a registered trademark of Visible Ink Press LLC.

Most Visible Ink Press books are available at special quantity discounts when purchased in bulk by corporations, organizations, or groups. Customized printings, special imprints, messages, and excerpts can be produced to meet your needs. For more information, contact Special Markets Director, Visible Ink Press, www.visibleink.com, or 734-667-3211.

Managing Editor: Kevin S. Hile
Art Director: Mary Claire Krzewinski
Typesetting: Marco Divita
Proofreaders: Larry Baker and Shoshana Hurwitz
Photo Research: Hobart Swaim
Indexer: Larry Baker

Cover images: Shutterstock.

ISBN: 978-1-57859-697-3

Library of Congress Cataloging-in-Publication Data

Names: Jones, Marie D., 1961– author.
Title: Earth magic : your complete guide to natural spells, potions, plants, herbs, witchcraft, and more / Marie D. Jones.
Description: Detroit : Visible Ink Press, 2020. | Includes bibliographical references and index. | Summary: "Earth Magic explores the world of natural healing and well-being through the use of plants, crystals, spell casting, rites, and rituals. Readers will learn the history behind using the natural resources of this planet, as well as how to make potions, use talismans, recite spells, and follow the practices used by witches, Wiccans, shamans, and other traditional healers. Physical, mental, emotional, and spiritual well-being are all covered to help readers reestablish their connection to nature and Earth magic" — Provided by publisher.
Identifiers: LCCN 2020004959 (print) | LCCN 2020004960 (ebook) | ISBN 9781578596973 (paperback) | ISBN 9781578597154 (epub)
Subjects: LCSH: Magic. | Healing—Miscellanea.
Classification: LCC BF1621 .J67 2020 (print) | LCC BF1621 (ebook) | DDC 133.4/3—dc23
LC record available at https://lccn.loc.gov/2020004959
LC ebook record available at https://lccn.loc.gov/2020004960

Printed in China

10 9 8 7 6 5 4 3 2 1

"Earth and sky, woods and fields, lakes and rivers, the mountain and the sea, are excellent schoolmasters, and teach some of us more than we can ever learn from books."

—John Lubbock

"For every human illness, somewhere in the world there exists a plant which is the cure."

—Rudolf Steiner

Also from Visible Ink Press

Ancient Gods: Lost Histories, Hidden Truths, and the Conspiracy of Silence
by Jim Willis
ISBN: 978-1-57859-614-0

Angels A to Z, 2nd edition
by Evelyn Dorothy Oliver and James R. Lewis
ISBN: 978-1-57859-212-8

Armageddon Now: The End of the World A to Z
by Jim Willis and Barbara Willis
ISBN: 978-1-57859-168-8

The Astrology Book: The Encyclopedia of Heavenly Influences, 2nd edition
by James R. Lewis
ISBN: 978-1-57859-144-2

Demons, the Devil, and Fallen Angels
by Marie D. Jones and Larry Flaxman
ISBN: 978-1-57859-613-3

The Dream Encyclopedia, 2nd edition
by James R. Lewis and Evelyn Dorothy Oliver
ISBN: 978-1-57859-216-6

The Dream Interpretation Dictionary: Symbols, Signs, and Meanings
by J. M. DeBord
ISBN: 978-1-57859-637-9

The Encyclopedia of Religious Phenomena
by J. Gordon Melton, Ph.D.
ISBN: 978-1-57859-209-8

The Fortune-telling Book: The Encyclopedia of Divination and Soothsaying
by Raymond Buckland
ISBN: 978-1-57859-147-3

The Handy Anatomy Answer Book, 2nd edition
by Patricia Barnes-Svarney and Thomas E. Svarney
ISBN: 978-1-57859-542-6

The Handy Astronomy Answer Book, 3rd edition
by Charles Liu, Ph.D.
ISBN: 978-1-57859-419-1

The Handy Bible Answer Book
by Jennifer R. Prince
ISBN: 978-1-57859-478-8

The Handy Biology Answer Book, 2nd edition
by Patricia Barnes-Svarney and Thomas E. Svarney
ISBN: 978-1-57859-490-0

The Handy Chemistry Answer Book
by Ian C. Stewart and Justin P. Lomont
ISBN: 978-1-57859-374-3

The Handy Christianity Answer Book
by Stephen A. Werner, Ph.D.
ISBN: 978-1-57859-686-7

The Handy Diabetes Answer Book
by Patricia Barnes-Svarney and Thomas E. Svarney
ISBN: 978-1-57859-597-6

Hidden Realms, Lost Civilizations, and Beings from Other Worlds
by Jerome Clark
ISBN: 978-1-57859-175-6

The Handy Islam Answer Book
by John Renard, Ph.D.
ISBN: 978-1-57859-510-5

The Handy Mythology Answer Book
by David Leeming, Ph.D.
ISBN: 978-1-57859-475-7

The Handy Religion Answer Book,
2nd edition
by John Renard, Ph.D.
ISBN: 978-1-57859-379-8

Lost Civilizations: The Secret Histories and Suppressed Technologies of the Ancients
by Jim Willis
ISBN: 978-1-57859-706-2

Native American Almanac: More Than 50,000 Years of the Cultures and Histories of Indigenous Peoples
by Yvonne Wakim Dennis, Arlene Hirschfelder and Shannon Rothenberger Flynn
ISBN: 978-1-57859-507-5

Native American Landmarks and Festivals: A Traveler's Guide to Indigenous United States and Canada
by Yvonne Wakim Dennis and Arlene Hirschfelder
ISBN: 978-1-57859-641-6

The New Witch: Your Guide to Modern Witchcraft, Wicca, Spells, Potions, Magic, and More
by Marie D. Jones
ISBN: 978-1-57859-555-6

Real Miracles, Divine Intervention, and Feats of Incredible Survival
by Brad Steiger and Sherry Hansen Steiger
ISBN: 978-1-57859-214-2

The Handy Nutrition Answer Book
by Patricia Barnes-Svarney and Thomas E. Svarney
ISBN: 978-1-57859-484-9

Real Visitors, Voices from Beyond, and Parallel Dimensions
by Brad Steiger and Sherry Hansen Steiger
ISBN: 978-1-57859-541-9

The Religion Book: Places, Prophets, Saints, and Seers
by Jim Willis
ISBN: 978-1-57859-151-0

The Spirit Book: The Encyclopedia of Clairvoyance, Channeling, and Spirit Communication
by Raymond Buckland
ISBN: ebook only

Supernatural Gods: Spiritual Mysteries, Psychic Experiences, and Scientific Truths
by Jim Willis
ISBN: 978-1-57859-660-7

Unexplained! Strange Sightings, Incredible Occurrences, and Puzzling Physical Phenomena,
3rd edition
by Jerome Clark
ISBN: 978-1-57859-344-6

The Witch Book: The Encyclopedia of Witchcraft, Wicca, and Neo-Paganism
by Raymond Buckland
ISBN: 978-1-57859-114-5

Contents

Author's Note

The herbal medicinals mentioned in this book are to be taken with some caution if you are pregnant or taking pharmaceuticals. Please check with your doctor or homeopathic doctor before taking anything to make sure it doesn't interfere with current medications or physical issues. Pregnant women and children are at a highest risk, so avoid taking anything new unless you have a knowledgeable practitioner to guide and monitor you. Natural remedies may be "natural," but that doesn't mean they don't come with some side effects. Herbal remedies may contain certain chemicals that can act as blood thinners, cause light sedation, increase energy, stimulate circulation and heart rate, raise or lower blood pressure, and a host of other effects of which you need to be aware. Be especially careful to check with your doctor about using any herbal remedy that is consumed before surgery because some herbs counter or increase the effects of anesthesia.

Photo Sources

Sergei Ivanovich Borisov: p. 2.

Kim Dent-Brown: p. 41.

Calvin Hennick: p. 8.

Midnightblueowl (Wikicommons): p. 80.

Shutterstock: pp. 3, 6, 9, 17, 18, 19, 20, 21, 22, 26, 28, 30, 32, 34, 36, 38, 43, 46, 48, 49, 51, 52, 53, 54, 55, 59, 60, 62, 65, 67, 68, 70, 72, 73, 78, 79, 82, 84, 86, 87, 91, 94, 98, 106, 111, 114, 115, 118, 120, 122, 124, 125, 127, 129, 130, 131, 133, 135, 136, 139, 141, 143, 145, 146, 148, 151, 154, 158, 160, 163, 167, 170, 171, 173, 177, 181, 182, 185, 187, 189, 196, 201, 204, 208, 214, 216, 221.

Veton (Wikicommons): p. 7.

Ycco (Wikicommons): p. 220.

Acknowledgments

I would like to thank Roger Jänecke and his amazing staff at Visible Ink Press. Roger, thanks so much for your belief in me, your ongoing support of my work, and for always coming up with great things for me to write about. It's an honor working with you! I would like to thank editor Kevin Hile for putting up with all my writing quirks and making my books absolutely shine. And of course, my agent Lisa Hagan for, well, everything!

Thanks always to my mom, Milly, for her love and support; and to my sister and best friend, Angella; my awesome brother, John; and my entire extended family. Thanks to my pop up in heaven who I know is watching me with pride. I'd also like to show my appreciation to everyone who has ever purchased or read one of my books, listened to me on the radio, watched me on TV, or engaged with me on social networking. Writers need readers. I so deeply thank all of mine.

Thanks to my girls; they know who they are. Without them, I'd be at the Funny Farm. I love them all dearly. Thanks to my writing and film friends and colleagues who educate, motivate, and inspire me, and even serve as my muses!

Most of all, I'd like to thank my son, Max, who is my hero. I am supposed to be his role model, but I'm pretty sure he's mine! The world is yours, Max. May you and your generation take good care of it.

Introduction

The earth is filled with magic and healing. Even as it gives us the food, water, and air we need to survive, it offers gifts far beyond the obvious. The earth can heal our bodies, minds, and spirits and has always provided the means to do so, long before the days of technology, computers, and pharmaceuticals became the things we turn to instead.

Working with the plants, herbs, stones, and even the energies and forces of the planet we live on provides us the opportunity to not only enrich our lives but also to do so in a way that is healthy, empowering, and doesn't harm or disempower others. Earth-based beliefs, practices, and traditions are at the heart of who we are as human beings and harken back to times when we lived off the land, or at the very least, close to it and always in harmony with it.

Yet few of us know which herbs, plants, spells, or incantations can help us and how to properly work with them. Even fewer are aware of the science and universal laws behind these practices and beliefs because we assume that something that evolved before the internet and modern medicine is "primitive" and backwards. Those are assumptions that are partially responsible for the physical, mental, emotional, and spiritual sicknesses that plague modern humans.

We got disconnected. No, the truth is that we disconnected ourselves. Bombarded with modern advancements and the distractions they bring, we lost touch with Earth and turned away from what she has to offer us, choosing instead to be on the cutting edge of progress, even if it didn't serve us on a deeper level. Now, we all feel a sense of uneasiness, a deep and protracted isolation despite having the world at our fingertips as we never did before. We ache and mourn for the days gone by when time was on our side and we lived more fully in the present. We long for the places in nature we once spent time in to rejuvenate and refresh before sitting in front of a television set or computer became the norm.

Imagine that everything you want and need to feel happy, fulfilled, strong, and healthy was right at your fingertips, dancing in a world unseen at the end of your nose? It still is, and all we have to do is open ourselves up to the knowledge, wisdom, and understanding that exists where the small voice within us speaks. Imagine feeling a part of everything and yet also possessing a secure and unique individuality that is always at home, no matter who you are with or where you go. Imagine coming home again to the mother that you cast out when you "grew up" and got connected to the digital world, forsaking the natural world you left behind.

Earth magic is everywhere around us, but it has become a lost art and science. We have forgotten our place within the greater picture that includes being more connected with, and reverent of, the planet we call home. Too often, we abuse the earth and her gifts and treat her as though her resources and wonders are something to be taken for granted. Disrespecting the earth is a more modern concept. Older nature-based traditions understood how important it was to treat Mother Earth with respect.

In this book, we will explore the history of Earth-based traditions from the dawn of humanity to these modern times. Earth traditions are making a comeback because people feel empty, alone, powerless, and cold, and they are beginning to awaken to the need to ground themselves and go back to their natural roots. It isn't about disregarding or casting aside the amazing progress we have made with technology but rather learning to balance that with the fact that we are vibrating energy living on a vibrating, energetic planet that serves as the foundation we build our lives upon. A weak foundation brings illness, despair, lack, and unfulfillment. A strong foundation brings well-being in all areas of our lives.

We will also explore the vast array of tools the planet offers for finding that well-being, including spells, potions, uses for herbs and plants, symbols and talismans, candles, and stones and gems and their special powers and meanings, grounding ourselves to the energy of the earth, discovering our animal and spirit guides, and finding wisdom in the stars and planets above. Oh, and so much more, such as the laws of the universe and the forces of science that allow us to align ourselves with our desires and intentions and use the energy that we cannot see to help us achieve them. The science behind Earth magic may surprise you!

Can you truly heal disease with a particular herb? Will a spell work to help you find your soul mate? How does knowing which stones to wear improve concentration and increase productivity? Is it possible to mix up a potion to bring more happiness into your life? Do the stars really hold secrets to your destiny based on where and when you were born on the earth below? These and other questions will be explored and answered in this book.

Then we will discover the rites, practices, and traditions people use to connect themselves to the planet, to the spirit world of the unseen, and to the energies that coarse through our bodies. Some people choose to learn and practice alone, while others love the idea of being a part of a group or coven or even just a social networking group with shared beliefs and interests. There are rituals that go far back into our historical past that are still being celebrated today, as well as rites of passage that bridge the past and the present in our traditional, organized religions with pagan roots.

Finally, we will be called to become more active in getting back to the Mother, using our newfound wisdom to help not just ourselves but those around us, even the planet. Earth is not dying, as you may have heard, but she is urgently calling out for help, and we must help her, or we will face dire consequences. This is where we live. This is our collective home. Unless we balance the masculine aspects and energies of existence with the rising feminine, we will continue to live lives that feel unharmonious and chaotic simply because we are giving too much energy to one extreme and not walking the middle road, allowing for both energies to express their strengths and benefits in ourselves and the world around us.

The world is on the cusp of great change. A shift is in the air and has been for years now. Perhaps it is time to return to the "old ways" even as we continue to exist in the new. Worry not, for you can still have your cell phones, laptops, gadgets, and modern advances. In order to experience what our ancestors once understood, you don't have to deny modern advancements and throw away your television sets. These are the gifts of the outer eyes, the things we see and make use of in our everyday lives on a surface level.

But Earth magic asks that we also use our eyes within and see the deeper, more profound things that are there glimmering, just beyond the veil, in the space called the liminal. Earth magic demands we use our hearts and souls to discern the highest and best good for ourselves and others, instead of always depending on the intellect and rational mind to guide our way. Surely, we need both the imagination and the intellect, the creative and the rational, but to be out of balance has caused great suffering and unhappiness for so many who long to stop blocking one way of expression for the sake of another.

While there are those who will scoff and say that casting a spell or mixing up a blend of herbs to create a particular outcome is silly, others know that these things work. Whether they work because there is a deep science behind these actions, or they work because of the power of belief in the practitioner—or perhaps a bit of both—is up for argument and debate. But they work. Just because something cannot be duplicated in a laboratory using the scientific method does not mean it doesn't exist or doesn't work. And perhaps it is this whole hidden part of reality that we have strayed so far from and long to return to.

Reality isn't just getting up and going to a job, or school, or tending to children and spouses and families. Reality is not just war and bad news and death and struggle. Reality is not just a paycheck and a stack of bills. There is a whole other level of reality—maybe many levels of reality—where magic occurs according to its own laws and rules. We may not understand it, or perhaps we've just forgotten how it works, but it's there nonetheless. Quantum physics tells us that the observer can change the outcome of the behaviors and actions of particles. It also tells us that "reality" is nothing more than a vibrating field of particles and waves in a state of superposition waiting to be collapsed into a fixed and measurable state.

It is in that field that all possibility exists, and from which magic—or what we call magic simply because we don't yet understand the laws behind it—arises.

This book is filled with tools, wisdom, techniques, and information all directed toward getting back in touch with the order of existence and learning to work with it to create external reality, both individual and collective. It is about learning to get back to nature and rediscovering her power and how we can utilize it—from the most mundane tasks in our lives to the grandest goals we can envision.

Whether you believe in these tools or this wisdom is your prerogative. No one will force you, dear reader, to become a neighborhood kitchen witch or a pagan goddess worshipper or an herbalist or modern shaman. And yet, if you stop the distractions and noise of your life just long enough, you might be surprised to find that you are all those things and more, and that you are capable of aligning yourself with the life force and the energies and laws of the earth. You might even realize you've missed that connection from childhood, or maybe you are lucky enough to know it already but just need a reminder or some new ideas for practicing a new way of living in the world.

The earth is filled with magical things. Things that await our rediscovery of the power they offer—the power to heal, to create, to unite, and to fully step into who we were always meant to be. Let it cast its spell upon you, and in turn you may find you have your own spells to cast by the light of the moon.

EARTH TRADITIONS

Long before the prominent religions we know of today came into existence, people worshipped nature. They began to attribute powers, positive and negative, to the world around them to understand their environment a little better and, perhaps, feel a little more in control of it. The most important thing was to survive and find food, water, shelter, and time to procreate and raise the next generation so that the species would continue. If something was of benefit to those needs, it was proclaimed good. If something hampered those aims, it was deemed bad. Thus, duality was born. But for our ancestral pagans who lived off the land and in accordance with the cycles of birth, life, and death, this duality was a part of their belief system and something to be revered, not feared. It was the way nature worked.

The worship of nature is not exclusive to old pagan traditions. Even today, we have neopagans and modern-day Wic-cans, witches, shamans, and druids as well as the long-standing traditions of Native and indigenous peoples the world over. The veneration of nature reaches even into Western traditions in their rites, celebrating birth, death, marriage, and fertility.

While many Earth traditions are goddess oriented or matriarchal religions, not all are, and most include gods among their pantheons. A strong bond exists, though, between women and the feminine aspect of duality and Earth traditions found in Wicca and witchcraft, where the Mother Goddess personifies Earth, and female deities represent the Divine powers of nature.

Modern societies often denigrate Earth traditions because they feel they impede the natural progress of humanity toward a more developed, materialistic, capitalist, antinature form of existence, yet, as we will see, the two are not exclusive of each other. One can respect the planet and still like progress. One can practice daily spell casting and still use a cell phone. One can worship the moon goddess and still drive a car to a job.

✧°✦✦✦ WITCHCRAFT AND WICCA ✧°✧✧°✦✦

Every year at Halloween, millions of people dress up as witches, usually as a caricature of the real thing. Pointy, black hat, warts on the nose, ugly, mean; the media has portrayed witches as something dark and evil.

For the rising number of women and men alike who call themselves witches, though, that portrayal couldn't be further from the truth. Witchcraft may be a great pop culture device, but for those who practice its rich traditions, it is a serious and reverent spiritual system that reveres nature, Earth, the feminine, and the masculine.

Witches have had a torrid past thanks to the mechanisms of the Catholic Church, which is hell-bent on keeping women from exercising their power and sexuality. They've been called demonic, associated with the Devil (despite not being Christians and therefore not believers in the Devil), barbaric, and cruel. During the medieval witch hunts, women were tortured and executed (as well as many men!) for having their periods, breastfeeding children, having unusual moles, being too attractive, and a host of other reasons that had nothing at all to do with dancing with the Devil in the dark of night.

Witches were the original healers and medicine women of European villages who used herbs, plants, and the gifts of the natural world to help bring about healing and the end to disease. Witches acted as midwives and helped new mothers nurse their babies. Witches cooked, cleaned, and gave birth as ordinary women did. Superstition and religious persecution resulted in the mass deaths of males and females accused of consorting with the Devil, and even today, the word "witch" often brings immediate, knee-jerk, negative connotations.

Wicca is a type of witchcraft, but the terms are often interchangeable. A mistaken assumption exists that Wiccans are "good witches" or "white witches," but again, the truth is that because of the beliefs of all witches in the Threefold Law, which states that anything you do comes back to you threefold, and the

Shaman women like this one shown in a 1908 photo from Khakas, Russia, were honored for their knowledge of nature, which could be used to help their fellow villagers who might be ill. They also recorded their knowledge in early books.

rule of "do no harm," no black witches exist who practice black magic. That is another thing entirely and should be labeled otherwise.

Some witches say that Wicca is the religion, and witchcraft is the spiritual practice. Witchcraft can be a part of Wiccan practice, but not all who practice witchcraft are Wiccans. It's confusing, to be sure. Outside of the Wiccan religion, people practice many other kinds of witchcraft such as the solitary road, Alexandrian, and Gardnerian traditions, but again, all are governed by the laws and forces of nature and a reverence and respect for Mother Earth and the goddess. Wiccans follow the Wiccan Rede, which lays down the rules and traditions that must be honored.

Witches usually meet and do their rituals in a coven, but today, some prefer solitary practice. Again, as with pagans, social networking has allowed witchcraft to not only flourish but grow in leaps and bounds as people come together online to build community and find common ground or explore different ideas and compare rituals and rites.

Real witches are as serious and committed to their practice as they are to their health, families, and careers and are not doing it for a quick way to get a lover or some cash.

Are witches magic? That depends on your definition of magic. They work with herbs, plants, spells, and rituals and know how to use the forces of nature to bend to their will. They understand how to achieve the alpha brainwave state and the meditative state of relaxed awareness, the best way to cast their spells, and how to bring about an altered state of con-

One obvious variation to come from early paganism was witchcraft and Wicca. Much of the belief set is in both, but the history of practicing witches is a dark one. Many were persecuted as happened, infamously, in Salem, Massachusetts, from 1692 to 1693.

The Wiccan Rede

Bide within the Law you must, in perfect Love and perfect Trust.

Live you must and let to live, fairly take and fairly give.

For tread the Circle thrice about to keep unwelcome spirits out.

To bind the spell well every time, let the spell be said in rhyme.

Light of eye and soft of touch, speak you little, listen much.

Honor the Old Ones in deed and name,

let love and light be our guides again.

Deosil go by the waxing moon, chanting out the joyful tune.

Widdershins go when the moon doth wane,

and the werewolf howls by the dread wolfsbane.

When the Lady's moon is new, kiss the hand to Her times two.

When the moon rides at Her peak then your heart's desire seek.

Heed the North wind's mighty gale, lock the door and trim the sail.

When the Wind blows from the East, expect the new and set the feast.

When the wind comes from the South, love will kiss you on the mouth.

When the wind whispers from the West, all hearts will find peace and rest.

Nine woods in the Cauldron go, burn them fast and burn them slow.

Birch in the fire goes to represent what the Lady knows.

Oak in the forest towers with might, in the fire it brings the God's

insight. Rowan is a tree of power causing life and magick to flower.

Willows at the waterside stand ready to help us to the Summerland.

Hawthorn is burned to purify and to draw faerie to your eye.

Hazel—the tree of wisdom and learning—adds its strength to the bright fire burning.

White are the flowers of Apple tree that brings us fruits of fertility.

Grapes grow upon the vine giving us both joy and wine.

Fir does mark the evergreen to represent immortality seen.

Elder is the Lady's tree burn it not or cursed you'll be.

Four times the Major Sabbats mark in the light and in the dark.

As the old year starts to wane the new begins, it's now Samhain.

When the time for Imbolc shows, watch for flowers through the snows.

When the wheel begins to turn, soon the Beltane fires will burn.

As the wheel turns to Lamas, night power is brought to magick rite.

Four times the Minor Sabbats fall, use the Sun to mark them all.

When the wheel has turned to Yule, light the log the Horned One rules.

In the spring, when night equals day, time for Ostara to come our way.

When the Sun has reached its height, time for Oak and Holly to fight.

Harvesting comes to one and all when the Autumn Equinox does fall.

Heed the flower, bush, and tree by the Lady blessed you'll be.

Where the rippling waters go cast a stone, the truth you'll know.

When you have and hold a need, harken not to others' greed.

With a fool no season spend or be counted as his friend.

Merry Meet and Merry Part bright the cheeks and warm the heart.

Mind the Three-fold Laws you should, three times bad and three times good.

When misfortune is enow, wear the star upon your brow.

Be true in love, this you must do, unless your love is false to you.

These Eight words the Rede fulfill:

"An Ye Harm None, Do What Ye Will"

sciousness to access knowledge, information, inspiration, and energies that exist beyond the confines of conscious awareness. They realize that everything is vibration and energy and that we can influence and alter those vibrations and direct the flow of that energy to our desire. They know and respect that the laws of nature they work with are available to anyone to utilize, so, in a way, we are all witches.

✻✳✶✶✶ OTHER EARTH TRADITIONS ✻✳✶✶✶

Native and indigenous cultures the world over have their own system of beliefs in the powers of nature and the deities associated with those powers. Native American peoples as well as those who populate Central and South America include medicine men and women, shamans, and spiritual wise elders who know the magic of Earth and use it for benevolent purposes. Even those who practice Voudon, or Voodoo, work with spirits that infuse the natural world and can be manipulated to influence human lives in terms of physical, mental, and spiritual healing.

In North America alone, over two thousand Native American and indigenous tribes exist, each with healing practices and rituals. Herbal medicine can differ from tribe to tribe, and customs and traditions may mirror one another, but they often are specified by region and tribal heritage. To Native Americans, good health of the body, mind, and spirit was a strong part of their beliefs, and they understood the gifts of the natural world to achieve that health. Though each member of the tribe was responsible for his or her own health, the tribal council and elders had much to offer in the way of guidance, direction, and knowledge of which herbs did what and how to work with natural forces for the benefit of self or of all.

Physical and spiritual healing dictated the use of specific herbal remedies that each tribe developed based upon the plants available in their locality. The environment was full of cures, whether it was the thick forest or the desert. Herbal plants were held as sacred, as was all of the natural world. Healing the physical alone would not lead to total healing. You had to cover the spirit, too, because spiritual maladies were as debilitating as those that attacked the body. The medicine man or woman was someone the tribe knew had the most extensive knowledge of herbs, plants, and medicines but also knew how to work with and heal the spirit. Even their tools came from nature in the form of furs, bones, shells, roots, and feathers. They might keep their herbal remedies tied up in a piece of animal hide or cloth called a medicine bundle, which would get passed down to the next medicine man or woman.

The role of elders and healers were intertwined and revered. The Great Spirit was accessible to all in the tribe, but the elders and healers knew how to communicate and obtain information that el-

Non-Natives in the United States have often been influenced by medical and ceremonial traditions of indigenous tribes. Many Americans find a greater spiritual connection to Nature by learning to practice these traditions.

evated them above the rest of the tribe in a high seat of honor.

Native American medicine and rituals could fill ten books, and because of the incredible diversity, suffice it to say here that if you feel called to it because of your Native heritage, a return to your roots will serve you well. A backlash has occurred against non-Native Americans who try to take on the customs, traditions, and beliefs of Natives, but no judgment exists here if you feel the call. For many modern people, Native Americans represent the longing to return to Earth that we all feel no matter what our background or bloodline. Even today, as their tribes fight against the loss of their traditions and customs, not to mention their land, the knowledge they have gleaned over the past continues to live on despite the onslaught of technology and modern medicine.

✿ ✿✿ ✿ ✳ ✳ ✳ ✳ SHAMANS ✿ ✿ ✳ ✳ ✳ ✳

The word "shaman" originated from the Tungus tribe of Siberia and was later adopted to refer to other similar cultural practices around the world. Modern New Agers have somewhat hijacked the tribal traditions and altered them for today's spiritual preferences, but for those who are truly a part of this indigenous wisdom and knowledge, the roots of shamanism run deep. The focus is on the connection with nature but also a belief in other realms the shaman can travel to, including the Lower World, Middle World, and Upper World. Each world is filled with different types of guides and spirits, and the shamans use chanting, drumming, and dancing as well as hallucinogenic methods to achieve access to these other worlds.

True shamans are the ceremonial leaders of their village and offer spiritual discovery and enlightenment as well as healing. They believe that healing must begin with the spirit. A sick or diseased spirit must be made strong and well before physical healing can be achieved. This understanding of the connection of body, mind, and spirit is behind all shamanic practices.

Medicine men and women of the Native American peoples can have different names according to tribe or region, but all are the highly respected chosen ones to give spiritual and physical healing and,

This Amazon shaman in traditional clothing is prepared to offer advice and aid to any of his fellow tribesmen in need of tapping his library of knowledge acquired through his long life.

like shamans, start with spiritual wellness as a focus. These traditions go back thousands of years and are practiced by over two thousand different tribes or indigenous populations in North America alone. They may use herbs, sage, roots, plants, and other natural objects in their healing. In general, many Native Americans are ethnobotanists, using the natural world of plants to do their spiritual medicine. They do not have to be medicine men or women, as this is a widespread practice just as kitchen witchery is a widespread practice among peasants and rural villagers in Europe.

Medicine men and women perform individual and group ceremonies and rituals used in their communities and rarely discuss or share their rituals outside of the tribal nation. They are not open to non-Indians taking their sacred practices and making them into moneymaking schemes or adulterized versions with New Age spins.

✳✳✳ VOODOO ✳✳✳

Witch doctors are African traditional healers, including those who practice Voudon, Vodou, or Voodoo as we know it, but they do not use that somewhat derogatory term and are truly healers and medicine men or women who originate from Africa or Caribbean nations. Vodou is the scholarly name for the religion, and the word means "force" or "mystery." Despite its negative portrayal in pop culture, Voodoo is not a cult. It is a real religion. It is not violent

Voodoo altars like this one in Boston can be divided into three parts: the righthand area holds offerings to Rada spirits, the top-left to Petwo spirits, and at the bottom are offerings to Gede.

and filled with witchdoctors and people poking pins in dolls. Voodoo practices vary according to region, but all originated in Africa with influences from the Yoruba religion of Southwestern Nigeria. Once Voodoo arrived on American shores, it had adopted many Haitian influences and blended with Catholic and Native American traditions to become new forms such as Santeria.

Voodoo is surprisingly focused on community and seeks enlightenment and experiential knowledge for both the individual and the whole group. Responsibility is part of the Voodoo beliefs, and those who practice it take it very seriously. The belief system centers on the understanding that, like other nature traditions, both physical and nonphysical, seen and unseen, worlds exist. The worlds are interconnected, and we can access them just as the spirits of our ancestors can access them and continue to be with us today.

Modern medicine treats the human body as a separate entity from the spirit and often looks at the body as a machine. Emotions are ignored in favor of "fixing the symptoms" and leave humanity reeling from rising numbers of anxious, depressed, and sick individuals. The Natives knew that you must not only treat the parts of the body but the whole of the individual inside and out. While some cultural traditions such as Voodoo utilize the sacrifice of animals as a symbolic gesture to the deities, others shun sacrifice or offer foods to the gods and goddesses.

However, one truly doesn't have to be labeled a witch, shaman, pagan, or Voodoo priestess to learn to accept, use, and benefit from the wondrous gifts of Mother Nature. We are all living on the same Earth and are all capable of accessing the laws that govern the planet and the stars above. We are all students of the same teachers, even if we don't all take the lessons to heart.

New traditions are springing up from old, and even the larger metaphysical and New Age movements focus on the "as above/so below" and "as within/so without" healing modalities for body, mind, and spirit. Often, they borrow from the older traditions while adding on new practices that suit today's busy, technology-obsessed, social world. No matter what, something can be learned from any and all of these traditions and schools of thought to assist our healing, enlightenment, and growth.

It's time to regain a sense of balance and relationship with the planet we live on and those we share it with: animal, plant, and human alike. It's time to find the power available to us and our connection to the greater whole, and it all begins with learning the laws of nature and the tools of the trade of working with those laws.

Longevity and a sharp but curious mind are what makes someone a tribal healer. Elders who are best at learning, remembering, and documenting become "The Chosen Ones."

UNIVERSAL LAWS TO LIVE BY

Whether working with spell casting, kitchen witchery, or candle magic, it is important to remember some of the universal laws and rules suggested by those who work with the natural world. Even if all we do is use plants and herbs to mix a potion for healing, we are behooved to remember these laws and use them to benefit our foray into the magic of Earth.

We can start with the basics. Popular idioms have much wisdom to share if we heed them. Some of those idioms we use every day include suggestions involving give and take and do and do not, and they speak of a reaction for every action we take. That actions have reactions is scientifically backed up, too.

Like attracts like.
You reap what you sow.
Where there's a will, there's a way.
Be careful what you wish for.

Religious texts such as the Christian Bible also include sayings such as:

Ask and you shall receive.
Judge not, lest you be judged in return.
Do unto others as you would have them do unto you.

Many of these basic wisdom teachings are repeated in older and newer religious traditions because they are universal, almost archetypal, in nature.

✧⁕✧⁕✧⁕✦✶✶ THE GOLDEN RULE ✧⁕✧⁕✶✶✶

The Golden Rule alone is a powerful and universally recognized saying that anyone in the world knows and understands, even if they don't particularly follow it. It is based on the ethics of the law of reciprocity, that what you give out comes back to you, and that ethically, we want to treat others just the same way we wish to be treated. Respect, compassion, acknowledgment, and, of course, using the rule for the good of all is a part of every major religious tradition. The reverse is also true. We don't want to do things to others that we wouldn't want done to us. Even in a less tangible sense, what we wish to befall others should always be aligned with what we wish to befall ourselves.

In the real world, people often forget this basic rule, which may date as far back as 551 to 479 B.C.E., when it appeared as a tenet of Confucianism. It then spread and became a tenet of Buddhism, Christianity, Judaism, Islam, Hinduism, Taoism, Sikkism, Brahmanism, Baha'i, pagan traditions, Unitarian Universalism, Zoroastrianism, Jainism, and Native American and indigenous traditions:

Respect, compassion, acknowledgment, and, of course, using the rule for the good of all is a part of every major religious tradition. The reverse is also true.

- Buddhism: "Hurt not others in a way that you yourself would find hurtful." (Udana-Varga 5:1)

- Christianity: "All things whatsoever you would that men should do to you, do ye so for them: for this is the law and the prophets." (Matthew 7:1)

- Confucianism: "Do not do to others what you would not like yourself. Then there will be no resentments against you, either in the family or in the state." (Analects 12:2)

- Hinduism: "This is the sum of duty; do naught onto others what you would not have them do unto you." (Mahabharata 5:1517)

- Islam: "No one of you is a believer until he desires for his brother that which he desires for himself." (Sunnah)

- Judaism: "What is hateful to you, do not do to your fellow man. This is the entire Law: all the rest is commentary." (Talmud, Shabbat 3d)

- Taoism: "Regard your neighbor's gain as your gain, and your neighbor's loss as your own loss." (Tai Shang Kan Yin P'ien)

- Zoroastrianism: "That nature alone is good which refrains from doing another whatsoever is not good for itself." (Dadisten-i-dinik 94:5)

When it comes to ethics in pagan- and Earth-based traditions and working with energy and natural forces to change and shift things, practicing witch and author Kirk White sums it up well in *Exploring the Pagan Path: Wisdom from the Elders*. He writes, "According to many Wiccan and Witchcraft traditions, it is unethical to attempt to manipulate, change, or affect any other person without their prior consent. This applies equally to situations to where you believe you have the other person's best interests in mind, such as healing work and protection spells." Even then, White believes that spells and energy work done without consent is questionable when it comes to ethics and gives the example of a parent wanting to cast a spell to prevent a child from doing something he or she feels is dangerous, even though the child might enjoy or benefit from it (like climbing Mount Everest or going to Europe alone).

In Wicca, witchcraft, and other pagan traditions, this translates to "An ye harm none, do what thou will" and other variations, which means do what you do without harming anyone else basically (and that includes yourself!) but also in the belief in a Rule of Three or Threefold Law. This law basically says that whatever you put into the world, positive or negative, energy or action, comes back to you threefold with the force of exactly what you put out coming back three times as powerful.

Not all witchcraft traditions go by the Threefold Law, even though they all recognize the basic Golden Rule. The earliest actual mention of this law comes from Monique Wilson, a witch who lived from 1923 to 1982 and interpreted the Wiccan Rede to include this ideal. It was then popularized by noted Wiccan practitioner and author Raymond Buckland in his writings and has become a mainstay for many who practice Wicca. Some scholars also point to mention of this law in a novel written by another hugely popular witch called *High Magic's Aid*, written in 1949. The law is mentioned

Rule of Three

This law basically says that whatever you put into the world, positive or negative, energy or action, comes back to you threefold with the force of exactly what you put out coming back three times as powerful.

as such: "Thou hast obeyed the Law. But mark well, when thou receives good, so equally art bound to return to good threefold." Although this law doesn't necessarily hold for all who call themselves Wiccans, witches, occultists, or pagans, it works for many and serves as a powerful deterrent against using the forces of nature for evil instead of good.

Living by these laws positively won't hurt, and it can help. At the very least, having these ethical foundations may keep people from having to live out the consequences of their actions if their actions usually fall on the side of good. All humans are dualistic, but by having a foundation of ethics to operate by, we can choose to remain more in the light than the dark and fight the temptation to use magic, spells, or anything else for the ego's selfish purposes. This world is not one size fits all.

Now that we know the basic laws and rules by which we should live when working with the gifts of Earth and the magic within, we can go directly to the tools of the trade. It's time to dig our fingers deep into the cool, rich soil.

Spell Casting

Words have power. The word "spell" usually refers to the order of letters required to make a particular word correctly, yet if we think of casting a spell, aren't we doing something similar? A spell is a group of words, letters, or phrases that have a particular intent whether to heal a disease or bring a love interest closer.

Like the Law of Attraction, a spell can be a focus of potent energy and attention to bring about a desired outcome. Casting a spell is not just something witches do; in fact, when we bless something or pray for someone, we, too, become spell casters, working with the power of the word and the forces of the mind and nature to bring out what we so desire.

The word "spell" is used as a verb to name or identify the letters in order of a word or phrase. "I can spell my name." "You spelled mayonnaise correctly!" However, it is also a noun and implies a word, phrase, or word formation that is imbued with magical powers and can bring about a state of enchantment or fascination. "The music cast a spell on me." "His singing put me in a spell." "I put a spell on you." The Middle English word *spell* comes from the Old English *discourse* and Old High German *spel*, which meant to recite or say something aloud. The Old French word *espeller,* which is of German origin, means to speak or talk. Thus, a spell is something spoken, basically, either as a verb or a noun.

Casting is a verb. To cast something means to throw it out or toss it out somewhere. Spell casting is the tossing of a blessing or intention into the aether, the universe, or the spirit to be made manifest. Performing a spell without casting it outward to be made real is pointless. It's like going fishing and only standing at the edge of the lake holding your fishing rod but never casting out the line. You don't catch any fish that way.

In the spell casting world, a spell is empowered with magic and often is called a "charm"; for example, "The beautiful woman cast a charm on the helpless man." Those who learned and cast spells understood that letters and words could invoke certain effects, especially in the form of incantations, which are spells used in a ritual format. The word "incant" means to enchant, and they have been used in some form as far back as the fourteenth century. They can be spoken, written, chanted, or sung and bewitch the person toward whom the incantations are directed. Spells can also be cast in general over nature, the weather, animals, and even situations to influence how they turn out.

Spell casting and charms come with connotations of witches and wizards, and pop culture has no doubt made people believe that only fantastical creatures of supernatural origin have spell casting ability, but think about when we bless something or say a prayer. These are terms often associated in religious connotations and are really the same thing. A blessing is given to someone or something because the blesser wants a positive outcome. We bless what we want to experience: happiness, love, success, and good health. We also pray for the same reasons: to use our words to ask for something of benefit to ourselves or another. On the dark side, we curse something in the same way.

It's all about using words and phrases that have meaning and power to influence the laws of nature and create a desired outcome. Hopefully, we do this understanding that the Threefold Law, the Laws of Attraction and Reciprocity, and just plain karma will give us back what we put out. Spells and charms to try to change another person, harm another person, alter a situation we have no business tampering with, win something that doesn't belong to us, or stop someone from having what they want are examples of the negative uses of spell casting.

Spell casting and charms come with connotations of witches and wizards, and pop culture has no doubt made people believe that only fantastical creatures of supernatural origin have spell casting ability but think about when we bless something or say a prayer.

✦✧✶✷✦ SPELL OR SUGGESTION? ✦✧✶✷✦

What is the role of the mind in spell casting? Is it the spell itself that works or the spell caster's belief that it will work? These are valid questions, and perhaps the answer involves both. Fetishism is the belief that certain objects have power, good or bad. Idolatry is the belief that statues and idols of gods, goddesses, or holy figures carry the ability to make prayers come true. However, is it the object itself that possesses power or the energies imbued upon that object through ritual and belief?

From worry beads and prayer stones to rosaries and lucky coins, we want to believe that items we find or own can bring us luck. Some believe that some items can curse us. Casting spells using an altar full of tools is no different. Those who practice magic and witchcraft as well as traditional and not-so-traditional religions and belief systems all have things they deem holy and sacred and things they deem evil and to be avoided at all costs.

Words themselves have power. Speaking words of good will causes a different reaction than words of ill will. Our thoughts create electrical impulses in the brain, and our words are expressed thoughts. Perhaps their energetic charges do have influence in the external world.

Whether we believe the spell or the spell caster has the power, it's hard to argue that some form of belief in one or both is mandatory for a spell to work. If you cast a spell you don't believe will work, it most likely won't. If you say a prayer your heart isn't really into, no doubt that prayer falls weak and ineffective. If you pray for another person and they can tell you don't believe it, why should they believe it unless their own belief can overcome your doubts? You, the one casting the spell, must believe in what you are doing, or why do it? If you're casting a spell to help someone else, but you do it without conviction, the person you intend to help may not believe it can happen. Doubt and disbelief are like roadblocks that keep the traffic from flowing steadily.

The power of suggestion is similar to the power of a placebo in medicine, something that is inert yet works because the person taking it believes it is real and will work. The placebo might work as well as, or even better than, a pill or medical intervention. The mind accepts as real that which it believes to be real.

That's not to say that an external force isn't being put into play. It's possible, but without the focused, committed intention of the person asking those forces to move on his or her behalf, it's doubtful that anything much would come of the request. Therefore, according to the power of suggestion, spell casting for the self requires self-belief, and spell casting for others requires that they believe it will work. When both the spell caster and the person being benefited truly believe, magic happens. Yes, the tools are important, as are the words chosen, but without a foundation of strong belief, they fall flat and fail to achieve the intention of the spell itself.

Those who practice magic in any form or any nature-based religion do believe that the forces and energies of Earth, sea, and sky are real and can be worked with and influenced for good or bad—hopefully good. The truth may lie somewhere right in the center as a combination of external forces and internal beliefs that trigger the flow of energy into creating the desired manifestation of the spell being cast.

When someone says "Bless You!" after a friend sneezes, they are spellcasting in the hope that their friend will not get sick, but, instead, stay well.

✳ ✳ ✳ BLESSINGS ✳ ✳ ✳

Blessings and prayers are offered to the deity or deities of each religion just as spells and charms might invoke a particular pagan god or goddess. Rituals may accompany blessing and spells because rituals are a powerful, structural form of getting into an altered state of consciousness via imagery, music, chanting, dancing, and other means. The altered state of consciousness allows the spell caster to connect more directly with the deities in question and with their inner power to assure that the spell has force behind it. This is no different from using a mantra during meditation or yogic practices to keep the mind focused and sharp.

Old German paganism involved blessings of home and hearth and were a holy part of the sacrificial customs of the day. Original Germanic blessings were marked with blood, and the word *blesian* dates back to the year 1000 C.E., meaning "mark with blood." Just like the word "spell," the word "blessing" can be both a verb or a noun. "George is such a blessing." "We are having someone do a blessing on our house next week." Also, just like spells and charms, bless-

A wife and spellcaster attempts to increase her husband's chances of a good job promotion.

ings are best used in a positive sense; otherwise, they become cursings.

The Old Norse had a word for spells and incantations: Galdr. Galdrs were mostly singing incantations to enchant or cast a spell and were constructed using a special meter to be used in rituals. Runes from ancient Norse cultures show that constructing a Galdr required some originality, and they were used for everything from helping a woman give birth to deciding whether a battle would be victorious or result in defeat. They looked and sounded poetic and often had up to nine stanzas.

Even monastic Christians recognized loricas, or special incantations or prayers designed mainly for protection. They were spoken like a request or command that someone or a group of people be protected. The word lorica traces back to the Latin word for "armor" or "breastplate" and referred to shielding the subject from harm or death. Knights might inscribe a lorica on their breastplate, then verbally recite it going into battle.

✿˳°✿˳°✿˳°✴✴✴ BLESS THIS HOUSE ✿˳°✿˳°✿˳°✴✴✴

To bless your own home, think of first setting the stage with uplifting music. Invite only those people who you know can hold positive energy, and be sure to include your children, as they will most benefit from a happy home. Stand in a circle, holding hands. Light a pink, white, or gold candle to bring friendship, love, peace, and prosperity. Say a prayer or intention, one you wrote yourself, out loud. End the blessing and break the circle, but keep the candles lit for a few hours. You may also carry the candles around the house and bless each room, setting an intention specific to the room and its occupants.

This can be done in hundreds of ways, so make sure the blessing feels right to you. For your prayer, you can find dozens of house blessings in books or online, but here is a simple template you can make unique to your needs and desires for your home. If you are blessing another person's home, ask them what they wish to include in the prayer or intention. Include them in the ritual if they are open to it. They have to live in the home, so it behooves them to participate.

"Divine spirit, as we light these candles and join hands, we summon the forces of friendship, love, peace and prosperity for this beautiful home and its occupants, and for all who enter within. Bless this house with white protective light, that those who live within may not come to harm in any way. Spread the light throughout the halls and rooms, that every inch of this house be clear of negative spirits, energies, and entities.

A newly completed home is being blessed by a monk who is drawing a talisman on the wall.

We hereby decree this to be done and thank you for these blessings and many more to come. And so it is."

You can change any part of the prayer or intention you want, but be sure to keep the tone positive and empowering rather than based on fear and sounding desperate. If candles aren't your thing, you can burn incense or sage or use smudge sticks as you walk about the house.

Here is a simple way to bless a kitchen. You'll need a large sprig of rosemary; a whole, large bay leaf; a strip of orange rind; and a long piece of twine or ribbon. Tie the bay leaf and orange rind to the base of the rosemary sprig with the twine or ribbon. Wrap it as many times as needed to keep it secured. Hang the sprig in the kitchen to keep negative energy out and good energy in.

Many blessings focus on a particular heritage. Here is a simple Celtic blessing:

"My fortress, my place of rest and peace, come bless my hearth and my home, and all who walk within."

The Caim, or protection prayer, is said as the spell is cast and an invisible but protective circle is drawn around the loved one.

Here is another:

"We ask only good to enter this home. We ask only love to come through the doors. We ask only abundance to fill its cupboards. We ask only happiness to echo through its rooms."

Here is a longer blessing:

"Divine spirit, bless each room and corner of this house. Bless the food and drink we partake, and the friendships we make. Bless us in our sleep, and the company we keep. Bless the days we live, and the love we give. Bless each and every wall, and bring peace and love to all."

Another type of "protection prayer" is the Caim, which comes from old Gaelic and also is used to keep someone from harm. Basically, it is an invisible circle of protection drawn around the body with the hand or a magical item to remind the person that they are protected and loved at all times. Old Irish and Celtic protection prayers involved making a circle out of stones and consecrating it as holy, then placing a written blessing within it. The shape of a circle is used in the majority of spell casting. Wicca, witchcraft, and other nature-based traditions use circles because they are closed, yet infinite, and represent the oneness of all things and the connectivity of all things. A circle is even used in darker spell casting and black magic to summon a demon and keep it contained so that it doesn't get away and cause havoc on Earth! Closing the circle once the spell caster enters is critical to working with any forces and energies that might get out of control. It is a big mistake of novice spell casters to forget this important step and expose themselves and others to possible negative influences.

Circles can be simple line drawings, or one can use stones, gems, objects, candles, and other sacred or charged markers. Elaborate circles often include geometric shapes such as a pentagram drawn within to represent the powers or deities one desires to work with or to draw down the specific energies those deities represent. Some circles might contain a particular sigil or symbol for a particular god, goddess, or even demon.

Once the spell is cast, the circle must be destroyed but not before the participants speak or chant a protection for themselves. Like the triangle, the circle is potent. The shape of a square, which represents the four directions of north, south, east, and west, is hugely symbolic to Native American peoples. The five-pointed star, or pentagram, is probably the most symbolic figure to witches, Wiccans, and pagans. Whether an amulet for protection or a talisman for power, numbers matter as much as words, images, and materials.

✿ ✿ ✿ ✿ ★ ★ ★ RITUALS ✿ ✿ ✿ ✿ ★ ★ ★

The use of rituals as part of a spiritual or religious tradition goes back beyond pagan times. Humans seem to have instinctively understood the power of gathering together and creating a sacred atmosphere to honor the gods or nature or even a situation like marriage or birth. Rituals are holy and formal and require certain steps be followed such as lighting candles or dancing. Those involved in the ritual entered a very sacred space where they communed more closely with the deities, or deity, and felt the presence of spirits. Like a moving meditation, ritual brings about a shift in consciousness and elevates the spirit to the forefront.

Rituals, whether simple or advanced, are a way to give meaning and importance to something and even add an emotional charge to them. The word need not scare anyone away because even brushing one's teeth before bed every night could be considered a ritual. Engaging in a certain type of dinner celebration every year is a ritual many religious traditions include with specific foods and drinks that hold great symbolic meaning. Religious texts may be read before dinner, songs sung, candles lit, or chants offered. Weddings, funerals, baptisms, graduations, First Commun-

ions ... all of these are rituals just as much as getting up every morning and doing yoga and then having chai tea before one goes to work.

One can find many existing rituals in books on witchcraft, the occult, Wicca, and Earth and nature worship, but don't be afraid to create one of your own that feels important and satisfying to you and the intention behind the spell you wish to cast. Strength in numbers may indeed exist, as

This Hindu religious ritual performed in Varansi, India, celebrating the light reflected from the river Ganges is a nice example of a yearly ritual.

witches who are part of a coven would suggest, but power also exists in solitary practice and highly individual symbolism that only you can understand. Secret societies such as the Rosicrucians, the Order of the Golden Dawn, and the Freemasons all use rituals, open only to those who are initiates, to teach and impart knowledge as well as to promote initiates to higher levels of achievement within the society.

With experience and skill, one can imbue magical words and rituals into their everyday language to the point where it becomes habit. This creates a charisma and "charm" that can be used in daily life whether on the job, at home with the family, or meeting new people for both personal benefit and to benefit the greater good and the planet.

✻ ✻✻ ✻ ✳ ✳ ✳ MAGIC WORDS ✻ ✻✻ ✻ ✳ ✳ ✳

Abracadabra! And so it is! Amen! Let it be! Sim sim balabim!

Magic words are a mandatory part of a powerful spell or incantation. They present a magical formula that is filled with symbolism and denote something that transcends ordinary speech. When we say spell casting, we need to know

"Abracadabra" is a word most people associate with magic tricks, but such magical words are all part of spell casting. It is important that one speaks with authority when saying the magic words or the effect may not be what is desired.

that the word "cast" is as important as the word "spell." To cast something is to toss it out or set it forward into motion, and that is what we want to do with our spells. We want to cast them forward in the right manner, and that means using magic words or formulas that symbolize something meaningful.

Magic words can themselves be powerful. Sometimes, it's the actual letters that make up the words that hold the power. Tone, placement, rhyming, capitalization, inflection, and emphasis all matter when coming up with the perfect magic formula for casting a spell. Also critical is the attitude of the spell caster. One does not meekly ask for a spell to be cast. One COMMANDS it! One demands the forces of the universe to do the bidding of the spell. Emotion and enthusiasm must be behind the demand or command. To cast a spell in a boring, flat, uninterested tone is a waste of time and energy.

Occultists use sequences of letters and words in their rituals and magical practices. Like words, letters and even numbers hold symbolic power and meaning and, when grouped together just so, can make or break an incantation or spell.

The word "abracadabra" isn't just something modern magicians and cartoon characters say when they want to pull a rabbit out of their hat. This ancient incantation dates back to the second century C.E. as a Hebrew declaration meaning "I create as I speak." An Aramaic version means "I create like the word." Both indicate that as one spoke a spell, chant, or blessing, that which they desired came into manifestation. This sounds a lot like an ancient version of the Law of Attraction!

While originally used on talismans and amulets to help bring about healing, the word was found in the magical formulas of both the early Gnostics and Puritan ministers. Even the notorious oc-cultist Aleister Crowley recognized the power of this word in his magical incantations (although he spelled it "abrahadabra.") Crowley claimed it was the word of the Aeon of Horus, which indicated that one had accomplished a great work of magic. Today, we hear the word thrown around in Disney movies and books about magic wishes, but according to Daniel Defoe in *A Journal of the Plague Year*, written in 1911, this word was instrumental in warding off disease during the Great Plague of London, although historians might argue that improved sanitation had a little to do with it.

✧₀✧✳✳✳ TOOLS FOR DIVINATION ✧₀✧✳✳✳

Your practice may or may not include methods of divining the future. This is entirely up to you, but for many witches and pagans, using various tools and methods for predicting future events for the self or for others is a part of their rituals and traditions. Our ancestors looked to the wise elders, shamans, witch doctors, or medicine men and women to divine the future, but the methods are open to anyone who wishes to learn them.

Divination tools can be anything from crystal balls to rune stones. The end goal is to obtain knowledge of future events by connecting with forces beyond the five senses, even supernatural forces, animal and spirit guides, or the gods and goddesses themselves. The tools are a channel through which your own intuition is expressed and spirit guides speak via symbols and images. The tools should fit the person, so choose one that makes you feel comfortable and that you resonate with. Pendulums, Tarot cards, astrology, numerology, palm reading, using a Ouija board, and scrying are all methods of strengthening your own ability to tap into the field of information in which the past, present, and future are one to access information, insight, and knowledge. This can be done via communication with the Divine or gods and goddesses via automatic writing, channeling, or meditating and allowing messages to come through.

A spell itself might be for insight and guidance or the ability to divine the future, but for those interested in going beyond basic spell casting, below are some of the most popular forms of divination. Each requires its own dedicated course of study and research to correctly learn the techniques, but here is a list of numerous methods to choose from. If you find one method that really speaks to you, read books, take classes, do research, and join groups and organizations online and offline to sharpen your skills. If you prefer a more solitary approach, the key to developing divination skills is just like any other skill—practice, practice, practice.

All forms of divination, whether reading palms, Tarot cards, tea leaves, or rune-stones, involve the basic steps of identifying and setting an intention, getting into an altered state of consciousness, allowing perception to notice everything without judgment, and recording everything without censoring. In divination, the third eye is open and "seeing" what our own two eyes cannot understand, and we must get out of our analytical brains to allow the images to take form or to be noticed.

- Aeromancy—Reading atmospheric conditions such as wind, rain, cloud shapes, meteors and shooting stars, and thunderstorms.

- Alectormancy—Observing birds like chickens and roosters pick through grains and marking each as a letter of the alphabet. For example, a chicken pecks two times, so that would be the letter B, and so on. This is quite time consuming unless you own chickens and roosters.

- Alomancy—Spilling salt and reading the shapes and patterns, much like tea leaf and coffee grind reading.

- Apantomancy—Using coincidences and chance meetings to interpret hidden meaning.

Long ago, reading tea leaves became a way for divining information based on the arrangement of those tea leaves after drinking from the cup.

- Arithmancy—Using numbers for divination. Includes *gematria*, which is a sacred Hebrew practice of numerology using numeric values assigned to letters, words, phrases, and passages in the Old Testament/Hebrew bible. Numerology, related to arithmancy, is an ancient practice of divination that uses birth dates and names to find master numbers, which are then assigned various characteristics and behaviors, much like astrology.

- Astrology—Reading the positions of the planets, sun, and moon in relation to the birth date and place of the individual. Western astrology is the most popular, with the usual twelve zodiac signs, but the Vedic astrology system is gaining popularity. In Vedic astrology, your sun sign is the sign before your traditional Western sign. If you are a Libra in Western astrology, you are a Virgo in Vedic astrology. Chinese astrology is another huge system involving animal symbols indicating behaviors and characteristics based upon your birth year.

- Belomancy—Shooting an arrow and interpreting its landing or position.

- Bibliomancy—Randomly choosing a page or passage in a book and interpreting it as indicative of future events.

- Carromancy—Reading the images found in melted candle wax.

- Cartomancy—Divination with a regular deck of cards (not Tarot).

- Chiromancy—Reading someone's future by examining their hands, fingers, fingernails, and palms. This includes palmistry, which is the reading of lines on the palm of the hand.

- Clairsentience—Reading information gleaned from the hidden sense or sixth sense. It includes clairvoyance (second sight imagery), clairaudience (hearing voices and words/phrases), precognition (seeing future events in visions, dreams, or during meditation), and psychometry (reading someone's future by holding or touching an object that belongs to them).

- Cyclomancy—Spinning bottles or other objects and interpreting their movements and end positions.

- Demonology—Summoning and asking demonic entities about the future.

- Dowsing—The use of wood or metal rods to find water sources.

- Fractomancy—Using fractal patterns to divine future events.

- Geomancy—Interpreting lines and images in the earth in the form of dirt, pebbles tossed onto dirt, sand formation, and other natural formations.

- Graphology—Interpreting someone's handwriting. This is also called handwriting analysis.

- Gyromancy—Walking or twirling in a circle surrounded by letters to point to words or phrases, similar to reading a Ouija board, but you are the planchette.

- Hydromancy—Reading signs in water and sources of water from fountains to pools, lakes, rivers, oceans, ripples, wave flow, etc.

- iChing—A sacred, ancient Chinese divination system that reveals patterns of change using *The Book of Change* and sixty-four different hexagram combina-

tions. It originated in the Han dynasty in approximately 50 B.C.E. The patterns of the hexagrams reveal insight, wisdom, and future potentialities.

- Iridology—Interpreting changes in the iris of the eye.

- Lithomancy—Divining with crystals, stones, and gems by placing them to the light and interpreting the placement of light waves.

- Metoscopy—Interpreting deep and shallow lines of the human forehead.

- Moleosophy—Interpreting moles on the body.

- Necromancy—Communicating with the dead to divine the future or ask for wisdom.

- Oculomancy—Divining by looking into the eye and interpreting its movements, color, size, pupils, etc.

- Oenomancy—Interpreting the color, texture, and how light passes through wine in a glass.

- Onomancy—Divination through interpreting a person's name.

- Ouija board—The pointing of a wooden planchette to letters to form words and messages for the user/s.

- Physiognomy—Reading a person's future by looking at their face and facial features.

- Podomancy—Reading a person's foot.

- Premonitions—Feelings or intuitions of something bad that will happen, like omens.

Necromancy is the art of communicating with the dead to divine the future or ask for wisdom.

- Prophecy—Allowing the gods or goddesses to speak through you as a channel.
- Pyromancy—Divining by reading fire, smoke, burning paper, burning items, torches, wood, leaves … anything having to do with fire falls under pyromancy.
- Radiesthesia—Divining with a rod or pendulum, which is also called pallomancy.
- Scrying—Staring or gazing into a mirror, crystal ball, water, fire, ink, wine, tea, or crystals. The object must be reflective or translucent.
- Selenomancy—Reading the phases of the moon.
- Sternomancy—Reading the bumps, moles, and marks on a person's torso/belly area.
- Tarot—Using Tarot cards to divine the future and seek wisdom. You can do a Tarot reading for yourself or ask a skilled Tarot reader for a more objective interpretation of the chosen hand of cards.
- Tasseography—Reading images in tea leaves, coffee grounds, or wine.

In this image, the divination tool is a quartz crystal pendulum that is used when questions about a person's future are asked.

- Zoomancy—Divination involving the appearance and behavior of animals.
- Zygomancy—Divining using weights or weighted objects.

In addition to the above, many methods of divining involve reading the excrement of dead animals, the bones of dead animals or humans, and even the placenta left behind after pregnancy. Those you may want to avoid trying.

Directly serving as a channel for information is a popular method, including channeling spirits during a trancelike or meditative state, and automatic writing, during which you go into a trance state holding a pen over paper and write without censoring, judging, or looking at the words. You can then interpret what was written in the trance state. These messages are said to come from your higher power, spirit guides, the Divine spirit, or dead relatives.

Keeping a dream journal can be incredibly insightful. Dreams often include symbols and images that point to future events. Writing down all memories of a dream immediately upon awakening is the best way to get them on paper before the conscious, awake mind takes over. The contents of a dream may not become relevant until a later date, which makes writing them down more important than trying to recall them from memory.

Dreams speak to the subconscious mind and have important information to convey. Over time, you may find you not only have a skill for interpreting your own dreams but also the dreams of others. Dream counselors help people understand patterns and recurring imagery pointing to physical, mental, and emotional changes that might be blocking the person from love, happiness, and success.

Divination methods can be divided into those that involve intuition and psychic abilities alone and those that require specific tools or items to be read. Tarot, astrology, and iChing require a study of objects outside of us to interpret someone's future outlook. It is hard to do a Tarot reading or astrology chart without an in-depth knowledge of the methods and techniques. Astrology is a perfect example of a divination method some think is nothing more than reading a magazine horoscope, but the true study involves an intensive understanding of the movements and placements of stars, planets, and the sun and moon as well as rising signs, nodes, various houses of influence, and more. This author had an astrology chart done years ago that was over forty pages of incredibly insightful detail courtesy of a stranger who was adept at her work. This was before the Internet, too, when you could Google information on someone ahead of time.

Precognition, visions, meditation, and psychic abilities require no necessary tools to divine the future, although they could help make the process easier. In any event, practice and learning make all the difference between successfully predicting future events or winging it and hoping you get at least a few positive hits.

You might wonder how much of divination requires actual divine intervention. Take channeling, automatic writing, and any method that involves making a choice (picking a Tarot card, finding a passage of a book in bibliomancy, choosing a card in cartomancy). Many argue as to where the information is being accessed from, whether by the gods and goddesses themselves, a higher part of our own being that exists beyond the dimensions of time and space we are restricted by, or via spirit guides in the form of angelic beings, dead loved ones, and totem animals. Physicists point to a field of information called the zero-point field that contains everything that has ever happened imprinted upon it in the form of energy, and we can learn techniques to access this information across the landscape of time and space. Other names for this information field include the morphic field, the akashic field, and the kingdom of heaven in the Bible that is described as being all through us, around us, and we are ourselves a part of.

Tapping into that field may be something individual to each person, but no matter how the information is being acquired, the key is to correctly interpret it for the benefit of the person you are reading for. The symbols and images received in the field are described as universal and archetypal, understood by people from all cultures, countries, and traditions. Archetypes belong to the collective unconscious written and taught about by noted Swiss German psychologist and psychotherapist Carl Gustav Jung, who believed that these archetypes originating in world myths and origin stories applied to every region of the

Zero-Point Field

Physicists point to a field of information called the zero-point field that contains everything that has ever happened imprinted upon it in the form of energy....

globe because they were foundational in nature.

Archetypes existed on the deepest level of mind, a sort of collective subconscious mind that every living thing was and is linked to. In this "field of information," if you will, elements are based on our personal, individual experiences but are also based on those of the collective. This collective level also contains the memories from our distant ancestors passed down from generation to generation.

Knowing archetypes allows someone to better read and interpret symbols in dreams, tea leaves, and clouds or images that burst into the mind during a channeling session or a candle scrying. Our pop culture is filled with readily identifiable archetypes like the hero, the villain, the innocent, the leader, the fol-

lower, the savior, the maiden, the mother, the wise elder, and more because we get them. We get them because they are a deep part of all of us, and the archetypal stories we love to watch on the movie screen (*Star Wars* is a perfect example of the hero's journey archetype as Luke Skywalker sets out to meet adventure, finds allies, meets the abyss, fights his demons, and returns to his home a hero) mirror our own lives and our own journeys.

In witchcraft, Wicca, and pagan traditions, the archetype of the mother, the maiden, the crone, the trickster, the explorer, the mentor, the educator, the leader, the wise elder, and the goddess no doubt will pop up in divination, spell casting, and general craft practices, so it helps to study archetypes and become familiar with them.

When using Tarot cards for divination, the archetypes revealed are universally understood and symbolic of specific traits assigned to them. Psychotherapist Carl Jung observed that these archetypes are in us all, and Tarot readings can help divine our future by analyzing these different archetypes.

Once a certain level of mastery is reached, as with anything, you will be able to divine more quickly and easily and be more accurate in your interpretations. Ultimately, divination is about sharpening your intuitive and interpretive skills. Don't be afraid to try several methods, and many practitioners like to master one, then learn another. William Shakespeare said, "It is not in the stars to hold our destiny, but in ourselves." Divination is about seeing the past, present, and future externally using our internal skills and gifts.

✧ ⚬ ✧✧ ⚬ ✧★ ★ ★ CANDLES ✧ ⚬ ✧✧ ⚬ ✧★ ★ ★

Part of setting the mood and creating the best atmosphere for spell casting involves lighting. Sure, just turning down the main lights helps, but using candles adds a whole new dimension to working with nature's energies. Candles are beautiful and hypnotic, and the flame represents the light and good amid the dark. Burning is cleansing, and as we watch a candle burn, we imagine ridding ourselves and our lives of the things that don't work and opening the doorway to that which we so desire.

> The color of the candle is probably the most important quality. Each color represents a different vibrational frequency and can amplify the outcome of the spell.

room on fire can spoil an otherwise perfectly good spell!

Many practitioners buy or make candles according to the specific spell they wish to cast, but you can stock up on several colors and even just do white candle magic if in a pinch. Some witches suggest beeswax candles because of their close connection to nature. You might want to do some type of blessing or consecration of the candle before you begin.

The color of the candle is probably the most important quality. Each color represents a different vibrational frequency and can amplify the outcome of the spell:

Some people like to cast spells only by candlelight and utilize specific colors, sizes, and shapes for their workings. Candle magic is an ancient part of ritual still seen today in most churches, temples, and shrines, where one goes to light a candle in honor of an ill or dead loved one. Because candles take a while to burn down, candle magic can be quick or take days to complete, but never leave an unattended candle burning overnight and keep it away from combustible materials at all times. Setting your living

- WHITE—Purity, healing, lightness, relaxation, freedom, truth, the goddess, higher self, peace
- SILVER—Joy, intuition, reflection, moon phase magic, the goddess, astral travel, intuition, dreamwork, telepathy
- RED—Love, affection, passion, ambition, power, control, sex, lust, fire, strength, career goals, driving force

- PINK—Love, romance, attraction, friendship, good will for humanity, caring
- GOLD—Financial increase, business success, power, influence, mastery over others, God, winning, male energy, happiness
- COPPER—Business, career, passion, money goals, professional issues
- BLUE—Peace, calm, understanding, unity, fluidity, water, wisdom, protection, inspiration
- PURPLE—Power, ambition, regality, mastery, command, courage, the third eye, psychic abilities, knowledge
- YELLOW—The sun, happiness, air, memory, joy, learning, expansion, intelligence
- ORANGE—Vibrancy, fun, openness, overall success, property, legal matters, justice
- GREEN—Prosperity, luck, nature, fertility, earth, physical healing, money, Mother Earth, the goddess, Pan, personal goals
- BROWN—Earth, tradition, groundedness, common sense, friendships, favors

Candles are a well-known part of spell casting and are believed to increase the possibility of an effective spell.

- BLACK—Dark, evil, harm, repulsion, the banishment of evil and harm, binding, protection

While black candles are often associated with dark or black magic practices, they have a powerful place in positive spell casting, too. Black candles can represent the death or necessary end to something negative such as old behaviors, habits, relationships, and patterns and are used to ritually "burn away" energies and influences no longer desired. Black represents the opposite of light, so a spell involving the banishment of any kind of darkness or a return to the light could involve burning a black candle down. Black also represents the night and can amplify moon magic when burned during specific phases of the moon. You can also burn more than one color if you need help in more than one area.

Size does matter, too. If the spell to be cast or the ritual is a short one, a votive candle works best because it will burn down quickly. Longer spells might require a bigger candle, including some that burn for a particular number of days. A candle sculpted into a particular shape can be very powerful. Some people prefer candles with no scent because they don't like the distraction of the odor, even if it's a pleasant one, but others might find that a scented candle helps to amplify the results. One thing all agree on is to use a brand-new "virgin" candle for a brand-new spell or intention so as not to mix energies, and it is not advised to repurpose unused spell casting candles on the dinner table or to freshen up a room! A candle used in spell casting will have attached to it the vibrational energies associated with the spell, positive or negative. If you need something to make your guest bathroom smell better, buy a new scented candle!

Once you've chosen your candles, you must dress or charge them. This is different from the cleansing or consecration, which prepares the candle by making it clean. Now you want to charge your candle with positive vibrations and energy and the intention of what you wish to manifest. One of the ways to dress a candle is with aromatic oil, which is rubbed up and down the candle while focusing on the desired outcome or casting the verbal spell. Stroking the candle seven times in one direction while casting the spell is one way. Using aromatherapy candles is another, which creates both a visual and sensual atmosphere.

To cleanse a candle, you can also submerge it in a sea salt and water mixture, being careful to avoid exposing the wick at the top. You can ask for a particular god or goddess to bless the candle. You can also inscribe something magical and personal onto the candle using a blade or athame. To draw something to you, you write from the top of the candle down to the middle, then from the bottom to the middle. To repel something from you, write from the middle of the candle to the top and the bottom.

Candles are a mainstay of many meditation practices for the same reason why they work so well in spell casting. They relax the mind, focus the attention, and bring about a sense of calm certainty. Like everything else, candles can be used for good and bad. The candle doesn't judge, it just burns. The spell caster must always remember the laws he or she is working with.

One of the ways to dress a candle is with aromatic oil, which is rubbed up and down the candle while focusing on the desired outcome or casting the verbal spell.

✴ SCRYING WITH CANDLES ✴

Scrying is a divination tool that can be done with mirrors, water, or candle flames. In many magical traditions, candles are the tool of choice. Two methods are used in candle divination: reading the wax and scrying the flame.

Wax reading involves putting a candle into a bowl of cold water. First, anoint or charge your candle (some call it "dressing the candle") by rubbing olive or grapeseed oil over the candle in said manner. Begin at the top of the candle, and rub downward to the middle. Then begin at the base of the candle, and rub upward to the middle. Do this for the whole candle, and as you do, envision the candle being infused with your energy and the intent of your spell or ritual.

Burn the candle and focus on the wax, which will harden quickly. Look at the shapes the wax forms and try to intuit or "read" the messages. You can first get into a meditative or trancelike state with chanting, burning incense, closing your eyes, and deep breathing. When you look at the wax, do not force the interpretation or judge what you see. Observe the shapes and take note of any images or words that come into your mind, then when you return your mind to the waking state, write it down immediately. This is the same process used to read coffee grounds and tea leaves. You can read the wax for a general message or ask the candle a specific question and then burn the wax to get a specific answer.

Scrying focuses not on the wax but on the flame. It's easy to scry, and you don't need anything more than a darkened room, a cozy cushion or chair, and some incense burning in the background. Oh, and a candle. You can choose the candle based upon the color and associations such as green for insight into money issues or red or pink for looking into your future love life. For general scrying, choose any candle that is large, thick, and lasts a long time. Spiral and decorated candles are fun, but always anoint or charge your candle first by rubbing olive oil or a scented essential oil on it. Patchouli oil smells great and adds to the slightly altered state of mind required for scrying.

Sit comfortably, take in some deep breaths, and begin to focus your attention on the flame of the candle. Stare into the flame. Become one with the flame. This is a form of self-hypnosis and will put you in a slightly altered consciousness, so you might lose the sense of having a body as you merge with the flame.

Look at the different subtle colors in the flame. Red, yellow, orange, green, brown. As you watch the flame, feel your body getting heavy and anchoring to the floor. Continue to breathe and focus until you feel your body just dissipate and you are nothing but mind, consciousness, and the flame.

Notice colors, shapes, forms, and images. Let them drift in and out of your awareness so as not to break the spell of the flame. Spend at least 10 or 15 minutes in this state of mind, then

Scrying is a good way to answer questions and determine what the future holds. This method of divination is practiced the world over.

breathe deeply and return to your waking state of consciousness.

Quickly write down or record the images that came to you. You may recognize their meaning immediately, or it may be days or weeks before your conscious mind understands what they are supposed to tell you. Trust that it works and that all will be revealed at the right time.

You can even do a question-and-answer scrying. Before you begin staring into the flame, ask or speak your intention out loud, and write it on a small piece of paper. Then, let the paper burn as you stare into the flame. Continue staring into the flame until you feel that enough time has passed and then come back to the waking state. Write or record immediately any words, phrases, or images that came to you. Again, their meaning will become clear when necessary.

> Scrying speaks directly to the subconscious mind, so don't be surprised if the images and words seem symbolic, even archetypal.

Never force your mind to see or hear anything, and don't dwell on a word or image for long when it does come, or else you block the flow of information being communicated to you. Pretend you are watching not only the flame but a giant movie screen, and let the words and pictures flow on by, taking note of them and knowing you will recall them once the scrying session has ended.

Scrying speaks directly to the subconscious mind, so don't be surprised if the images and words seem symbolic, even archetypal. These are universal symbols that your mind understands on a very deep level. You want to avoid analysis and judgmental interpretation. Let the words and images come, write them down without censoring and criticizing, and wait patiently and expectantly for their meaning to be made clear.

✦°₀°°°₀°°✶✶✶ INCENSE AND SAGE ✦°₀°°°₀°°✶✶✶

Scent is a powerful amplifier for spell casting. Incense can be used to create an aromatic atmosphere as well as to cleanse and purify the air before setting forth a spoken intention. As many types of incense as spell casters exist, and each evokes a different feeling or reaction. Incense is made of aromatic plant materials combined with essential oils. It is used in many religious and spiritual traditions during rituals, prayer, and meditation and even church services such as weddings and funerals. Whether it comes in stick, paste, cone, powder, or bud form, incense is a wonderful way to create an atmosphere during a ceremony or ritual by appealing to the sense of smell's ability to shift the brain into an altered state of consciousness.

Though humans are visual creatures, smell is more powerful than any other sense for evoking mood, memory, and emotions. It is probably easier to recall a memory from childhood based on a particular smell than on a sight or sound. Smell transports the mind to another place, another reality, which is why it was so important in ancient rites and rituals. Incense works by calming and preparing the mind first via the sense of smell. In witchcraft and spell casting, it can draw down spirits from the air and also, once the spell has been cast, send the intention up into the aether, where it can manifest physically. It is a powerful tool in spiritual work and can create an altered state of consciousness during meditation and prayer work.

Ancient Egyptians, Babylonians, and Romans all used incense to either clear up or cover up putrid scents, much like we use scented sprays today, or to deter demons or welcome positive entities and forces ... depending on the smell, of course! Resin balls were found in prehistoric Egyptian tombs, and the oldest incense, burning device dates back to the fifth dynasty of Egypt. India and East Asia used oil forms made of flowers and roots as well as herbs, seeds, and parts of trees. The ancient Chinese used incense extensively in their worship ceremonies, and Buddhist monks utilized the aromas for purification rites for new initiates. Some types of incense were used, and still are today, to ward off and repel mosquitoes; think citronella. Others, like frankincense, were only used for grand occasions in the past; think the Three Wise Men.

Today, we can choose from an abundance of incense types and aromas. It can be burned before spell casting as a way of purifying the air or during the spell to help focus the mind or create a heightened conscious state. Incense is considered an aphrodisiac in many cultures and was said to be used by gods and goddesses in ancient Egyptian and Roman myths. It supposedly heightens sexual attraction and desire and can be a great addition to spell casting for love, romance, and sexuality or simply be-

The burning of incense and sage has long been a major part of divination and helps focus the mind into a better state for divining information gathered during a ceremony.

cause it smells great and is fun to use, especially if you choose a fun and funky burner to put on your altar! Incense should never be overused though because of health risks from excessive inhalation of gaseous pollutants such as carbon monoxide, nitrogen oxides, sulfur oxides, and toxic organic compounds.

Some of the most commonly used types of incense are:

- Blueberry—Keeps negative energy away from you and your home
- Blue Rose—Burn this to honor the goddess in rituals
- Carnation—A healing incense for body, mind, and spirit
- Cherry—Burn to honor the goddess of love, Venus, and to attract love
- Cinnamon—Helps attract prosperity and success

- Frankincense—Burn to attract sun energy, positivity, and to consecrate a room or altar
- Honeysuckle—Brings health, happiness, and increases psychic abilities
- Jasmine—Brings luck and love
- Musk—An aphrodisiac that increases courage and physical vitality
- Myrrh—Protects and purifies the spirit and the home
- Passionflower—Calms the mind and aids in sleep
- Patchouli—Brings money and abundance of all good things
- Sandalwood—Heals the body, mind, and spirit and brings positive energy into a room
- Vanilla—An aphrodisiac that sharpens the mind and increases memory recall

✻ ☆ ✻ ☆ ☆ ✻ ✻ ☆ ✻ ★ ✶ ✶ SMUDGING ✻ ☆ ✻ ☆ ☆ ✻ ✻ ☆ ✻ ★ ✶ ✶

The burning of herbs and plant materials like sage is also a tool for rituals and spell casting. Much like incense, it is designed to both cleanse and banish negative energies and restore a balance and sense of calm to the user. Burning sage and "smudging," which is the act of doing so, is an ancient practice among indigenous peoples. Although it has been adopted by the New Age and pagan communities today, its roots, pun intended, go deep.

The original intent behind smudging was to unlock the hidden powers of the plant or herb to be used in healing ceremonies or, again, to rid a person or community of something undesired. The smoke is considered to be medicine, and scientific research can back this up. A 2006 study published in the *Journal of Ethnopharmacology* titled "Medicinal

Smokes May Have Broad Range Therapeutic Applications and Benefits" looked at the smoke from both single-ingredient and multiple-ingredient herbal and nonherbal remedies across fifty different countries. The researchers involved found that globally, the medicinal smoke was used to address pulmonary issues 23 percent of the time, neurological issues 21 percent of the time, and also dermatological issues on a smaller scale.

The study found that the use of medicinal smoke was worthy of more research because of its ability to be rapidly delivered to the brain, which meant more efficient absorption by the body and lower production costs. Our ancestors obviously knew smudging worked by simple observation and experience. The use of dried white sage is over two thousand years old and is still used by Native Americans today. Sweetgrass was a favorite of shamans as well as dried sage plants burned on a fire during rituals and healings.

Smudging is a typical part of yoga and meditation to keep the energy channels clear and the spirits lifted. Both the scent and the medicinal effects on the brain are at work to create a sense of sacred spiritual connection and communion with our ancestors as well as a sense of higher consciousness. Like incense or candles, burning herbs and plants can alter one's state of consciousness just enough to make their ritual work or ceremonial work more effective, whether they are healing a sick person or doing their daily yogic routine.

It's become quite easy to buy "smudging sticks" and to make them on your own, and it is common to hear people today talking about having to "smudge" a location considered to be haunted or harboring negative spirits!

Sacred sage (*Salvia apiana*), also known as white sage, bee sage, and California sage, is an evergreen shrub native to the American Southwest that is commonly used in smudging.

The smudging stick can be burned while walking around or in a ceremonial bowl or cup. Some smudging ceremonies require no more than a wave or two of the smoke, and others burn it continuously. Like incense, it should be treated with respect, and, if too much smoke is inhaled, it could present problems for anyone with respiratory issues such as allergies and asthma.

The main focus of smudging is to cleanse, whether it be a person, a location, or a situation. Smudging a new home, a new place of business, a body wracked with illness, even your "aura" are all common practices, something akin to taking a cleansing energy shower that alters the composition of ions in the air to create a greater sense of calm and balance. Sage or any type of smudging herb or plant can be a part of spell casting to create a more powerful and conducive environment and get the user into a more harmonious mental and physical state.

Tree resins are popular smoke tools for spell casting. The resin is the hardened sap; a few examples are copal, myrrh, and frankincense. Tree resin smoke is considered more powerful than the use of flowers or floral-based smokes, but for making a room brighter, clearer, and cleansed of negative energies, a floral smoke provides a nice scent. Roots of a plant (ginger root, galangal root) are stronger than the flowers, buds, or leaves, so they are used for more serious banishment spells and ridding strong negative energies. Wood also has a signature smell and purpose and is stronger than floral but weaker than resin for particular spells.

Working with smoke, incense, or sage involves identifying which items you have most available access to, what smells appeal to you, and the strength required to fulfill the intention. If you don't have time to make your own smudging sticks or incense, even burning a few bay leaves can bring relief from anxiety, reduce inflammation, boost the immune system, sharpen memory and alertness, open the nasal passages and decrease congestion, and assist in mindfulness even when not meditating.

✧ ✿✧ ✧✦✦ ✦ ESSENTIAL OILS ✧ ✿✧ ✧✦ ✦ ✦

The use of essential oils can also be a big part of spell casting and natural healing, and aromatherapy has become a hugely popular modality for reducing stress and increasing balance and well-being. Essential oils are described as concentrated liquids of volatile aroma compounds from plants and flowers. Volatile simply means that the liquids are quickly evaporated at normal room temperatures. The oil comes from the plant or flower and is distilled using different methods such as steam, cold pressing, resin tapping, solvent extraction, and wax embedding.

For basic spell casting and working with intention, aromatic oils, like anything else, can add to the sensory experience and assist the user in getting into the right frame of mind.

The use of essential oils in aromatherapy is considered a viable form of alternative medicine due to the healing influences of particular combinations of oils. Though no solid research exists to back up any claims of oils having actual medicinal benefits, plenty of subjective experience and support by those who use the oils does. The inclusion of oils in rituals and ceremonies, even medicinal use, goes back to a physician, chemist, and pharmacist named Ibn al-Baitar, who lived from 1188 to 1248 C.E. in Spain during Muslim rule. Over time, other cultures began to utilize oils and compounds, depending on which plants and flowers they had access to.

Some of the most commonly used oils are those that include lavender, peppermint, menthol, anise, camphor, patchouli, tea tree oil, eucalyptus, and citrus. The plant parts used include the roots, stems, leaves, flowers, bark, wood, peel, and petals, distilled in a device where it is steamed over water. The steam vaporizes the compound, which is then returned to liquid form and collected in a vial or container for use.

Because some oils can cause allergic reactions and because some oils are to be used for particular effects over others, it is "essential" that the user gets to know which oils have which properties if they are to become a bigger part of spell casting and herbal medicine use. If it's all about how they smell, then look out for skin reactions, but ingesting essential oils can be dangerous if you don't know what is in them and how they will affect your body. This is especially important if used for children, pregnant women, and those with compromised immune systems. Always get a good education first on oils and oil compounds and which are safe to ingest or consume.

Interestingly, some oils are used as natural pesticides. Though usually considered nontoxic for mammals, they can stunt growth and reduce reproduction rates for certain insects!

For basic spell casting and working with intention, aromatic oils, like anything else, can add to the sensory experience and assist the user in getting into the right frame of mind. Oils can be rubbed on candles or placed in a bowl on altars during spell work or even worn on the skin as a perfume. A few drops of oil can be kept in an aroma locket worn around the neck. They are not meant to be ingested and could be dangerous if done so for the purposes of casting spells, but they can be another tool to help center the body, mind, and spirit for casting intentions in a more powerful and effective way.

Burning fragrant oils is not only great for a nice, hot bath, but they certainly affect the mind, and some will find certain oils too strong or repulsive. Menthol, spearmint, citrus, and even cloves are examples of oils that might not sit well with some yet bring calm and healing to others. The author of this book cannot stand the smell of anise, yet others find it pleasurable. Again, it's about experimenting first to see what works and what doesn't. Rosemary oil is a commonly used botanical that sharpens memory and increases memory recall. Even in its raw state, the herb can boost memory capacity just by smelling it. With the Internet just a few keystrokes away, it's easy to purchase oils online or at any Whole Foods outlet or health-food store. Doing it in person allows you to sample the scent and see what effects it has on you.

Some of the other common and easily obtained oils used in spell casting,

The use of essential oils can be traced back to a very early age, and the use of these oils in both spell casting and aromatherapy has become a normal tool to enhance our sense of well being.

botanical healing, and kitchen witchery are:

Almond	Lavender
Avocado	Mineral
Bay	Myrrh
Cedarwood	Olive
Cloves	Peppermint
Coconut	Pine
Evening Primrose	Rose
Frankincense	Sandalwood
Ginger	Sunflower
Grapeseed	Tea Tree
Jojoba	

These and other oils can be used solo or blended to create special oils, depending on personal preference. You can make infused oils that contain flowers, plant parts, or even foodstuffs that apply to the spell you are casting. One example from Amy Blackthorn's *Blackthorn's Botanical Magic* is olive oil infused with Chinese hot peppers. This, she suggests, can be a great oil to use for banishing spells. It is best to use dried materials in infused oils to keep mold from forming. She also suggests working with "conditioned oils," which are oils that are exposed to low heat. The low heat removes water from the mixture while preserving the oils in the plant and will have a stronger fragrance and energy signature. Throw your mix into a crockpot, slow cooker, or tabletop infuser on low heat. Keep on low heat for at least 8 hours, then let the oil mixture cool before bottling. Let it sit a few weeks before using in your spell casting.

Also, think about using a carrier oil to dilute essential oils, so they can safely be applied to the skin. Their purpose is to dilute the essential oils, so they can be easily absorbed by the skin and not cause allergic reactions and other negative effects while keeping the therapeutic integrity of the essential oil. Carrier oils

are vegetable oils and have a neutral scent or a very light scent. They do not evaporate and are not volatile oils. The best are cold-pressed plant oils. Aloe vera gel and unscented body lotions can be used as carriers, too. These oils do not interfere with the main essential oil in the mixture and should always be stored in a cool place like the refrigerator, preferably in a dark glass.

Carrier oils can nourish the skin and also increase the shelf life of essential oils. Some absorb into the skin better than others. All are labeled by the Food and Drug Administration as cosmetic oils, but some edible cooking oils can be used. All carrier oils are vegetarian sourced but do not use butter, lard, or vegetable shortening as a carrier oil.

The most popular carrier oils are coconut oil, jojoba oil, apricot kernel oil, sweet almond oil, olive oil, argan oil, rosehip oil, black seed oil, grapeseed oil, and avocado oil. Try a few on for size, so to speak. Grapeseed oil has a lighter consistency than sweet almond oil, which has a medium consistency. Both leave a slight oil sheen on the skin and are great for massage therapy and dry skin. Olive oil has a thicker consistency and a much stronger aroma. Coconut oil can start out solid and turn to liquid upon the skin but leaves a nutty scent behind.

These oils can be used alone, but if mixing with essential oils, follow these instructions before you do anything else:

1. Add a small amount of carrier oil to the inside of your wrist and cover with a loose bandage.

2. Check the skin after 24 hours.

3. If any irritation occurs, cleanse the skin with water and never use the carrier oil again.

Don't be overwhelmed when working with essential oils. Start with a few you really like and can easily find, and go from there. Experiment with mixing oils, and don't use any that give you an allergic reaction or turn you off. Some people will be more sensitive to the smell and feel of certain oils. Stay away from any oils that smell rancid. Go to a health store and smell a few oils. Many stores have samplers you can use. When you buy, be aware of expiration dates and shelf life (average for oils is three to six months) and cycle out older oils with newer ones. If you are getting close to your expiration dates and are not planning any spell casting, you can always use oils for massages, skin and facial treatments, or anointing and cleansing your tools and candles.

When thinking of things to add to your essential oils for an extra power infusion, remember that just as they are great for spells, they also work magic on the body, mind, and spirit. Try dried lemon or orange peel for bringing happiness, love, and light into a dark situation. Vanilla bean shavings or even a sprinkle of cinnamon can add a little oomph to a spell for healthy sexuality, vigor, and energy. Lavender oil mixes will soothe your anxiety and calm you down and can also treat a headache or insomnia and lower blood pressure. Peppermint oil will pick you up and lift your spirits, but it also treats upset stomachs and in-sect bites. Peppermint oil even reduces the spasms in the gastrointestinal tract associated with diverticulitis.

Eucalyptus oil blends will be strong in odor but work wonders on colds, flu

Dilution Guidelines

When mixing carrier oils with essential oils, follow these dilution guidelines (for adults):

2.5 percent dilution—15 drops of essential oil per 6 teaspoons of carrier oil

3 percent dilution—20 drops of essential oil per 6 teaspoons of carrier oil

5 percent dilution—30 drops of essential oil per 6 teaspoons of carrier oil

10 percent dilution—60 drops of essential oil per 6 teaspoons of carrier oil

For children: 0.5 to 1 percent dilution— 3 to 6 drops of essential oil per 6 teaspoons of carrier oil

bugs, and sinus infections, as eucalyptus has antibiotic and antiviral properties. Tea tree oil is another infection fighter, alone or in a blend, and, when used as a topical oil, fights athlete's foot. Always use dried materials and think about the symbolism they represent. If something feels light, use it for lighter spells. If it smells sensual and earthy, use it for grounding and improving sexual health. If it smells minty, try it for extra clarity and energy. A calming scent is great for a spell for improved sleep and relief from anxiety. An exuberant scent will serve best to give you the motivation and boost you need to tackle a big project or challenge.

Diffusers are a great way to fill a room or altar area with essential oils, but if you don't own a diffuser, you can make a nice room spray to spritz before you spell cast. This can also be used during meditation and yoga practices. Notice the smell the next time you go into yoga class. Most often, you will recognize patchouli oil coming from a room diffuser! One warning with sprays: they can stain clothing and cloth furniture, so be careful where you spray them.

If buying oils online or at a store, don't be concerned with price. Read the label and see how diluted the oil is before you buy or ask for recommendations and look at reviews from other users before buying. Yes, some companies will want to sell you their premixed oils at a high price with a fancy label, so buyer beware and do your research!

✩₀°✴ ✳ ✳ ✳ ATHAMES AND CHALICES ✩₀°✴ ✳ ✳ ✳

Ceremonial blades called athames are often used in magical spell casting, especially in the Wiccan tradition. An athame usually has a black handle and can be simple or rather ornate, single or double bladed, but is only used for ceremonial and ritual purposes. The use of athames dates back to the time of King Solomon and is a part of the grimoire known as "The Key of Solomon" from the Middle Ages. The handles are often decorated with important symbols and images chosen by the owner.

Athames are tools for banishing negative forces and energies. They are not used to cut or harm the spell caster or anyone else and certainly not for sacrificing anything! They are also not to be used for everyday cutting purposes, so find something else to slice your steak with.

Some witches claim the athame is a symbol of fire or air and represents an elemental force in nature. Others include the wand and pentacle with the athame and the chalice or cup to represent the four elements. Again, it is up to the practitioner what makes sense or feels right, as some may prefer only using wands, but others may like to have one of everything on their altar.

The athame is a symbolic ceremonial knife, but it represents many other things in addition to a simple knife.

The chalice or cup also represents feminine Divine energy. The chalice is a receptive tool and represents receptive energy. The cup of the Holy Grail is believed to be symbolic of the Divine feminine, and cauldrons have long been associated with witchcraft and mixing potions and magical formulas.

It has been said the chalice is the vagina to the phallic penis of the wand, blade, or athame. Pagan traditions have long revered symbols of the penis and the vagina and the act of sexual intercourse as the most powerful force of creation, something to be revered as sacred. The creative and the receptive are dynamic forces that are found in all religions in some form or another because the act of creation itself is universal. Rituals might involve the athame or wand to represent the male and the chalice to represent the female to balance or harmonize the dual energies and bring about unification of male and female energies or to draw forth one energy that is particularly needed for a spell. This act is called the Great Rite, or the *Hieros gamos*, which is the ancient Greek term for a sacred marriage. It can be done as a real sexual intercourse ritual or symbolically, depending on the coven or tradition.

In rituals, casting a circle is done with an athame or sword as a masculine symbol of protection for anyone within the circle. The athame's association with fire and the sun purifies the circle and cleanses it of negative energy and spirits. The chalice is associated with water and the moon, and its receptive and creative nature allows magic and energy to come into the circle. Both the chalice and the athame should be consecrated and purified beforehand by rubbing with a soft cloth and essential oil mixed with salt and water. The essential oil can be made up of favorite herbs or particular herbs that are sacred to the god for the athame and the goddess for the chalice.

✧｡✿✧｡✧✦✦✦ THE ALTAR ✧｡✿✧｡✧✦✦✦

Whether you just use a dresser or tabletop or an elaborate display of magical, symbolic items, an altar is a place for worship, prayer, and spell casting. Altars go back to pagan traditions that often created a sacred spot in nature, perhaps under a specific tree or near a rushing river, to carry out magical practices. The altar itself could have been created from rocks, dirt, or leaves, but today, they can be as simple or as expensive as the person desires as long as they are regarded as holy and sacred. Altars are as individual as, well ... individuals.

M. Matcha Nightmare, author and member of the Reclaiming tradition of witchcraft, writes in *Exploring the Pagan Path: Wisdom from the Elders* that an altar's appearance might change with the purpose of the ritual or spell. "Our purpose suggests which items we put on our altar, which incense we burn, what color candles we burn, what Deity(ies) we invite, and who we seek as witness or aid in our ritual." Performing a moon ritual will require different tools than holding a ritual for blessing a new baby or a Yule celebration. It is perfectly okay to have fixed items on an altar but equally okay to change things up when necessary. It's about looking at the altar as a foundational place upon which the added items and tools are placed according to the will of the practitioner.

Ancient Greeks created altars in the entryways and courtyards of their homes as well as in public places such as sacred groves and country locations, but they also built grand city altars with burning fires and stone sculptures of the powerful gods and goddesses they were meant to honor and invoke. Roman altars were similar, but when Christianity spread, worship and ritual were done in the home with altars relegated to churches. Original altars were made of wood, but eventually, more and more were built of stone, including marble. Sometimes, the remains of saints and martyrs were ritually buried underneath the altars.

Special cloth covered most altars along with holy objects such as crosses, candles, holy water, and images of those being prayed over. Today's altars are as vast and varied as their owners, with the common theme being the inclusion of meaningful objects and ritual items to be used during spell casting. In some cultures, altars are a burst of bright color and trinkets. Other cultures are simpler with a white cloth, white candle, and not much more.

A typical modern spell caster's altar might contain candles, incense, crystals, oils, an image of the intended object, a prayer or written spell, and perhaps an athame or consecrated knife. Make sure all items are positively charged before you put them on your altar, and never use anything with a negative or painful connotation.

Some choose to keep a book of spells on their altar at all times for quick reference. This is called a grimoire, and it could be a handwritten book or one from the store, it doesn't matter, although again, the original, handmade items always have more personal power attached to them. Find a colorful journal or lined

Any flat surface, whether it be a flat rock in nature or a well-built table containing all your spell casting tools, can become a perfect altar. More importantly, it is what you have on your altar that helps define the type of Wicca you feel confident performing.

paper book and write your spells in varying colors of markers. You might want to go even more elaborate and make one with leather bindings covered with jewels or special symbols. Grimoires have been a staple of occult and magical practices for hundreds of years. They are not to be shared with others and are personal collections of magical musings, insights, and incantations. They also contain instructions on how to make items and charge them and specific rituals. Some grimoires focus on how to communicate with the dead or with angels and spirit guides.

Your grimoire is your book of magic. Make it your own; fill it with symbols, prayers, blessings, and spells that are unique and important to you. If you are worried about prying eyes, buy a large locking diary and fix that into a nice, private book of spells. Hopefully, those who live with you will respect you and your sacred space enough to keep their hands off your magical tools, as their energies could directly influence them, maybe not for the better.

If you are short on space, consider an altar you can set up and take down and store in a closet such as a nice tray or small folding table, or find a small corner where you can set up the altar where it won't be messed with by spouses, kids, or pets. Even the back of a large closet could suffice!

Get creative and put your mark on your sacred space. This is where you will come to calm your mind, focus your intention, and work with the magic of the universe. Plenty of images of altars have been created by others online, or use your interior design skills to build a special spot that is yours and yours alone.

CRYSTALS, STONES, AND GEMS

The use of crystals, gemstones, and other stones with magical properties is an ancient practice, one that is even more popular today. Whether it is a symbolic or actual physical property, stones can be utilized to amplify and cast spells, heal, and bring about balance, harmony, and restoration.

Though most of the proof that crystals work in healing and spell casting is subjective, quartz crystals in particular are said to have the ability to amplify frequencies and vibrations that affect the user's physiology. Perhaps it's the natural geometric structures of crystals that cause them to retain information and emotion, but that same structure allows for the flow of energies and even health-promoting negative ions outward into the person holding them and their immediate environment.

Crystals and gemstones provide a healing modality to cure illnesses and ailments as well as ward off negative charges and energies. Most doctors and scientists would claim these stones hold no power and that perhaps it is the placebo effect at work in those who believe they do, but again, subjective experiences abound of those who benefit in body, mind, and spirit from using rocks, minerals, gems, and especially crystals.

Beautiful, multifaceted stones of varying colors and shapes can alone be enough to bring calm and healing to a stressed mind. Believing in the power of crystals and gems no doubt adds to any potential healing properties they may have. One of the most interesting aspects of crystals is the electric charge that accumulates inside of them, called piezoelectricity. This charge comes from pressure and latent heat that occurs when crystals form and is used in electronics, computers, and a wide variety of scientific and engineering techniques. Piezoelectricity converts mechanical pressure into electricity. While no definitive studies have proven that this type of electricity is detected by humans and even amplified by your own electromagnetic fields, many believe it is exactly this link that gives crystals their power to aid in healing.

The use of crystals to heal and enlighten goes back over six thousand years to the ancient Sumerians of Mesopotamia. They worked with crystals to promote healing and wisdom as well as provide a connection to inner enlightenment. The ancient Greeks, Romans, Egyptians, Chinese, and Indians all adopted crystals as powerful aids for working with psychic abilities and attracting good and prosperous energies. Quartz crystals are some of the most stable of the crystalline structures, are hugely popular in metaphysical and spiritual practices, are used in transistors and integrated circuits, and are the foundation of computer chips. Crystals are used in everything from telephones to radios to laser optics, timekeeping, and just about every electronic device you can think of.

Claims have been made that crystals can absorb dangerous radiation and high-intensity electromagnetic waves and protect the body from being penetrated by negative and even dangerous energy fields. Many crystals and stones do not interact well with water and therefore should not be put into water to be cleaned. These include calcite, mica, turquoise, hematite, obsidian, selenite, halite, pirite, and malachite.

✧｡°✦✶✦ CRYSTALS AND STONES ✧｡°✦✶✦

A huge variety of stones, gems, and crystals are used in spell casting and rituals, but some of the most popular are listed below in A to Z order:

There are many different stones, gems, and crystals that have properties that are helpful for spell casting.

• Agate—Agates come in a variety of colors and patterns and are made of silica and quartz that intertwine. Colors include black, red, blue, green, brown, white, pink, and gray. They are associated with keeping the eyes and heart healthy and are said to improve circulation. They are protection stones, too, and offer extra courage and strength to the wearer. Agates are among the oldest types of healing stones on the planet and are considered grounding and centering.

• Amazonite—A turquoise-colored stone that brings confidence, increases self-love, and allows for more creative expression.

• Amber—Not a stone but fossilized resin of coniferous trees over thirty million years old, usually containing something that has been trapped inside like an insect or leaf. It is found in many countries and was said by ancient Greeks to possess electrical properties. It is used to cleanse the air, aid in childbirth, strengthen courage, improve eyesight, attract love, and offer protection from evil energies.

- Amethyst—A very powerful and ancient magic stone made of quartz, usually purple, reddish, or violet in color. It is basically quartz with iron added and is found in geodes. The name comes from the Greek word for "not tipsy" and was thought to help sober up the drunk! It is most associated with enlightenment, wisdom, intuition, healing the nerves, the brain, clarity, ESP abilities, and producing calm. It is one of the most popular stones in terms of jewelry and home decor.

- Angelite—This crystal is used to communicate with angels, and access the angelic realms, and increase mental telepathy, psychic powers, and mediumship abilities. It can also aid in opening the throat, third eye, and crown chakras and alleviate headaches, inflammation, and heart issues. It is the stone of Divine love, healing, and kindness.

- Aquamarine/Beryl—Known as beryl, this stone is made of aluminum silicate and, when in its bluish forms, is called aquamarine. It can be found in Russia, Siberia, the United States, and Madagascar and is considered protection and a luck stone for fishermen. It supposedly aids in digestion and bloating and also increases psychic abilities. Because of its aqua colors, it is often associated with the sea and sea goddess energy.

- Aventurine—A type of quartz that can be gray, yellow, brown, or green with silvery mica slivers and is found in Brazil, India, and Russia. It is said to attract luck and prosperity and to increase psychic abilities. In healing, it focuses positive energy on the eyes, eyesight, and gifts of inner sight.

- Azurite—Usually medium or dark blue, this copper, carbonate-based stone makes beautiful crystals that were used in ancient Egypt as enlightenment stones to raise consciousness. It is a divination stone, often used for precognition, ESP, and remote viewing, and is said to be good for the brain and brain development. It is associated with the third eye and intuition.

- Bloodstone—This type of quartz belongs to the same family as chalcedony and is dark in color with a greenish tint and spots of red. It is found throughout Germany and India and is named after the ancient Greek city of Chalcedon. As an amulet, it is said to stop wounds from bleeding and, because of its color green, is considered a prosperity stone. It also gives good luck and extra courage to the wearer.

- Calcite—A carbonite mineral, this soft stone amplifies energy and is great for all kinds of healing. It comes in pink, light green, orange, gray, yellow, and white and is also a great stone for students, as it aids in learning.

- Carnelian—Another member of the chalcedony family, this stone is clear red or brown-red in color and is found in India and South America. It is easily cut or engraved, so it is often used for jewelry and as necklace beads. It is said to cleanse the blood, offer healing, and improve attitude. It also dispels fears and anxieties and can purify the blood, cure impotency, and increase fertility. It also represents passion, sexual energy, and creativity.

- Celestite—A high vibrational crystal that increases intuition, psychic abilities, and astral projection skills. This is a calming crystal that works with the throat chakra to help speak truth, communicate clearly, and attract love and clarity.

- Citrine—This glassy yellow, golden, or greenish type of quartz is perfect for spirituality, intuition, and opening the third eye. It looks sunny and warm, promotes and stimulates clarity of the mind, and is good for healthy kidneys, liver, color, and digestive organs as well as the heart. It is said to bring luck and raise self-esteem.

- Dalmation Stone—A speckled stone that brings loyalty, family bonding, and a spiritual connection with the animal world.

- Diamond—Probably the most desired stone, the diamond is a form of the element carbon with atoms arranged in crystalline structure called diamond cubic. It is the most natural substance in existence and can be clear, green, blue, red, black, orange, pink, or brown. It is associated with wealth, power,

The Dalmatian Stone is aptly named because of its similarity to the fur of the canine of the same name. Naturally, it has a connection to the animal world.

strength, and beauty and can protect from evil spirits, disease, and negative energies. The word diamond comes from the Greek word for "invincible."

- Emerald—A type of beryl, this stone is famous for its gorgeous green shade and is a desired gemstone for jewelry. It can be bright green, bluish green, yellow, red, pink, and even white, although in any color other than green, it is referred to as beryl. Emeralds bring love and attraction and was associated with the goddess Venus in ancient Greece. It also brings prosperity and business success and aids in mental and spiritual perception and clarity.

- Garnet—Known as the "poor man's ruby," this rich, deep red stone is said to bring good luck and to stimulate the body, mind, and spirit. It also helps increase sexual stamina and energy. It has been said that if you sleep with a garnet, you will have vivid, memorable dreams. It is also associated with fertility and menses. Garnets protect against negative energy and balance the root chakra. Garnet keeps our thoughts and emotions in balance and harmony with our intentions and in spell casting can aid fertility, passion, sexual issues, and love affairs.

- Hematite—This iron oxide can be gray, red, brown, or black and is a mineral, not a stone. Often, it comes in a color similar to blood, and the name itself is Greek for "bloodlike," thus making it a healing tool for blood disorders, purifying the blood, and for winning legal arguments and lawsuits! It is often worn as a ring or necklace and is iron-based, can ground the body, mind, and spirit, and remove illness and stress from the body. Use it to ground your power and center yourself in inner strength.

- Jade—Jade is the green version of tremolite, which can come in gray, yellow, pink, and lilac shades as well. It is a hugely popular stone for rings and necklaces, especially beaded, and brings good luck and prosperity to the wearer. Jade carvings are kept in homes to attract good energy, luck, happiness, and wealth. To the ancient Mayans, jade was more priceless than even gold! Some cultures used it to raise the dead, and others see it as a protection stone. Putting jade near plants can help them grow and flourish!

- Jasper—Jasper is another member of the chalcedony family and is usually brown or greenish in color. It is called "Egyptian marble" for the interplay of dark and light browns and greens and was said to be good luck for Native American tribes. It is used in grounding and centering rituals and has a stable, earthly energy.

- Lapis Lazuli—This gorgeous, sky-blue stone is a type of silicate with sulfur. Its traditional name is lazurite, and it comes in ranges of blue from light to deep and even green and violet-based blues. It is light in weight and is more compact than in crystal form but is a hugely popular stone for jewelry in ancient Egypt. It has been said to help with the pain of childbirth, open the third eye, and bring about altered states of consciousness in ritual and trancework. It is an attractor of spirituality and love and sharpens ESP skills and vision work. It is said to bring health to the pituitary gland, eyes, ears, and brain.

- Lepidolite—A pink, speckled stone that brings relief from stress and assists in emotional balance and harmony.

- Malachite—This stone is made from copper carbonate and comes in shades of green. It often has bands of darker and lighter colors and is considered both an ore and a gemstone. It can aid in spell casting, magical works, business success, and prosperity. It balances energies in the spleen, pancreas, solar plexus, and heart area. It also helps with sleep issues and brings balance and harmony to the body and spirit. It is the stone of individuality and wealth.

- Moonstone—This gorgeous stone looks like moonbeams with a silvery or bluish sheen. It can have a gray, blue, green, brown, yellow, or white cast or sheen to it. Moonstones are sometimes called "cat's eyes." This is a stone to be used in moon magic, and it has a strong association with goddess energy. It is also used in love spells and is healing to women's bodies, hormones, and organs. It can also give someone the gift of ESP, prophecy, and inner sight and amplifies feminine aspects of the personality. Black moonstone is associated with the third eye and the crown chakra and con-

Due to malachite's green color, it is often tied to spells about money and acquiring wealth.

nects us to the Divine feminine and intuition. It assists in contacting spirit guides and protects from negative forces. Holding black moonstone also grounds us to Earth and your powerful center. Sleep with black moonstone under your pillow to aid sleep and bring relief to nighttime indigestion.

- Obsidian—Made from the flows of volcanic lava, this mineral is stunning— black, shiny, and glassy. It can also be smoky with transparent edges or mahogany, dark gray, or dark green but most often is black. Its name means "mineral" in Latin. It is used as a divination or scrying stone, to see into the future or to read fortunes, and as jewelry. It is a protective stone and also symbolizes going deep into the inner realms of mind and consciousness. It gives courage to the meek and anxious and cleanses the liver of toxins. This volcanic glass absorbs negative energy and, when brushed lightly over the body, can help release old patterns and cut energetic cords with toxic people. Snowflake obsidian is a gorgeous, black-and-white, speckled stone that offers spiritual protection and assists in spiritual transformation.

- Onyx—Another black stone and member of the chalcedony family, it gives strength, courage, and self-control. It inspires the mind and heals the body down to the bones. Carrying onyx helps keep away bad energies and relieves anxiety and stress. It is called a "power stone."

- Opal—Opals are delicate stones made of silica, iron, and aluminum. They come in shades of white, pink, red, gray, blue, and clear with specks of color. They have a pearlescent look to them and make wonderful jewelry pieces. The opal is a stone for luck,

and because it contains all the colors of other gems and quartzes, it has overall general healing powers. It is also said to give the gift of invisibility if you know the correct spell for it! It is known specifically for bringing healing and balance to the spirit and emotions. It has been called the stone of the gods because of all the colors it embodies.

- Pearl—Although they are not stones, pearls are often used in spell casting and healing to represent light, purity, and the sea and are called "sea gems." Pearls are the hard, glistening, round objects produced from the soft tissue of a shelled mollusk. They are made of calcium carbonate deposited in layers. They come in a variety of colors and shades and bring protection, luck, good energy, and healing. They are also known for their calming effects.

- Peridot—This visionary stone is found in meteorites and is a powerful tool for accessing the higher self, the spirit world, and other states of reality. It is a great stone for manifesting prosperity and abundance, too, and for healing the heart and stomach areas, glandular system, adrenals, liver, spleen, and blood. It is both a calming stone for the body and a stimulating one for the mind.

- Quartz—Quartz of every color and shape plays a huge role in magical works, spell casting, and working with the energies of Earth. It is both an amplifier and absorber, used to work with the electromagnetic properties of Earth and to amplify psychic and healing energies. Quartz comes in every color from clear and light to dark and smoky and are purifiers and grounding tools. Different types of quartz work with different parts of the body and the seven chakras, or spiritual meridian points, of the body. Quartz crystals are clear and work especially well to cleanse, detoxify, and heal the body, blood, brain, and mind and activate the pineal and pituitary glands. Quartz may be the most important stone in the spell caster's collection for all the properties it has to balance, empower, and strengthen the body, mind, and spirit as well as increase dream recall, ESP, precognition, harmony, channeling abilities, and a host of others.

• Rose Quartz—This stone represents unconditional love and friendship. It calms and soothes anxiety, stress, and emotions. Rose quartz aligns the heart chakra and cleanses the body and spirit of all negative energies while restoring self-love and self-worth. Carrying rose quartz keeps the heart open to love in all its forms. It heals broken hearts and restores trust and positivity. In love spells, it assures balance, harmony, and beauty in all loving relationships.

• Ruby—This gorgeous, red gem is prized in fine pieces of jewelry. It possesses powerful healing for the blood, immune system, and the entire body. Rubies awaken passions, courage, and power and assist with circulation and blood flow. This is the stone to wear to gain positive power and remove blocks to happiness and success. Rubies come from the mineral corundum and can range from pink to deepest red in color and tone. Along with sapphires, emeralds, amethysts, and diamonds, rubies are a "cardinal" gem. The word *ruby* is Latin for "red."

• Sapphire—Another member of the corundum family, sapphires are usually thought of as deep blue but can also be pink, green, violet, gray, and yellow, too—even black. It is one of the hardest gemstones, right behind the diamond. Sapphires are considered royal and Divine stones beloved by the gods and goddesses and are associated with spiritual enlightenment and the third eye. In spell casting, they aid in sending forth powerful energies to manifest spoken desires, and as healing stones, they are overall protectors of the body and especially the immune system. They attract love, loyalty, clarity, creativity, and awareness.

• Serpentine—A uniquely colored, green and dark green/black stone that increases the power of observation and allows you to discern hidden mysteries.

• Selenite—The Greek word means "moonstone"; selenite is a colorless and transparent form of gypsum. It's a softer stone that can be found in different size crystals and is used most often to heal the psyche and spirit rather than the physical body. It is also said to magnify the properties of any other stone placed on top of it. It has a soothing, calming effect and is also known to open dialog with spirit guides and Divine beings.

Quartz stones come in many colors with each having different powers. The example pictured here is a clear quartz stone, which can be used for healing the body and mind.

- Shungite—This gun-metal-gray stone, named after the Shunga village in Russia where it was first discovered, is considered very rare and powerful. It goes back over two billion years and is a mineral with healing powers and the ability to purify, charge, cleanse, cure, protect, stabilize, and promote growth when worn on the body. Made up of over 88 percent carbon, it also purifies the water content of almost all organic compounds, metals, pesticides, bacteria, and micro-organisms. It can clean and purify even the dirtiest tap water, as it draws out contaminants.

- Sodalite—High in salt, manganese, and calcium, this stone can strengthen confidence, self-worth, and self-esteem and is a harmonizing, soothing stone to the body and spirit.

- Tiger Eye—This distinctive, yellow-brown, semiprecious quartz is striped or banded like a tiger, thus its name. It is a popular stone used in jewelry and in spell casting and rituals; it rep-

The striking, semiprecious tiger eye stone has many qualities, including everything from helping with energy and happiness to warding off evil spirits.

resents courage, happiness, strength, and emotional healing. Tiger eye is worn for good luck and to ward off evil spirits. It balances emotions and increases vitality, willpower, and energy. It also promotes prosperity, wealth, and success.

- Topaz—This golden or blue stone is a powerful protector against depression, fear, anger, sleep problems, and emotional turmoil. It stimulates the intellect and is a favorite stone for artists, writers, philosophers, and scientists. Some people use it to protect against colds, flus, and respiratory bugs because it is associated with the breath and lungs. It also detoxifies the blood and body and brings calm, peace, and balance.

- Tourmaline—Pink on the inside and green on the outside, this beautiful gemstone is often referred to as the watermelon stone. It is found all over the world and is used in jewelry when sliced or cut into facets. It helps bring about calm, peace, and relaxation and is most associated with balancing and healing the heart and working with the heart chakra energy center.

- Turquoise—Turquoise is a mineral that can be blue, bluish-green, or green in color. Gem-quality turquoise is hugely popular in jewelry, belt buckles, and even carvings for home decor. It is used for protection and worn to keep bad energies and danger away. Native Americans of Southwestern tribes in the United States use it as a powerfully symbolic stone in rituals and wear it on their bodies for protection and strength. It is considered an elemental gemstone to the Pueblo Indians along with coral, jet, and abalone shell. It is worn by healers to amplify their healing gifts and energies.

- Zircon—Zircon is a mineral in the form of a prismatic crystal. It can be brownish, blue, green, rose, or clear and is not to be confused with the man-made "cubic zirconia." Zircon can strengthen the mind and intellect and also balances the pineal and pituitary glands. It brings balance to subtle body energies and balances emotions. Zircons are said to have similar healing properties to diamonds and quartz crystals, which they look similar to.

Dozens of other types of stones, crystals, gems, and minerals hold various properties. The use of stones is both universal and personal, and it is important to use stones that make you as an individual feel good.

✧₀✧**✶✷✷ CLEANING YOUR CRYSTALS ✧₀✧✶✷✷**

Before using crystals in any kind of spell work, you want to make sure they are cleansed of any negative energies from other people who have handled them. Crystals store energy, and that includes your own, so it is even recommended that you cleanse them before each ritual or spell.

Immersing them in a saltwater mix is common. If you live near the ocean, use seawater, but if not, simply mix purified water with sea salt to get the same effect. Fill a bowl with enough water to submerge the crystals and leave them in the solution for at least an hour. You can leave them overnight for a good cleansing. You might wish to add some sage, basil, or lavender to the water.

If you have certain crystals that are high in water and metal content, they

Crystals can be cleaned in a dry salt bath or in saltwater.

may be too porous for salty water, so get to know your crystals and how best to cleanse them.

Holding the stones under running water works, too, but beware of hard water minerals that may be in your tap. It's best if you have a water filter to keep the cleansing purer.

You can also do a dry salt bath, simply placing the crystals in a bowl of good salt and immersing them for a few hours before removing.

Saging or smudging your crystals also works to rid them of negative energy. Simply hold the crystal over the smoke for a while. Incense works, too, although it produces a lot less smoke to work with.

Once the crystals are cleansed, either use them immediately or wrap them in a fine, silk cloth and set on your altar for when you are ready. If you don't have access to sea salt, water, or anything that smokes and smells good, you can remove negative charges from your crystals by doing a meditation with them in your hands, visualizing all negative energy leaving the crystals and being replaced with light.

✮ ˚ ✶ ✳ ✦ ✦ STORING YOUR CRYSTALS ✮ ˚ ✶ ✦ ✦ ✦

Crystals can be wrapped in silk or another soft, gentle cloth and set into a box or container when not in use. Some people choose to display them in glass cases, so they can enjoy looking at them. Small velvet bags with ties work well, too, to keep the crystals protected from scratches and pets that might think they are shiny, new toys.

Your crystals should be stored in soft, velvet drawstring bags to help keep them safe for transport.

It is best to keep them stored in natural containers such as wood or cloth of any kind rather than a plastic box. Natural fabrics, chosen for their aesthetic appeal, are a great way to keep them clean and protected. Try not to throw them in a box or wrap together, as they will chip or crack against each other.

You can even keep them in a nice ceramic bowl, spread out enough so they aren't touching. Take the one that most appeals to you each morning and carry it with you for extra good energy! Sacred spaces such as yoga and meditation rooms are wonderful places to keep crystals on display, as they create a grounded and calming presence. You can place crystals on your body during yoga for extra healing powers.

Crystals that are not going to necessarily be used for spell casting, of course, make beautiful decorative displays around the home and allow you to benefit from their good vibrations all the time. Even larger-sized healing crystals are being used as paperweights, end table features, and coffee table pieces that will no doubt become conversation starters. Amethyst, because of its healing properties and positive energies, is often found on display in homes as well as large pieces of rose quartz and smoky quartz, but anything that beautifies your home and makes it feel more peaceful will do. You might want to be sure to keep some calming crystals near the bathtub or jacuzzi tub along with some scented candles or incense.

✳✳✳ CHARGING YOUR CRYSTALS ✳✳✳

You can wear them for seven days to build a personal connection, or you can carry them in a small pouch or bag. Charging them with positive energy can be done by doing a special ritual over them, where you state the intention to only use them for the highest, best outcomes. You can do a quiet meditation holding the crystals and visualize them being charged with healing light and love. Intention is important here, as you want the crystal to be open and ready to amplify how you plan to use it. Dedicate your crystals out loud for extra effect, as the spoken word has vibratory power that the crystal will pick up.

Another way to charge crystals and stones is to wait for the next full moon, then collect water by placing a bowl under its light. You can then cleanse and charge your stones in the full moon water, which will be infused with special energy from the goddess herself.

✿ ✿✿ ✿ ✳✳✳ GEMSTONES ✿ ✿✿ ✿ ✳✳✳

Gemstones are precious and semi-precious stones that are often used in jewelry. Basically, a gem is a piece of mineral crystal that is cut and finely polished to look glassy and shiny. Some nonmineral rocks can also be made into gemstones, such as lapiz lazuli, opal, pearl, amber, jet, and others. Gemstones have been used for thousands of years in jewelry and physical adornments as well as on decorative items such as vases and statues.

The terms "precious" and "semiprecious" refer to rarity of the stones and is a traditional way to classify gems in the West. Precious stones include diamonds, rubies, sapphires, and emeralds, which are the most highly desired gemstones. The rest are considered "semiprecious" stones. The study of gemstones is called gemology, and a gemologist is a must to truly identify the stone's rarity and worth. Unlike diamonds, no grading system exists to de-

While it costs a bit more in the short term, a good rock tumbler like the one in this photo can make having clean, smooth gems a bit of an adventure.

termine the worth of gemstones, although with precious stones, size does matter, with a large ruby being far more expensive than a tiny one, but for spell casting and healing, it really comes down to which stone has what properties and holds appeal to the individual.

Gems can be purchased already cut and polished, which can be somewhat expensive, depending on which stones you choose, or you can buy them uncut and unpolished and invest in a good rock tumbler that uses grains of sand and rock to polish the stones over the course of a few days. This author owned a rock tumbler as a child and still has little velvet bags full of delightful, shiny stones that look way more expensive than they probably are! Watching a dull rock turn into a smooth stone before your eyes is very special, much like growing your own food or making your own candles.

Using gems in spell casting can consist of little more than casting the spell onto the stone and wearing it for three days, or gems can be a part of a ceremony or ritual and kept on an altar. Because they are not as porous as crystals, they can be cleaned by immersing them in water and drying on a soft cloth to avoid scratching.

✦°✧✶✶✶ STONES OF THE ZODIAC ✦°✧✶✶✶

Each birth sign has a corresponding birthstone that amplifies the positive qualities of your astrological sun sign. Stones can be worn in jewelry form or kept loose in a medicine/magic bag on your altar. Each sign has two types of stone. The first is the zodiac birthstone, which corresponds to the astrological sign. The second, which may or may not be the same, is the stone that corresponds to the actual calendar birth month, which is called the modern birthstone. We today tend to use the modern birthstone chart.

✶ MODERN BIRTHSTONES ✶

- January—Garnet
- February—Amethyst
- March—Aquamarine
- April—Diamond
- May—Emerald
- June—Pearl/Moonstone
- July—Ruby
- August—Peridot
- September—Sapphire
- October—Opal/Tourmaline
- November—Citrine
- December—Topaz/Turquoise

✶ ZODIAC BIRTHSTONES ✶

- Aquarius—Garnet
- Pisces—Amethyst
- Aries—Bloodstone
- Taurus—Sapphire
- Gemini—Agate
- Cancer—Emerald
- Leo—Onyx
- Virgo—Carnelian
- Libra—Chrysolite
- Scorpio—Beryl
- Sagittarius—Citrine
- Capricorn—Ruby

- Garnet—Positive: Friendly, humanitarian, wise, honest, loyal, original, inventive, independent. Negative: Contrary, immovable, unpredictable, sketchy, detached, cold.

- Amethyst—Positive: Sensitive, regal, imaginative, compassionate, kind, selfless, intuitive, empathic. Negative: Selfish, weak-willed, secretive, idealistic, escapist, unrealistic.

- Bloodstone—Positive: Energetic, enthusiastic, adventurous, courageous, innovative, confident, dynamic. Negative: Selfish, brooding, bad-tempered, impulsive, impatient, testy.

- Sapphire—Positive: Patient, reliable, warm, loving, persistent, determined, calm, balanced. Negative: Cold, jealous, obsessive, compulsive, resentful, greedy, inflexible.

- Agate—Positive: Versatile, open-minded, adaptable, witty, eloquent, youthful, energetic. Negative: Anxious, tense, superficial, inconsistent, manipulative.

- Emerald—Positive: Emotional, loving, caring, intuitive, imaginative, creative, shrewd, cautious, protective. Negative: Moody, tense, overemotional, oversensitive, clingy, codependent.

- Onyx—Positive: Generous, courageous, bold, warm, caring, expansive, faithful. Negative: Arrogant, patronizing, bossy, dogmatic, intolerant.

- Carnelian—Positive: Witty, modest, reliable, practical, diligent, steadfast, smart, analytical. Negative: Fussy, overanxious, critical, harsh, perfectionist, conservative.

- Chrysolite—Positive: Diplomatic, charming, romantic, sociable, easygoing, idealistic, urbane. Negative: Flighty, indecisive, gullible, self-indulgent, flirtatious.

- Beryl—Positive: Emotional, determined, intuitive, powerful, passionate, exciting, magnetizing. Negative: Jealous, obsessive, compulsive, secretive, stubborn.

- Citrine—Positive: Optimistic, free, joyful, witty, honest, intellectual, philosophical. Negative: Careless, unrealistic, superficial, restless, irresponsible.

- Ruby—Positive: Practical, ambitious, disciplined, hardworking, humorous, reserved. Negative: Pessimistic, fatalistic, miserable, complaining, unhappy.

Using the knowledge of the properties of the stones, spell casters can work magic to find balance when negative aspects are out of proportion.

Using the knowledge of the properties of the stones, spell casters can work magic to find balance when negative aspects are out of proportion or overwhelming. Spells can focus on increasing the influence of the positive aspects while banishing or minimizing the negative.

Birthstones can be different according to many charts you might come across, but in general, the stones of the zodiac signs rarely change. These stones can be worn to protect you from evil and ward off negative energies just like any other charm or amulet. You can wear any sign's stone, but your own sign's stone's will be the most powerful and effective.

✧✦✷✷✷ THE POWER OF COLOR ✧✦✷✷✷

Finding the right stone often comes down to the properties of the specific color the stone is. Color is not just aesthetically pleasing but has its own range of influences on the body, mind, and spirit.

- Blue stones—Blue stimulates the throat chakra and assists with glandular issues, throat and mouth diseases, and illnesses of the throat area. It is soothing, yet stimulates energies required for healing and balance.
- Red stones—High-energy red is all about blood and the root chakra and governs imbalances with blood disorders, fertility, sex drive, menstrual cramps, and impotence and frigidity. It is the stone that brings courage and boldness.
- Black stones—Just like red stones, black stones represent base/root issues with sexuality, reproduction, and lack of courage and willpower. Black stones are powerful and stimulate the base energies.

- Yellow stones—Like the sun, yellow is bright and brings balance and healing to the stomach and solar plexus area. It is great for working with food allergies, liver and kidney problems, and muscle strength. It is soothing and warms the spirit but also gives energy, like the sun.
- Purple/violet stones—These healing stones work well on headaches and stress with their comforting properties and also help boost focus, concentration, and mental acuity.
- Green/pink stones—These are considered the heart stones and help with emotional issues as well as depression and anger. Use for any issues with chest pains from stress and anxiety.
- Orange stones—These increase your energy, brighten your outlook, and balance any issues around the stomach, kidneys, and sacrum at the base of the spine. Orange is stimulating!

✧✦✷✷✷ CHAKRAS AND STONES ✧✦✷✷✷

The seven chakras refer to seven energy centers in the body in Hinduism and Tantric Buddhism. The Sanskrit word *chakra* means "wheel," and the balance of these seven swirling wheels of energy is critical to well-being. These seven centers regulate every aspect of the body and the spirit, too, and must be kept open, clear, and in proper alignment. Blocked or imbalanced chakras mean that energy is not flowing through the body properly and with ease and result in disease of the mind, psyche, and body. Chakras became hugely popular during the 1970s and the rise of New Age practices, but because of their far older roots, they are a mainstay of alternative healing and achieving a harmonic system. Chakra work is a big part of yoga, meditation, and Ayurvedic medicine today, but one of the ways to work with the chakras to keep them in perfect balance is to work with corresponding stones (the stones and properties are listed above). Each stone mentioned has specific properties that help open, clear, and balance the chakra.

- Root Chakra—Muladhara: The root chakra is considered the foundational chakra and is located at the bottom of the spine and end of the tailbone. The corresponding color is red, and the element is earth. A blocked root chakra can mean you are living in fear and anxiety, and your survival feels at risk because of lack of money, food, or shelter. In order to feel grounded and centered, this chakra must be balanced and strong. The corresponding stone to work with balancing the root chakra is hematite.

- Sacral Chakra—Svadhishthana: The sacral chakra is where your creativity comes from. Located in the center of the abdomen about two inches below the navel, it governs sexuality and the imagination and is home to doubt and low self-worth when out of balance. The color is orange, and the element is water. If this chakra is not clear, you feel off-balance and blocked, uninspired, and even resistant to change. You can also suffer from sex-related issues. The stone for the sacral chakra is carnelian.

- Solar Plexus Chakra—Manipura: This chakra is the home to self-worth and self-esteem, autonomy, and personal power. If clear, it leads you to success and independence. If blocked, you feel constant failure and low self-worth and have difficulty in social settings. The color associated with this chakra is yellow like the sun, and the element is fire. Blocks here lead to issues with security and ability and include digestive disorders. The stone associated with the solar plexus chakra is citrine.

- Heart Chakra—Anahata: It's all about love, intimacy, and compassion for the heart chakra, located directly above the heart. Its color is green, and its element is air. Blocked heart chakras lead to intolerance, a lack of compassion, and the inability to trust and love yourself and others. If you want inner peace, self-love, and to be able to love others and be loved by them in return, this chakra must be open and balanced. The associated stone is rose quartz.

- Throat Chakra—Vishuddha: This chakra governs expression of self and how we convey our authenticity out in the bigger world. If we are always afraid to speak up and be ourselves, our throat chakra is out of balance, if not blocked entirely. Located where the vocal cords are, its color is blue, and its element is aether. Blocked throat chakras lead to feeling stuck, invisible, unheard, and unacknowledged by others. Pain in the neck area and throat issues are common to those with blocked throat chakras. The stone to work with is sodalite.

The seven main chakras are invisible wheels of energy that, when in balance, provide for a well-adjusted body that is healthy, vibrant, and feeling alive.

- Third Eye Chakra—Ajna: This is a powerful energy center associated with intuition and your alignment with the universal energies. It governs gut feelings and knowingness, connection to your higher power, and self-trust. Located in the center of your eyebrows, its color is indigo, and its element is light. It also governs your ability to have faith in your purpose and your choices as well as your ability to sleep well and learn new things. The stone to work with is amethyst.

- Crown Chakra—Sahasrara: At the top of the head sits the crown chakra, which is the highest and most connected to spirit and spirituality. It is where energy enters and leaves the body during Kundalini and allows for the experiences of connection, wisdom, enlightenment, and higher consciousness. Problems and blocks lead to headaches, dizziness, and lack of motivation or purpose. The color is violet, and the element is thought, which is itself a form of energy. To work with the crown chakra, use the stone clear quartz.

Chakra-balancing exercises can be done during yoga, meditation, prayer, or anywhere you can find some peace and quiet. Hold the stone during the exercise, which can consist of simply visualizing balancing energy and light entering that particular chakra and bringing the scales back to equilibrium. You can also keep the particular stone on your physical body to help achieve balance and harmony. Some people even eat particular foods that are associated with the color of the chakra such as red peppers or oranges. Guided visualizations are a great way to work with chakras, and you can record your own to use later or find one on the Internet.

Pictured are some of the stones useful with the Third Eye Chakra, including healing crystals angelite, fluorite, amethyst, iolite, and lepidolite.

POTIONS, INFUSIONS, AND BREWS

Creating a special brew or potion to assist in healing or spell casting often brings up images of scary witches dressed in black, hunched over a cauldron filled with some awful boiling concoction of bird's beaks, frog's toes, and lizard's gizzards, but the use of potions, liquids, balms, and even salves goes back thousands of years. Even in the New Testament, Jesus is often anointed with various oils and salves, and potions differ little from a spoonful of modern medicine when it comes to what ails you. Most potions and liquid concoctions are edible, and many quite delicious, in the form of hot and cold drinks or added to juices and other drinks. Some people even add a touch of alcohol to their infusions and drinks, although whether or not they do this for fun or for spell casting is open to debate.

The cauldron, like the crockpot or cooking pot, is nothing more than a tool for mixing together natural blends for cooking or drinking. Our ancestors most likely never used heads of newts or wings of bats but instead chose to utilize the living things that grew locally for culinary and medicinal purposes. Therefore, a witches' brew or magic potion probably included ingredients they grew themselves.

✧⚬✧⚬⚬✧★★★ POTIONS ✧⚬⚬⚬✧⚬✧★★★

A potion is specifically a liquid that can be imbibed or used topically like a lotion or cream on the skin. Potions can be made of a variety of herbs, plants, liquor, juices, spices, and even crystals or other nonedible items that the potion is steeped in. Obviously, you don't drink the crystals or nonedibles and must remove them before drinking the potion, but they can add some extra oomph to your spell or healing ritual (just be sure whatever you choose doesn't leech any toxic chemicals). The great thing about potions is they don't require having to go to some obscure store to buy the ingredients. You can use what you have around the house or items you can easily buy at your local grocery store.

It is important to mix up potions in a symbolic cup or bowl to add to their effectiveness. If you want to go all out, look for a cast iron cauldron and a nice stirring spoon. If you like to heat up your potions, you can find a little decorative bowl with space for a tealight candle under it. It really is up to the individual spell caster or healer. Some choose to buy ornate, little bottles to fill with various potions, then mark each bottle according to what it is effective for. These must be kept according to whether they require refrigeration, a cool and dark place, or are fine being shelved for future use with no concern of expiration dates. Do be aware of anything that might trigger an allergy if you drink it or put it directly on your skin.

The classic mixing bowl for mixing potions is the cast iron cauldron to be sure your results are the most effective.

Potions meant to be used as lotions or creams or used with candle magic don't require the same concerns as those meant to be imbibed, but certain ingredients can become rancid if left exposed or unused for too long or kept in the sun or heat. Potions are charmed or enchanted both by their ingredients and by the actual spell they are to be used for. You must charge or bless your potion before using it, or it's just plain liquid. Lotions can be made with corresponding gods and goddesses in mind and charged during a ritual to that deity.

One type of potion is "spell oil," made with essential oils and herbs. These spell oils have been a mainstay for gypsy recipes for love and attraction and can be kept in little vials and put into mojo or magic bags along with a symbolic trinket or stone. Spell oils are not meant to be used as drinks, but they can be put on the skin like perfume or scented lotions as well as dabbed on doorways, window ledges, and other places in your home or office you want to give a little protection from negative energies.

Here is a potion to bring about the manifestation of your desires. You need a tea sac, a pinch of sage, a pinch of cinnamon, a pinch of thyme, rose petals, lavender flowers, and peppermint leaves. Blend the herbs together, grinding them up if you can. Put the herbs into the tea sac and boil a cup of water. Steep the tea sac in the water for 10 to 15 minutes. Take out the tea sac, and use your ritual athame to stir, repeating three times:

With these herbs I ask of thee,
God and Goddess come to me.
Let me bend thy will to me
To manifest my goals to be.
As I drink this sacred tea,
My intentions come to me
Blessed me and blessed be,

I thank thee for my destiny.
So mote it be.

Now drink the tea and ponder the happiness of knowing that your intentions are on the way to becoming realities. Asking a deity ensures that your intentions will happen in the highest and best way, as the deities are protective and loving.

Here is a potion that also serves as a herbal bath and a "glamour" spell to make you more attractive: Start a bath full of warm water. Add a handful of rose petals, some lavender oil, a handful of lavender flowers, and a handful of chamomile flowers, and let them steep in the warm water. Light some sandalwood incense and soak in the bath while imagining yourself becoming more and more beautiful and sensual. If you don't want to add the flowers directly to the water, use a sachet or sac.

This power potion can be made before an important event or meeting where you need an extra boost of confidence. Fill a glass of purified water with a pinch of ground allspice, a pinch of ginger, a few drops of vanilla extract, and a squeeze of fresh lemon. Using a red pen or marker, draw a large pentacle on a piece of white paper, and in the center, write the following:

By this potion, I do ask
For the power for this task.
Herbs and spices, color red
Set into play the spell I've said.

Wrap the red ribbon or yarn all around the glass and tie it off. As you do, focus on the best positive outcome of the event you will be undertaking. Take one big sip of the water. That's all you need to work the spell. Let the glass of water sit on a windowsill, where moonlight can strike it until the event has passed. Then pour the water outside. Do not pour down the sink or toilet.

Here's a passion potion to bring the lust back into your stale relationship. Take a pinch each of thyme, rosemary, and nutmeg. Add two teaspoons of black tea leaves, three mint leaves, three rose petals, and a pinch of orange or lemon zest. Boil three cups of water and add the ingredients. Let it steep, add a touch of honey or natural sweetener, then drink a cup and give a cup to your lover to rekindle the fires within.

Potions are obviously made to drink or imbibe, so be careful to avoid any toxic herbs that may be for topical use only.

This love potion is easy to make with a few ingredients. Take a cup of organic milk and add two teaspoons of raw, organic honey. Pour into a small pot on very low heat just to warm it up. Add three drops of vanilla extract and two drops of orange oil or orange juice, then hold half a teaspoon of coriander powder in the palm of your hand as you think of the intention of the spell. As you add the coriander, say, "Bring to me the love I seek" and repeat as you turn up the heat until it boils. Drink a cup with fresh rose petals in it, and if you are with the one you love, have him/her drink a cup, too. The spell will not force that person to love you but rather encourage the feelings that may already be just below the surface.

Potions are obviously made to drink or imbibe, so be careful to avoid any toxic herbs that may be for topical use only. Creating potions with any toxic herbs can be for carrying around for luck, success, love, or money in tiny jars or containers or put on the windowsill or in the garden under the light of the moon to intensify the energy of the intention. Potions can be dedicated to a specific god or goddess and include corresponding herbs, stones, and flowers.

Other types of concoctions include:

- Elixirs—Sweet liquids for healing and energy made from powders and extracts dissolved in a water base, sweetened with honey, syrup, sugars, or fruits. Elixirs are like syrups but not as thick in texture.
- Wines—Mulled wines, dandelion wines, and berry wines are great during holiday rituals and special occasions.
- Brews—Infusions or mixtures in liquid form meant to be consumed, usually thick or fermented such as homemade ales and beer.
- Tinctures—Extracts of scented liquids mixed with ethyl alcohol and infused with dry herbs or plant parts, but they don't have to contain alcohol.
- Infusions—Liquids made from steeped herbs or plant parts added to balms, salves, ointments, and lotions (teas can be considered infusions, too).

- Salves/Balms—Pastes, balms, body butters, creams, and ointments made with healing herbs and plants plus beeswax or a vegan wax.
- Poultices—A soft, moist healing mass of herbs/plants that are often heated and placed on body parts to relieve pain and swelling.
- Philters—Potions usually used to obtain love.
- Powders—Ground mixtures of herbs and plants, which may or may not be for consumption. They can be spread around the house, office, yard, on altars, or in spell pouches and boxes.
- Sachets—Pieces of porous fabric or netting filled with aromatic herbs and plants or flowers to put under the pillow or in an herbal bath.
- Scented Oils/Perfumes—Homemade scents from herbs and plants for specific spells or healing purposes or to anoint and scent the body.

Always consecrate or charge these concoctions before use. You can bless them in a ritual devoted to an associated deity, or use your crystals and gemstones to charge them with the spell energy you require, and, it goes without saying, test anything that you plan to touch your skin beforehand by rubbing a little on the inside of your elbow.

✧✦✶✦✦ LOVE POTION HISTORY ✧✦✶✦✦

Love. Since the dawn of humanity, men and women have desired love in all its forms and often looked to nature to help manifest love. The idea of love potions and concoctions abounds in books, art, movies, and music, but it's all based on a long history of believing in the power of magical assistance. Whether in the form of a liquid or a special cake baked with alleged aphrodisiacs, the desire to obtain another person's love has manifested itself as more important than health or wealth. Every culture has gods and goddesses, even saints and holy figures, devoted to love and rituals, including love potions that were often carried out in their honor, asking for their assistance to bond two hearts as one.

It's the tactics and methods that prove surprising. Love potions of the past included some gruesome and disgusting ingredients. During the Byzantine civilization, newlyweds received love cakes made from a mixture of donkey milk and honey. Later, during medieval times, love cakes included the sweat of the person making them. The cake dough would be rubbed against every possible orifice of the person doing the spell casting, including armpits and genitalia. They believed giving the cakes to the one they loved would cause them to fall in love.

The ancient Roman author and naturalist Pliny the Elder wrote in his *Historia Naturalis* about love concoctions made from some questionable ingredients, including hyena eyes, which he believed to be an aphrodisiac. The popular European "Spanish fly" or "blister beetle" dates back to the time of Hippocrates, when the beetle was considered a sacred aphrodisiac. The potion was made from ground-up beetles and sold on the open market. It still is, despite it causing potentially permanent liver and kidney damage! In sixteenth-century France, blood was a powerful love potion ingredient, especially menstrual blood mixed with mandrake. This potion would bind in love any man and woman who drank it and prevent them from leaving one another. Menstrual blood was considered a potent ingredient for fertility, and mandrake root was known as a powerful aphrodisiac and fertility plant thousands of years ago, perhaps because the root resembles the human shape. According to folklore,

the root would shriek like a human when it was pulled up out of the ground and cause the person pulling it to go insane. Henbane was also popular during medieval times to attract love when worn on the body. If consumed, it had a powerful narcotic effect that would sedate the one desired into falling in love, but too much caused delirium and death.

Curative agents taken during medieval times might turn out to be deadly. Ground-up corpses, snails, animal dung, insects, and even toxic mercury were thrown into potions and brews, and people took them without hesitation just as modern humans take pills prescribed by their doctors without asking about deadly side effects. It was also about

The history of the human race is full of references to love potions. It was obviously highest on the list of desired spells, elixirs, and potions.

using what you had around, too. Ancient Egyptians mummified their dead and used some of the corpse materials to make into a powder to heal various ailments. Romans believed they could acquire vitality and vigor by drinking potions made of the blood and vital organs of gladiators. England's King Charles II used powdered skull mixed with alcohol in his own tincture, "King's Drops." Potions used human body parts such as bone, hair, fingernails, pubic hair, and organs of the dead to secure love.

Even the excrement of animals and humans was included in ancient love potions. Medieval practitioners believed that the white coating on dog dung known as Greek white could cure sore throats and lung ailments. The dung of individual animals could cure individual illnesses. Mice dung was good for killing internal worms and parasites. Sheep dung apparently cured jaundice. No evidence exists measuring these strange prescriptions against the power of suggestion, yet we might venture to guess that those taking the dung really believed it would do the trick.

That's not all, though. Since people were obsessed with romantic love, they took whatever they could afford and believed it would work, despite any proof to the contrary, including snail slime, human and animal urine, and toxic mold. Yes, mold. Ancient Greek and Roman doctors believed different types of mold could cure different ailments. At least they got that one right,

as the mold on bread (*penicillium glaucum* mold) was later discovered to have an antibiotic effect and became the forerunner of what was later called penicillin.

We've come a long way from those garish folk rituals, but today, we have social networking and sexting to replace the bizarre methods our ancestors used. Certainly, some herbs and plants have aphrodisiac properties, but it took a lot of trial and error of early medicine, old wives' tales, and crazy superstitious beliefs with some pretty disgusting starter ingredients to figure that out.

Potions were not just for love. Our ancestors sought good health, success in all endeavors, wealth, better sleep, and happy, healthy children. A potion existed for everything, if not a dozen, and plenty of wise elders and knowledgeable shamans, witch doctors, and herbalists were around to create a spell for any need. The desire for a quick and easy fix to something that ordinarily might take a lot of effort and hard work is as old as humans are. Today, we have self-help books, videos, pills, remedies, and gurus galore for finding a mate, improving relationships, having more and better sex, making more money, falling asleep more easily, getting in shape, losing weight, and everything else imaginable, each with their own products and prescriptions. Times may change, tactics may change, but the desire for easy change remains.

> Medieval practitioners believed that the white coating on dog dung known as Greek white could cure sore throats and lung ailments.

When it comes to potions in particular, people usually are looking for help with love, luck, success, happiness, and protection, but you can make a concoction for just about anything, such as a job interview, finding a new home, or even acing an exam or test. The ingredients should be symbolic in some way, and you can find potion recipes in books and on the Internet by the thousands. The only warning when it comes to mixing something suggested by a stranger is to make sure the ingredients can be consumed if you plan to drink it and that you aren't allergic to anything! When this author was little, she used to make a "motion potion" in the bathtub out of bubbly water poured into a colorful plastic cup. The potion served no real purpose (motion of what?) other than to have fun, but the act of creating drinks that infer magic and make things happen is inherent in us from the start!

A simple potion for clear skin might include actual healthy ingredients such as honey, water, and lemon mixed with a symbolic herb or collagen powder, known to promote a vibrant complexion. If you are using potions, you may as well create them with the body and spirit in mind; the difference is that you drink them consciously as you proclaim your desire for clear, youthful skin. The drink and the word create the actual spell when it comes to potions. A beauty potion like this one could be consumed two or three times a week and com-

Through the years, many potions have been concocted that amplify the desires of the consumer and instill an emotional quality or bring about a desired change. Stories exist about the effect of a potion, and there are recipes for various desired effects, but caution should be taken to check for any allergic reaction to the ingredients.

bines herbal remedies with actual nutrition, something many a "kitchen witch" knows all about.

Your potions will also be based on ingredients you can easily acquire. If a potion you find in a book asks for some obscure herb found only in Jamaica or Milan, you may wish to substitute it with something readily available unless you can order it online.

SPRAYS AND SPRITZERS

During hot summer months, you may want to cool down with a spray or spritzer that is also good for your skin. You can mix plenty of herbs with lukewarm or cool water and place the mixture into a small pump spray bottle. You can use essential oils, dried herbs, fresh herbs, or even mild herbal teas mixed with water. Try these suggestions, or experiment with your own:

- Chamomile—soothing, calming
- Lavender—refreshing, relaxing
- Eucalyptus—sharp, head-clearing, stimulating
- Mint—cooling, stimulating
- Rose—relaxing, sensual
- Sandalwood—warming, uplifting
- Peppermint—invigorating, clears the sinuses
- Jasmine—sensual, summery

Avoid the eye area when spritzing the face, and always test on the inside of your elbow for potential allergies.

SACHETS

Making a sachet is easy, even if you don't know how to sew or don't own a sewing machine. You can find beautiful fabric scraps or use a scarf or piece of cloth you find at home, stitching three sides together. Make it small enough to keep in a drawer or under a pillow. Place dried flowers or herbs of your choice inside the sachet and stitch to seal it. If you want to get more creative, stitch a cord around the third open side, so you can refill the sachet and tighten the cord to seal. Simply mix the ingredients, and put them inside the sachet.

Good Night Sleep Sachet: combine two tablespoons of dried lavender flowers, two tablespoons of dried chamomile flowers, one vanilla bean broken into tiny pieces, and one spoonful of Epsom salt.

Energy Sachet: combine two tablespoons of dried peppermint leaves, two tablespoons of dried rosemary, and two tablespoons of rosehips (minus the seeds).

You can see how easy it is to make sachets since you are using dried plant parts. Try different blends using cloves,

Sachets you make yourself are a great way to enjoy a variety of scents that have medicinal qualities.

rose petals, and other aromatics to see what you like and how they affect your energy. Sachets can be used to add scent to socks and underwear drawers or to keep with stored clothing. They also make wonderful homemade gifts or craft items you can sell online or at craft fairs. Holiday sachets can be made with appropriately decorative cloth and filled with seasonal herbs and plants like pine needles and dried cranberries for Yule or pumpkin and cloves for Samhain.

Make a stash of herbal sachets to be used in herbal baths, and keep them in a bowl or container by the tub. Use muslin for these, as herbs will pass through the finer cloth into the water more easily, but most types of thin, porous material will do. You can make a few foot-soaking sachets, too. If you are moving or putting clothing into storage, put some scented sachets in to keep things smelling fresh.

BITTERS

Bitters are a cocktail staple: bitter-flavored extracts made from infusing aromatic herbs, bark, plants, seeds, roots, flowers, and berries with alcohol. Much like a tincture, bitters result in a concentrated liquid that can be added to mixed drinks, usually just a dash or two because of the potency. Bitters are found at most grocery and liquor stores, but you can also make them by infusing them yourself if you have the time and wherewithal to learn. They date back to ancient Egyptian times when herbs were infused with wine and put in jars. In the Middle Ages, bitters became popularized as an herbal tonic and a part of herbal medicines used by the local apothecary.

Though bitters were used more for fun than for healing purposes, depending on the plant parts included, they also helped stop cold and flu symptoms and added energy as well as cured seasickness, stomachaches, and nausea. Digestive bitters were a part of mealtimes in many cultures to help digest a big dinner. They were consumed straight or with ice.

Pick your favorite types of herbs, spices, and plant parts to use as your ingredients. Decide if you will use vodka or whiskey. If you prefer a hint of vanilla, you can add vanilla extract, or, for a little sweetness, add molasses.

Combine the plant parts with the alcohol in an airtight jar and keep it in a cool, dark place for about a month. Shake it once a day. After a month, strain out the liquid into a clean jar with a piece of cheesecloth. You can also heat up the solid plant parts that you strained out in some water on the stove, then strain and add to the first batch you made for extra potency.

TINCTURES

Tinctures are liquid extracts from herbs that are taken orally and usually are extracted in alcohol. They can also be extracted in apple cider vinegar or vegetable glycerin if you are making them for children. They are easy to make and can be kept in small vials to carry with you to work. The extraction liquid serves to make the herbal properties stronger and more effective and helps them enter the bloodstream directly. Some tinctures work immediately, but others may require a buildup in the bloodstream over time to work effectively.

Tinctures are made similarly to tea, but the tinctures don't have to brew. They can be taken by the spoonful or a couple of medicine droppersful (called a "squeeze") and carry the same amount of effective herbal medicine as a cup of tea. A dropperful is the equivalent to approximately thirty drops. Adults can take two droppersful two or three times a day. Children under twelve can take one dropperful twice a day but check first with their pediatrician for counteractive herbs and medicines they might already be taking. They are not recommended for children under the age of two. After taking a tincture, it is best to not eat or drink for half an hour to let the ingredients get into the bloodstream first. Two droppersful can be added to a cup of warm water to make a tea.

Pregnant and nursing women can only take small amounts of tincture due to the alcohol content, or you can avoid that issue by making them without it; the same goes for children or those with an intolerance to alcohol. Many over-the-counter medicines contain alcohol, some in surprisingly high percentages.

Tinctures made with alcohol have a shelf life of several years if kept in a cool, dark place. It isn't necessary to refrigerate them. The great thing about tinctures is that they require only a clean, glass jar with a lid, preferably at least pint sized, herbs of your choice, and either vodka, rum, apple cider vinegar, or vegetable glycerin. That's it. Once you pick your herbs, you fill the jar one-third to one-half full with those herbs, then pour in some boiling water to dampen them (optional) or just fill the jar to the top with your alcoholic or nonalcoholic choice and stir the mixture. Put the lid on the jar and store it in a cool, dry place. Shake the jar daily and keep for at least three weeks, although some prefer even longer "steeping" times. Once you wish to use it, strain it through a cheesecloth. Store the liquid in dropper bottles or a clean jar. You can dispose of the used herbs in your compost pile.

Here are two easy recipes that can serve as templates for your own experimentation.

Peppermint Tincture: Place half a cup of dried peppermint leaves and ¼ cup of ground ginger root in a quart-sized glass jar and pour 1½ cups boiling water in the jar, covering the herbs. Fill the rest of the jar with your alcoholic (1½ cups vodka or rum) or nonalcoholic (apple cider vinegar or glycerin) choice. Put the lid on the jar, and store for two to six weeks. Shake the jar daily. When ready to use, strain out the liquid and store in smaller jars or droppers. Adults can take one dropperful or one teaspoon with or without water as needed. Children can take ten to twelve drops of the nonalcoholic tincture.

Application of a homemade liquid herbal extract tincture is usually done with a dropper on or under the tongue, but it can also be added to a beverage.

Maceration Versus Percolation

Tinctures can be made in two ways. Maceration is the process of soaking or steeping herbs or plant parts to make them soft and help separate the compounds out. Percolation is the process of seeping water through herbs or plant parts, filtering them via a porous material like a cloth or coffee filter. These two extraction methods are both popular but have different applications that may determine how you wish to make your tinctures.

Maceration soaks the herbs and involves biological and chemical processes to soften them and allow more of the active compounds to enter the liquid used in the tincture. Alcohol helps this process and is a mainstay in many tinctures. The problem with maceration is time and control. Once you've chopped or ground up your herbs or plant parts, you put them in a jar, cover them with a solvent made of alcohol and water (or just plain alcohol for a stronger tincture), then let the mixture sit for up to a month before straining the parts from the liquid, which serves as your tincture or extraction. This method takes time and a little bit of effort, but no equipment or tools are needed beyond a jar and some type of cloth or filter to strain out the parts from the liquid.

Percolation is faster and easier. You grind the dried herbs and plant parts, moistened with water and alcohol or just alcohol, into a porous cloth, cone, or strainer sitting inside a jar, then let the mixture sit for 12 to 24 hours. Think about a coffee percolator and how the water goes through the grinds and into the pot below in a dripping process. With percolation, it's all about gravity pulling the liquid down through the herbs. This will allow the ingredients to moisten through the herbs/plant parts so that the liquid drips down from the bottom of the filter and into the jar below. This is your tincture. Percolation results in a stronger tincture because the ingredients are fresher and have not been distilled for weeks as with a maceration. Both are perfectly fine ways to extract the compounds from herbs and plants and create a potent tincture. Use the one you resonate most with or have time for.

Tinctures are popular items online and in health stores, but they are so easy and inexpensive to make that it's better to make your own and avoid unnecessary ingredients or high packaging costs. They also make great gifts for friends and family, and you can order vials, droppers, or boxes to put them in, or you can make them in larger amounts and give

Continued...

them in small, decorative mason jars. Though it is often the alcoholic content that adds to their potency, it is not a necessary ingredient. If you prefer something other than vodka or rum, experiment.

Chamomile Tincture: Use the same process as above but with ½ cup to 1 cup of dried chamomile flowers. This makes a soothing, calming tincture that works well for children and can even be given to infants (minus the alcohol, and use just a few drops!), but always check first with your doctor or your child's doc- tor. Try the same tincture with lavender flowers instead of chamomile. Make sure that whatever herbs or plants you use are edible! Feel free to mix and match and to try using more than one herb or plant in a tincture to see what flavors complement each other.

HERBAL POPSICLES

On those hot summer days, you can enjoy your herbal infusions and syrups in cold teas or popsicles. Kids love to make and eat them, and they are incredibly easy. You can try the lazy way and buy herbal tea bags already prepared or make your own. Once the tea has cooled a bit, pour it into popsicle molds and stick in the freezer. Here are a few recipes to try, but don't be afraid to get creative. If you are afraid that they won't be sweet enough, add in a touch of honey or natural sweetener. You can use any variety of herbal teas on the market to make all kinds of popsicles.

Easy Raspberry–Peach Popsicles: Boil two cups of water, pour into a bowl, and steep six raspberry tea bags for 6 to 8 minutes. Boil two cups of water, pour into a bowl, and steep six peach tea bags for 6 to 8 minutes. Let the teas in both bowls cool for a few minutes. Add sweetener to taste during this step. Pour into popsicle molds. Add fresh raspberries and peach slices or chunks as desired. Put into freezer. Once almost solid, put in popsicle sticks if they are not a part of the mold. Put back in freezer.

Elderberry Popsicles: Put a handful each of elderberries, rosehips, and hibiscus flowers into a tea bag or ball strainer. Place into a pot of boiling water. Remove from heat and let the pot sim-

Herbal popsicles are a great way to beat the heat and to give your family a healthy treat to help them cool down while restricting sugar in their diet.

mer. Steep the plant parts for 12 to 15 minutes. Remove the tea bag or ball strainer and add a touch of honey or sweetener to taste. Put the liquid into the popsicle molds. Freeze. Remove before solid if you need to stick in the sticks. Freeze again and enjoy!

Lavender and Lemon Balm Popsicles: Boil four cups of water in a saucepan, and pour over six whole, fresh lavender blossoms and ¼ cup fresh lemon balm into a quart-sized glass jar. Steep for 15 minutes, then strain out the plant parts with a mesh cloth or sieve into another clean jar. Add in two to four tablespoons of honey or sweetener, seal the jar, and shake it up. When mixed, pour into the popsicle molds.

You can always add ice cubes to cool the tea faster. Why not make herbal ice cubes while you're at it, or get a slushie machine and make herbal slushies? Kids won't hesitate to get their daily dose of beneficial herbs when you make them a slushie! If you don't have time to make the teas, you can buy organic, chemical-free juices of all kinds to mix with herbs, even lemonade. Avoid drinks high in sugar, though. The idea here is to get kids to take their medicine and love it without getting them hooked on sugary drinks that will lead to future health problems. You can also add in some sparkling water to make herbal spritzers. For adults, add in red or white wine with bubbly water to make spritzers, herbal sangrias, or grown-up popsicles.

HERBAL GUMMIES

Gummies are all the rage and a great way to get children to take their herbal medicines and syrups. They can be purchased online or make them yourself. Let the kids choose the flavor and help. Gummies are made with various ingredients mixed with gelatin, a translucent, colorless, and flavorless food derived from the collagen from animal parts. You can buy vegan gelatin substitutes as well as grass-fed, animal-based gelatins. You will also need a gelatin mold or ice cube tray. Kids like animal shapes, so look in your local craft or cooking store for gummy molds or fun-shaped ice cube trays. Gummies should keep for a few weeks. Let kids enjoy up to three a day for an extra immune system boost. Adults can eat them, too.

Herbal Tea Gummies: Bring one cup of water to a boil. Steep two herbal tea bags in the hot water for about 4 minutes. Pour 1½ tablespoons of gelatin into another cup of water and mix. Com-

bine the gelatin water with the tea water and add 1½ tablespoons of honey or sweetener (or to taste). Mix ingredients together. Pour ingredients into your mold or ice cube trays. Put into the refrigerator and let it set for at least an hour before using.

Gummies are a great way to sneak a more "good-for-you" treat to your kids.

Elderberry Syrup Gummies #1: Combine half a cup of dried elderberries, ⅓ cup of dried rosehips, ¼ cup of cinnamon stick chunks, and three cups of apple or grape juice in a small to medium pan and bring it to a simmer. Let it simmer for 20 minutes, then remove from heat. Strain the liquid. Measure two cups of this liquid and add more juice to taste if needed. Put half a cup of the juice into a glass bowl and refrigerate until cold. Then, sprinkle three tablespoons of gelatin on top, and let it sit for a minute. Heat the rest of the juice until hot, but not boiling, and pour over the cold, gelatin-covered juice, mixing thoroughly with a spoon or whisk until the gelatin is dissolved. Add honey or sweetener. Pour into molds or trays and let refrigerate.

Elderberry Syrup Gummies #2: Prepare your molds or ice cube trays using one tablespoon of coconut oil, so the gummies will slide right out. Take ¼ cup premade, cooled elderberry syrup, and put it into a two-cup measuring cup. Stir in ¼ cup of gelatin and whisk thoroughly. Add half a cup of hot (not boiling) water and keep stirring until smooth. Add another ¾ cup of elderberry syrup, and mix. Pour into your molds or trays and refrigerate until firm. You can add a touch of honey or sweetener to taste if it isn't sweet enough for the kids.

Passion Fruit Tea Gummies: Put ¾ cup of hot water and three passion fruit tea bags into a saucepan and let the tea steep for 10 minutes. Take half a cup of that tea liquid and transfer it to a glass bowl along with the gelatin. Set this aside. Heat the rest of the passion fruit tea and water just to a simmer, then remove the tea bags. Add six tablespoons of gelatin and water mixture to the tea and stir thoroughly until it is fully dissolved. Take the pan off the heat and add in two to three tablespoons of honey or sweetener to taste. If any white foam rises to the top, remove it with a spoon, and do not use it. Pour the liquid into your mold or trays and refrigerate until firm. You can replace the passion fruit tea in the recipe above with just about any tea.

Herbal gummies are a snap when you learn how easy they are to make, and you can mix and match herbs, flowers, teas, and even a touch of spices like cinnamon, cloves, and pepper to create unique flavors, each with their own healing properties. The prep and cook time for gummies rarely takes more than half an hour, and most of these recipes make a good-sized batch of gummies, depending on your mold size. You can add a tiny bit of food coloring to the mixture if you wish to make them more appealing to kids.

WITCHES' BOTTLE

A witches' bottle, or witches' jar, is not the bottle or jar you put your herbal teas and tinctures in. It is a powerful, magical tool used to break a curse or negative spell that someone has cast upon you. The bottle/jar is filled with items like urine; old, rusty nails; dirt; glass shards; sharp pins; and other nasty objects that you hide somewhere on your property, preferably buried in a hole in the ground and away from places children might dig it up. It keeps negative and evil energies and people away when buried near your home. If you already suspect that someone has cursed you, toss the entire bottle/jar into a fire. When it explodes in the flames, that means the curse on you has been lifted.

Depending on your intention, you can fill your bottle or jar with whatever objects make sense to you to carry out your will or spell. A love bottle would include things like flower petals, red wine, rose quartz, and other items associated with love. You would leave the bottle open in your bedroom or under your bed to draw love to you. A money bottle would be filled with a green liquid, a four-leaf clover or lucky charms, and some small coins.

You can even use the bottles to heal. If you or someone else is sick, fill the bottle with items that represent healing such as particular stones, teas, infusions, herbs, charms, etc. and then leave it in the room, lid off, of the sick person to absorb their illness. Then, dispose of the bottle by either dumping it out or burying it.

If you don't consider yourself a witch, these bottles and jars are also known as spell jars and work according to the same principle of filling them with appropriate items to aid in spell casting. For those involved in herbal medicine and healing, these jars come in handy for steeping infusions and decoctions (more on this later) and storing herbs and plant parts for herbal teas, baths, syrups, and other uses. Always keep bottles and jars of every size on hand.

CASTING THE SPELL

Now that we've looked at many of the tools of spell casting, we can get down to the actual methods of creating and manifesting the outcomes we desire, using the forces and laws of nature to the benefit of ourselves and anyone involved. Remember the Laws of Reciprocity and Attraction. Remember the Threefold Law and the law of karma: "An ye harm none, do what thou will." It's time to bend the will of nature to do our bidding.

Natural magic is exactly what it sounds like. It is the practice of working with the laws of nature and the natural forces that govern our world. It is considered an occult practice, even though it has roots that date back to the earliest humans on the planet. Natural magic is where all other belief systems sprung from because as we learned more and more about the scientific laws at work in our world, our beliefs evolved, too.

However, a few people today are still around who know the power of working with the laws of nature and the gifts of the natural world whether in divination, summoning guides and spirits, healing, ceremonial magic, rituals, astrology, alchemy, numerology, and a host of other studies and traditions that focused on working in alignment with nature, not against it.

Natural magic was the foundation of modern sciences of botany, which came from herbology, and even astronomy, biology, and chemistry. We first learned about nature by directly interacting with it before we became adept enough to try to dissect the scientific laws and mechanisms behind it.

✶✶✶ FOLK MAGIC ✶✶✶

The term "folk magic" refers to the practices of common folk and is interchangeable with natural magic, kitchen witchery, botanical magic, and practical magic. Folk magic was practiced by European pagans who were often persecuted for witchcraft, even though they were using plants, herbs, roots, and nature to heal and cure. We might even call them herbalists today. Their education came from getting hands-on experience with the plants that grew in their environment and over time whether it was for medicinal or magical purposes.

In the villages they lived in, those who practiced folk magic were the doctors, nurses, pharmacists, and overall healers for anyone with an ailment of the body, mind, or spirit. Folk magic is also a part of African American Hoodoo, the nineteenth-century magical practice that combines some elements of African and Haitian Voodoo or Voudon with Amer-

icanized folk magic influenced by Native Americans, Europeans, and even Christianity, with many rituals involving images and statues of Jesus or the saints alongside curious items specific to folk magic. Hoodoo folk magic spread into the American South, where it took hold in rural areas mainly such as the Bayou Country of Louisiana and in the Appalachian Mountain range.

Eventually, Hoodoo folk magic became known as conjuring and included working with spirits and entities to assist the living and the dead. One could conjure a spirit to assist a dead villager to the other side as well as protect those alive in the village. If someone was sick, they visited the local conjurer to see what kind of root, herb mixture, tea, or spell could heal their maladies. Some of the favorite flowers used in Hoodoo healing include:

- Bluebonnet—For protection
- Lily—For resurrection of body or spirit
- Thistle—For fidelity and loyalty
- Rose—For love
- Violet—For forgiveness
- Magnolia—For commitment and devotion

Folk magic in any form utilizes many of the same tools as witchcraft, Wicca, paganism, and Earth-based traditions. Plants, herbs, spices, roots, stones, crystals, powders, infusions, and tinctures were all utilized in spells and conjuring work by those who were considered the wisest and most experienced (usually the village elders and women). Folk magic would also be requested for love, money, luck, success, banishing negative people and spirits, breaking a curse or hex, cleansing homes, winning legal battles, finding a new job,

Working with nature and visible, natural laws led early men and women to gradually expand their knowledge and understand the glories of the world around them.

protection against violence and gossip, and even some darker desires such as inspiring lust, getting someone to fall in love with you, getting revenge on someone, breaking up with someone, and dominating another person.

Divination and psychic development were also the goals of the Hoodoo practitioner either for himself or herself or at the request of a client who came to ask for assistance from spirits on the other side. This type of folk magic employed cards (such as Tarot), tea leaves, seashells, or bones that were cast and read to seek guidance, direction, and, at times, warnings of pending dangers.

✱✱✱ BOOK OF SHADOWS ✱✱✱

Whether you call it a journal, a diary, an herbal recipe book, a grimoire, or a spell book, having your own sacred and private Book of Shadows allows you to keep all your knowledge, experience, and wisdom in one place. A Book of Shadows is a spiritual and personal collection used by witches, pagans, and Wiccans to keep track of their magical journey and undertakings. The end result is a valuable resource you can turn to for spells, herbal remedies, rituals, infusion directions, favorite essential oils and blends, and information at your fingertips gleaned from your own practice that includes your own creative and imaginative touches.

Once called grimoires, perhaps related to the Old French root words for "grammar" and "glamour," a Book of Shadows is a magical textbook that has been used for thousands of years by those who practiced the craft, from sorcerers to witches, and understood that words have incredible power (thus the use of spells and written intentions). Putting words down on paper made them more powerful still as if binding them for all eternity in the same manner as the texts used by traditional religions. Keeping everything in one book also made it a lot easier to spell cast without having to remember recipes and chants, much in the same way people keep recipe books to avoid leaving out a key ingredient.

Making a Book of Shadows involves finding or creating a journal-style book that you can decorate to your heart's content with symbols and images that mean something to you. You can buy blank journals of every size, style, and cover design, or you can make one yourself with paper and binding of your choice, ranging anywhere from fancy parchment to embroidery or cloth. Tons of styles are available in specialty shops and online if you are not the artistic type, so fear not. Some people like the idea

Making a Book of Shadows is similar to keeping a personal journal except you are keeping notes about your craft.

of using a three-ring binder, so they can easily add or remove pages and recipes. You can make one of these as a "travel Book of Shadows" to take to rituals or coven meetings while keeping your private book at home. Find a few pens that write easily and match the cover in some way. Yes, any pen will do, but this is what you will be writing important things with. Make it as special as the book itself.

Decide if your Book of Shadows will be a daily journal or an organized, categorized collection of spells, recipes, and rituals with cool dividers. Anything goes, but the most important thing is that the book is easy, comfortable, and feels right for YOU. If you have been practicing for a long time, you will no doubt have more than one Book of Shadows, as one gi-

gantic, heavy book will be difficult to take with you for outside spells.

In addition to the usual spells and herbal recipes, think about including your own musings and comments on how they worked, or didn't, for you. Perhaps you may want to pass this collection down to your child, so think about writing it in an intimate and personal style, describing things in enough detail that they can be understood by someone else. If you make your own tools, add a section on crafts and tool making with pictures and diagrams. If you are into correspondences, add tables and charts with colors, planets, zodiac signs, gods and goddesses, moon phases, etc., for easy reference. Include a dedication page to the gods and goddesses or a special person who helped you on your journey

A Book of Shadows (BOS), or grimoire, is like a diary in which you store information for later reference. The above photo is of a Book of Shadows owned by Gerald Gardner, a key figure in reviving Wicca in the twentieth century. Your Book of Shadows should be where you track what works best in your life.

and a section for the laws and traditions your coven follows or that you follow as a solitary practitioner. This can include the Threefold Law, the Charge of the Goddess, and the Wiccan Rede. An entire section can be a list of herbs and plants and their various uses in spell casting and as medicines. Make notes of which you prefer and how they helped heal you or a loved one.

This is how information gets passed down to future generations, so don't rush. Even if you decide to never show anyone your book, it behooves you to be thorough and dedicated to capturing every aspect of the craft and every nugget of information you've gained even if only to make it easier on you later when your memory needs the boost.

A Book of Shadows is a wonderful photo memory book of rituals and celebrations, so add pictures you print out that you can one day look back on to see how far you've come. Record recurring and symbolic dreams, inspirations and intuitions, and insights you've gleaned from rituals and meditations. A whole section can be devoted to your favorite blessings, chants, songs, prayers, and mantras.

This will be one of your most important and sacred tools, so cleanse and purify it often and keep it clean and free from coffee stains and food. Treat your Book of Shadows with reverence and respect, for it is an ongoing representation of your personal journey with your chosen practice.

✳ ✳ ✳ ✳ ✳ ✳ SIGILS AND SYMBOLS ✳ ✳ ✳ ✳ ✳ ✳

Symbols have as much power as words. Our subconscious minds respond to symbols and archetypal images that have universally understood meanings. What the conscious mind may not comprehend, the deeper levels of mind do. Sigils are personal symbols used in a special form of magic called, appropriately, "sigil magic." They are as simple or ornate as the individual using them and have a long and ancient history dating back to medieval ceremonial magic.

Similar to talismans and amulets, sigils incorporate imagery that has an occult or hidden meaning from anyone but the practitioner. The word is derived from the Latin word *sigillum*, which means "seal." During medieval times, seals and sigils incorporated darker images such as demons and entities as well as angels. *The Lesser Key of Solomon*, an anonymously written gri-

moire on demonology compiled in the mid-seventeenth century, lists seventy-two different sigils that represented the hierarchy of hell for magickal rituals alone. Each sigil summoned a different entity or spirit and often incorporated the name of the entity in Latin.

Today, many witches and pagans enjoy having a personal sigil that best represents who they are. Sigils might be drawn or designed by the practitioner, or an artist might be hired for such purpose. A personal sigil could be the image of a power animal or spirit guide, a particular phase of the moon, a god or goddess, or anything else that meant something and amplified the ability to spell cast. They could be described as visual mantras.

Just as corporations today have their logos and brand images, sigils represent the person and the outcome they want to achieve. It is not necessary to have just one sigil. You can have as many as you want to work with. They can be any shape, size, or color and be made from metal, wood, cloth, or stone. The key is to make the imagery count. If doing a general sigil for yourself, think of something you might get as a tattoo. Do you resonate with wolves? Butterflies? The sun? The moon? Coming up with a singular sigil is difficult because it requires you to dig deep and intuit the correct symbol you feel represents your authentic self. You can always do several if it's too hard to pin down one characteristic.

For particular spells or intentions, a sigil for wealth might be a dollar sign. For love, perhaps a rose, a heart, or two heart halves that make a whole. For success, a house or big car. The sigil itself can be the written intention within a pentacle or circle. Whatever you choose, it

A modern way of showing a performing artist that you enjoy them is to create a sigil with your hands to form a heart, arguably the most familiar symbol of love.

must have a deeper effect on you than just being pretty or cool to look at. Because sigils were occult symbols, they often hid the real meaning behind the imagery or used letters and numbers to convey meaning. You can come up with some kind of code such as a sentence describing your intention minus the vowels or use the number correspondences to the letters of a short intention. Some people resonate more with images and others with words. Find out what you resonate with most. Think about the essence of what you want it to convey. Perhaps a happy, smiley face can be used to describe and capture the essence of joy or a joyful heart instead of writing the word "happiness."

If you are not the artistic type, you can easily find someone to design the perfect sigil or find one that already exists but speaks to your heart and soul. The best way to figure out what you want is to go into a meditative state and ask for the right sigil to appear on the screen of your mind. Ask the deities for signs. Look for repeated words, images, or numbers. Pay attention to images and words you see on television, computer screens, cell phones, billboards, or even restaurant menus. Before you go to sleep, tell yourself you will dream of the sigil. It will come to you. Don't force your sigil to appear. In the meantime, you can use intention sigils for sigil magic the same way you use candles for candle magic. Your own personal symbol may still be evolving as you are with your practice and your craft.

Once you've settled on your sigil or sigils, you want to charge them as you would any other magical tool before spell casting. This imbues the right energy into the symbols, so they can carry out your desires. You might look at each one and visualize the meaning as you burn incense or take an herbal bath. You can meditate on it, dance with it in your hands, chant over it, light candles, or stand under a full moon and ask the goddess to impart her energy upon it— anything goes, as the charging ritual will be as individual as the sigil itself.

Then you can place a sigil on your altar, carry one on you in a charm or in a mojo bag, or bring one to work and place it on the wall. If anyone asks, you don't have to tell them what it is. If you're concerned about the boss getting too nosy, keep it in your desk drawer. Think of royal houses of kings and queens and their crests or the symbols of knights upon their shields. This is your personal crest. You don't have to explain it to anyone.

Say you desire to be a famous and successful writer. You might have a sigil with a pen and paper or an old-fashioned typewriter on it, or you might do a paper sigil containing the words, "I manifest a successful career as a novelist now." Keep it present, keep it focused, but don't get too vague or specific. Don't say, "I want to be a writer" because the sigil may attract a job for you writing something you have no desire or talent for. You can cast a spell for the perfect writing jobs in your field to appear using the sigil or for an increasing income of a certain amount (always add this or something better) from your existing writing trade. Incorporate the sigil into the spell itself for more power and impact. Hold it in your hand, visualizing the perfect writing situation. Set it into a decorative bowl, and light a green and gold candle on either side to spell cast for making a prosperous and fulfilling living as a writer. Sigils are not meant to simply be looked at; they are channels of the natural forces you are working with and, when activated, can help spells manifest more quickly and accurately.

Once you've settled on your sigil or sigils, you want to charge them as you would any other magical tool before spell casting.

Sigils are not black magic or white magic. They are symbols to be used in whatever way the practitioner chooses. They are tools for affecting change and influencing natural forces. Use them wisely, and don't be afraid to choose a new sigil as you evolve and change. Your magical practice should always evolve with you.

✦ ✦ ★ ★ ★ JOURNEYING ★ ★ ★ ✦ ✦

Shamans journeyed into the Upper World and Lower World to find guides and spirits for those who came to them. The shaman might meet up with a bright, glowing angelic being or a wolf or black bear. The shaman would return to reality and tell the person who or what their guide was. The person then could build a relationship with that guide either via the shaman's journeying or their own attempts at communicating and connecting through a spiritual practice.

Human and angelic beings usually inhabit the Upper World with animal guides in the Middle World and Lower World. That did not mean that animal guides were any less important, though, as animals were often considered symbolic, even archetypal, of the qualities and characteristics the person sought in the first place. As an example, the author of this book took part in an intensive, three-day shamanic course that involved finding a partner from the group and taking turns journeying to find their animal guide, sometimes referred to as "totem." This author's partner found a black bear, and when he returned to a conscious, awakened state, he informed her. Immediately, the negative qualities of a black bear came to mind—belligerence, aggressiveness, and directness—but during the course of the event, so did the dawning realization that other black bear qualities—positive ones such as courage, strength, and personal power—needed to be worked on. To this day, this author can call upon the black

Find a natural place where you feel relaxed and at peace so you can request a spirit guide to join you while you are journeying.

bear within herself for guidance, direction, and general strength.

If you don't have access to a neighborhood shaman, you can find your own guides by doing guided visualizations or meditations that involve finding a sacred, quiet place where you invite your guide to appear to you and then engage in connection. You ask the guide to come to you whenever you appear in your sacred space. You can simply visit with your guide and be present to any insights that arise or ask the guide a specific question. Many guided visualizations are available online and offline for you to try, or you can make up your own.

Find a place where you can be alone and relax into a deep meditation for at least half an hour. Close your eyes, and imagine you are walking down (or up) a staircase. You are not afraid because the staircase is well lit and you feel totally safe. As you descend the staircase, count from ten back to one. When you reach one, you are at the bottom of the staircase, and a door is in front of you. You open the door and go through it into a beautiful, peaceful sanctuary. Imagine this sanctuary as a place you want to return to again and again. Make it look any way you wish, but it must be inviting and make you feel totally safe.

Find a spot to sit down, perhaps a bench or at a table. Now look around your sanctuary and take it all in, breathing deeply. Say out loud, or in your head, "I now invite my guide to come sit with me in my sanctuary." Maybe repeat it three times. Then, be patient and allow anything that happens to happen without judgment or censorship. If nothing happens, invite again. If still nothing happens, thank your guide and say you will be back again another time and you hope they will reveal themselves to you. Your guides, like you, may need a little bit of coaxing.

If someone or something appears, welcome it. Ask it to sit by you. Ask it if it has a name. Listen to what the guide tells you. Become comfortable communicating. Ask your guide something specific you seek to know or for general life advice. Listen for the answers. Don't judge.

Once about half an hour has passed, you will begin to feel restless or notice that your guide is, so go out the door back to the staircase. Counting from one to ten, rise a step at a time until you reach ten. Open your eyes and return to a waking state.

It is helpful to notice how you feel when you open your eyes. Do you feel blocked? Tight in a particular part of the body? Fearful or anxious? This helps you identify possible blocks and obstacles that are keeping you from accessing your guide or getting the answers you need, or your discussion with your guide may have raised some deep, subconscious programming and issues that now need to be dealt with. Take notice.

When someone comes into your sacred space, do not be alarmed if they don't look like the typical "guide" you were hoping for. It might be an ugly troll or a giant. It might be an old man or a beautiful child. Welcome the guide to sit with you in your space and ask them if they have a name. Open the lines of communication. Speak with your guide until you feel it is time to go or you can sense that they wish to leave.

If a deceased ancestor or loved one appears, even if it was someone you didn't know well or like much, allow them to offer what wisdom and guidance they have. Sometimes, the people we didn't get along with have the most to teach us.

These guides will be spirits you can call upon at any time, including during spell casting, rituals, and in quiet prayer and meditation. As you grow and evolve as a human being, your guides might come and go, changing as you do, so that you are always working with the right guides for where you are in your spiritual evolution. Consider them like friends who move away to be replaced with new friends, yet the old friends are always around if you seek them out.

> If a deceased ancestor or loved one appears, even if it was someone you didn't know well or like much, allow them to offer what wisdom and guidance they have.

✧✦✶✶✶ SPIRIT AND ANIMAL GUIDES ✧✦✶✶✶

The belief in spirit guides in human, angel, or animal form is as old as belief itself. When someone or something died, our primitive ancestors had no sci-entific understanding of the finality of death in a medical sense, that the person or body was no longer functioning. The person or animal wasn't around anymore in a physical sense yet beyond death was another realm of existence filled with those who once walked in this world. Those beings could still be communicated with (usually by the wise elders) in rituals and ceremonies.

Even something as simple as a prayer could be turned into a plea for help from the spirit realm. Nothing was ever really dead and gone; it simply changed form and went from physical to aethereal. Beyond our dead ancestors and animal friends, the belief in angels and higher spirits/deities meant that the possibility still existed for us to talk to them, to ask them for guidance and direction, to petition them for healing.

Finding and using spirit guides have become mainstays of most nature traditions from Native American to Wiccan. Honoring the dead and honoring the other levels of reality beyond our physical plane went hand in hand and still do. Anyone can access their guides in the Otherworld. Even traditional religions have their angels, saints, and gods to help mortal men and women by directing and guiding them or providing comfort and strength in times of need. It's the adult version of a child's imaginary friend.

ANIMALS

Once you meet your guide, or guides, as you might have more than one, you have access to them at any time by turning within and finding that center, that quiet place. Don't worry if an animal shows up when you were hoping for an angel. Animal companions and guides are a powerful part of Native and

We see animals as fellow travelers on Earth, and we form bonds with them. After they have left this earth in body, a spirit remains that can be called upon for guidance.

indigenous traditions that honor the creatures of the sky, land, and sea as much as they honor two-legged guides. Animal guides allow us to transcend our human limitations and see things from a different perspective. As a hawk or eagle, you can fly above and get the bigger-picture view of your life. As a wolf, you can learn the skills of being alone or working with a pack. As a horse, you can come to appreciate your physicality more. As a beaver, you can find your inner productivity and industriousness.

Michael Harner, who lived with shamans for years to study their ways and traditions, wrote in *The Way of the Shaman*: "Shamans have long believed their powers were the powers of the animals, of the plants, of the sun, of the basic energies of the universe. In the garden Earth they have drawn upon their assumed powers to help save other humans from illness and death, to provide strength in daily life, to commune with their fellow creatures, and to live a joyful existence in harmony with the totality of nature." Harner reported that shamans utilized "power animals" in all of their rituals and traditions and were convinced that animals and humans were interrelated. They believed that animal characteristics were commonly portrayed in human form. The coyote might represent the mischievousness of humans. The raven was their wisdom and keen insight.

Native American and other indigenous cultures also revered animals for their powers and symbolic nature in the human world. The Lakota Sioux elders would see and speak to animal spirits during visions. Aborigines encountered and interacted with animal spirits in the dream world. The idea that humans and animals could coexist and even help each other evolve is as old as time but,

sadly, one that doesn't resonate strongly today except in pagan and Earth traditions.

Animals impart wisdom to us via feelings, symbols, images, and their specific characteristics. A cold-blooded critter might teach us how to adapt to certain changes in our environment. A whale or dolphin might be the playful part of us we are ignoring or indicate that we are social, playful creatures at heart when we have been too serious. Animal guides are often not our favorite animals but those that have something to teach us or bring out in us. However, deceased pets can be guiding spirits, too. That leads us to a familiar subject.

FAMILIARS

Witches of legend and lore have been associated with animal companions called familiars. Usually black cats, familiars were supernatural creatures that assisted the witch in spells and rituals and provided companionship, too. These familiars were physical creatures but possessed otherworldly abilities that were either benevolent or malicious, depending on the owner's intent.

Familiars became popular in folklore, fairy tales, and stories, and today's pop culture continues to portray the evil witch with her black cat or flying monkeys and the good witch with white doves and sweet, little mice scampering around her feet. The familiar could be demonic in nature or a fairy presence, personal totem, or alter ego to the witch or practitioner. The familiar might be an astral creature or a fully physical one, but it always served the witch and enhanced the witch's powers and abilities.

The familiar also had healing powers and could protect its owner with magic,

which made it the perfect best friend and companion, especially if the witch was working with negative energies or was in danger of someone else's black magic or curses. Familiars could pick up on sensitive

The most common familiar, at least in popular culture, is the black cat, but any animal can be a familiar, such as an owl, rat, or raven.

Questions to Ask Your Spirit Guide

Whether you seek a spirit guide in angel, human, or animal form, here are some important questions to ask yourself:

• Does my intuition/gut trust this person/animal/entity?

• Does a particular bird or animal keep showing up in my life?

• Am I drawn to a certain animal or creature?

• Do I associate myself with a particular animal or creature based on their traits?

• What parts of me do I wish to build up, and what type of guide could most help me?

• What kind of guide would make me too afraid to be comfortable?

• Am I open to this guide and not afraid to reveal my deepest secrets?

• Does the name of a person keep coming into my mind for no apparent reason?

• Do I identify with a particular type of person or animal based on my traits?

• Have I dreamt of a person or animal over and over?

By pondering these questions, you allow your mind to become receptive to the answers and hopefully guide you right to your perfect familiar or spirit helper. You cannot choose your helper. They must come to you and choose you. Ask them to make themselves known. Ask the universe for dreams and signs to help you readily identify them and validate your intuition. Don't force a relationship with an entity or animal just because you like them. Working with magic is a deep craft, and the ones you seek direction and assistance from are critical to your success.

vibrations and could read people to quickly identify whether they were good or bad.

Lest you think only cats made good familiars, African witches had monkeys, lizards, leopards, jackals, and snakes among their chosen animal guides. Even an insect could be a loyal familiar if it did the job of assisting the witch. Witches preferred familiars found in the animal and creature world to humans because of their close relationship with nature. To choose the proper familiar, a witch might cast a spell for insight or perform a ritual to invite the familiar to appear. The witch would intuit whether what did appear was a friend or foe.

If you seek your own familiar, you might start paying attention to the animals and creatures that show up in your life. You can invite the familiar in via meditation, guided visualization, spell casting, or intention setting. Speak a prayer out loud asking your familiar to come forward. You may find that more than one familiar comes forward. Having more than one loyal assistant and companion is perfectly fine if it suits you.

The most important thing in choosing a familiar is comfort and a sense of trust, for this familiar will accompany you on your astral journeys, into the ritual circle, and on the journeys of life if you ask it to. As with any companions, make sure you get along.

ANIMAL QUALITIES

A particular animal's symbolic characteristics can be interpreted in many ways, but here are some traits that may resonate with you when attracting an animal guide.

Alligators—Strength, cunning

Anteaters—Curious, troubleshooters

Antelopes—Active, alert

Ants—Productive, industrious

Armadillos—Grounded, trusting, peaceful

Badgers—Courage, aggressiveness, problem-solvers

Bats—Mysterious, intuitive, secretive

Bears—Strong, bold, courageous, protective

Beavers—Industrious, resourceful

Bees—Helpful, positive, creative

Birds—Able to see the bigger picture, free, soaring

Buffalo—Strong, bold, determined

Butterflies—Transformative, love change

Cats—Psychic, intuitive, solitary, resourceful

Coyotes—Wise, aware, quick thinkers, tricksters

Cranes—Graceful, balanced, wise

Crows—Creative, powerful, magical

Deer—Nurturing, peaceful, sensitive

Dogs—Loyal, capable, committed

Dolphins—Playful, communicative, expressive

Doves—Peace, gentleness, harmony

Dragonflies—Change, new perspective, thriving

Eagles—Powerful, wise, insightful

Fireflies—Luminous, free, light givers

Foxes—Clever, resourceful, agile

Frogs—Wise, peaceful, healing

Goats—Playful, diligent, resourceful

Gorillas—Strong, dominant, powerful

Hawks—Aware, honest, wise

Horses—Graceful, free, wild

Hummingbirds—Resourceful, lucky, healing

Jaguars—Powerful, exotic, cunning

Kangaroos—Friendly, resourceful, honest

Lambs—Innocent, gentle, happy

Lions—Proud, wise, protective

Lizards—Cunning, sly, aware

Mice—Resourceful, able, curious

Otters—Industrious, playful, joyful

Oxen—Strong, determined, stubborn

Peacocks—Proud, self-confident, glorious

Pelicans—Lucky, playful, resourceful

Porcupines—Humble, hardworking, curious

Possums—Fun, curious, clever

Rabbits—Productive, efficient

Raccoons—Curious, family-oriented, playful

Rams—Proud, strong, determined

Ravens—Wise, mystical, knowing

Salmon—Determined, persistent

Seagulls—Free, solitary, soaring

Seals—Happy, family-oriented, clever

Snails—Undeterred, persevering, focused

Snakes—Cunning, powerful, protective

Spiders—Resourceful, connected, industrious

Squirrels—Hardworking, insightful, forward-thinking

Swans—Graceful, beautiful, calm

Tigers—Fierce, knowing, instinctual

Turtles—Wise, intuitive, knowing

Whales—Intelligent, wise, leaders

Wolves—Loyal, wise, powerful

The characteristics of animal spirits and guides help us understand what we most need to bring ourselves into balance and harmony or what traits most complement our own. Often, the guide that shows up is one we may not expect yet, on a deeper level, realize is the perfect one for where we are at in our lives—even creepy, crawly spiders. In his book *Animal-Speak: The Spiritual and Magical Powers of Creatures Great and Small*, author Ted Andrews writes, "By studying and reading about the animals, birds, fish, insects, reptiles, etc. you encounter in your life, you can understand more about the circumstances you also encounter." These allies become a part of our team that we meet and work with not just when we cast spells or do rituals but throughout our lives. Imagine having a dragonfly show up to help us learn to gain a new perspective or a lion appear in our dreams when we most need the courage to overcome a challenging situation; that is the power of animal guides. Andrews goes on to say, "You will learn how to draw upon those energies most effectively in dealing with life situations."

Sometimes, we might be drawn to a type of flower, plant, or tree. Yes, tree spirits and spirits of the green do exist, so don't count out the possibility that nature is filled with unusual guides. Even mountains, streams, rock formations, and the ocean can offer insights and direction if we stop long enough to listen for it. Honor whatever shows up, and embrace the messages meant for you no matter what form they arrive in.

The characteristics of animal spirits and guides help us understand what we most need to bring ourselves into balance and harmony or what traits most complement our own.

✧ ✿ ✦ ✷ ★ ★ ★ SPELLS FOR LOVE ✧ ✿ ✦ ✷ ★ ★ ★

In any love spell, it is critical to be open to a result you have not imagined. The gods and goddesses, universe, and forces of nature all may have in mind someone for you that you may not envision as the great love of your life. Whether you already know this person or haven't met him/her yet, focusing on a specific person is a recipe for disaster should you get that person only to be reminded that some wishes should never come true. Say the spell, believe in the intention, but be open to the end result.

Love Bath Spell: Combine a love spell with the benefits of a herbal bath. Add rose petals and lavender flowers into a warm to hot bath. Light red and pink candles for love, friendship, and passion. Get into the bath and lie back with your head resting on a bath pillow. Close your eyes and breathe deeply. Now envision yourself happy and in love with the perfect person. Don't necessarily imagine a particular person or face because you must let the forces of nature dictate the best partner for you, who may not be the person you want or think of. Simply feel the joy and happiness of having a loving, caring, and passionate mate. Hold that vision, and repeat this or a modification of this chant three times:

> Merry meet my one true love,
> merry meet again.
> Bring to me the perfect love in the
> highest and best way possible,
> to no one's harm.
> I am worthy. I am ready. I am love.
> So mote it be.

After your bath, continue to visualize yourself with this person and feel the emotions you will feel when he or she comes into your life. Repeat daily, "I am worthy. I am ready. I am love."

The Love Jar: In a small jar, place rose petals, jasmine flowers, rose quartz, and a piece of red construction paper with this written on it: "Love come to me. Love with me be." Drip some apricot oil onto the paper. Place the paper in the jar, and seal it. Bury it under the light of a full moon. Each day for thirty days, repeat, "Love come to me. Love with me be." On the thirtieth day, dig up the jar, remove the paper, and read the spell out loud. Your love should be on the way if he/she isn't already in your life. Be open to signs and signals.

Twin Flame Spell: Find two candles, one a male shape and one a female shape, preferably pink or red. Under the shape of the lover you wish to attract, write five traits you want him/her to have on a piece of paper. Place the candle on top of the paper. Burn both candles while visualizing being with the perfect person and feel the feelings you will have in their presence. Repeat, "Let this flame be my twin flame to me" three times, ending with "So mote it be." After 10 minutes, take the piece of paper and burn it, and blow out both candles. You can modify this same spell by cutting out the shapes of male and female dolls and placing one beside the other while saying, "As I bind these dolls side by side, so will my true love bind to me" three times, followed by "So mote it be."

Love Draw Spell: Get a picture of a pink or red rose; a small, white envelope and a stamp; and a red pen or marker.

Enhance your love spell by preceding it with a love spell bath to help get you in the right frame of mind.

Take the picture of the rose and write "my perfect lover" on it in red pen or marker. You can also write "my ideal partner." Fold up the picture and put it inside the white envelope. Stick on the stamp, write your name and address on the envelope, and mail it from a spot far from your home. When the letter arrives in the mail, place it under a pink or red candle, and burn the candle while saying "my perfect lover is on the way" over and over. Do this for 5 minutes, blow out the candle, hide the letter, and keep your eyes and heart open for your perfect love to appear soon.

Solid Marriage Spell (adapted from spellsofmagic.com): Get a beautiful, pink candle. Use an essential oil or incense you love, perhaps rose or patchouli. Envision the other partner as being with you in spirit. Anoint the candle with the essential oil, and light the incense, then light the candle, and envision you and your partner in loving and fun circumstances. Take as long as you need to fix those images in your mind, then say the spell:

> God and Goddess,
> As you are joined with each other,
> So am I joined with (name of person)
> In faith and hope and love.
> Help us to work together.
> Toward a happy, healthy relationship,
> Balanced and equal,
> In work and compromise and love.
> Let our union be harmonious,
> Productive, caring and filled with joy
> And let us overcome life's difficulties
> With cooperation, communication and love.
> God and Goddess,
> Watch over this union

> And let it grow stronger every day
> With passion and joy and love,
> So mote it be.

Cut the Cord Spell: If you can't let go of a past love and want to welcome in a new love, you must first cut the cord. Take two candles, one pink or red and one blue or purple. If you are female, you will be represented by the pink or red candle, and if you are male, the darker candle. Take a white ribbon or cord for purity and cleansing and tie it in a figure eight around the candles. Light the candles. Visualize saying a final goodbye to this person and holding a pair of scissors that cut a cord between your hearts. You can also visualize a huge cord or ribbon that entwines you being untied. Do this as you untie the ribbon around the candles and let it fall loose, freeing the candles, and saying, "As I lose this ribbon/cord, so do I lose you from my heart." You can repeat it as many times as you need to feel that inner click that says you are free, and keep visualizing the separation getting bigger and bigger between you and your ex-lover. When you feel ready, blow out the candles and say, "It is done, the ribbon/cord is cut, so mote it be."

Always perform spells of release and letting go with a grateful and compassionate heart filled with love for the lessons taught by past lovers and experiences. If you do the spell angry and hurt, no matter what was done to you or how justified you feel, you really aren't letting go and will take that negative energy into the next relationship or situation you're involved in. Life only changes when we let go of what doesn't work to make room for what does. Allow the past to float or burn away like the ash from the paper, thanking it silently for the gifts of strength, wisdom, and insight, but be firm in your intention to not live in the past anymore.

Heal a Relationship Spell: This is a beautiful spell found in Wicca for repairing a marriage or broken relationship. Get a white candle, a pink candle, a bowl or dish, matches or a lighter, two pieces of string, two pieces of paper, and a pen or marker. Begin by writing two letters. The first letter will describe the problems you are having in your relationship and how you feel about them. You can unload your anger, hurt, grief, and sadness onto the letter because no one will ever see it but you and the god or goddess. Now take another piece of paper and write what you envision your relationship should be like, how you want to be treated, how you want to feel, and what would be the ideal, happy scenario. Make both letters as detailed as you like. Then stop and meditate to get grounded before continuing with the spell. Gather your ingredients and cast a sacred circle around you. Light the candles and take the first letter, the letter describing your problems, and burn it in the bowl or dish. Feel the negative aspects of your relationship burn away as you say:

> Sacred flames, carry these energies away,
> Let our relationship begin anew today.

Now take the second letter and the pieces of string. Read the letter again, and visualize a great and happy outcome for your relationship. Tie the two pieces of string together to make one longer piece of string and then fold up the letter and wrap the string around it. Say:

> God and Goddess above,
> Help me reunite with my love.
> Bring us loving harmony and peace,
> May the strength of our bond increase.

End the spell with "So mote it be," close the sacred circle, then bury the

Release the Past Spell

A nother variation to release pain or past memories is to write down the word "past" on a piece of black paper. Burn it over the flame of a white candle while breathing deeply, exhaling loudly as if to exhale the past from your body. Say, "I let go of the past and let it burn away. I now live for today. And so it is." Let the candle burn as long as you wish. This is a spell you may have to repeat a few times to really be done with the grip of a past hurt or grievance, and that is perfectly okay. You can write the name of a person you are saying goodbye to on the black paper and perform the same spell. Simply say their name in the spell: "I let go of _____ and let my ties to him/her burn away. I now live for today." The great thing about spells is that they can be modified for personal use without diminishing the basic structure or goal.

string-wrapped paper near a tree. Oh, and blow out the candles, too!

Moon Love Blessing: Perform your favorite love spell under the light of a full moon for extra power. Here is a lovely blessing for your own life or for the love life of another you are spell casting for. Light a pink candle to represent affection, love, and friendship (red is good for a more fiery, passionate love). Take three basil leaves and draw a heart upon each with a red marker. As you say the following, hold each basil leaf over the flame until they are all burned. Watch your fingertips!

Upon the moon's full light,
Bring to me this night,
A love so wild and free,
A perfect love for me/thee.
So mote it be.

SPELLS FOR HEALING

Spells to heal yourself or a loved one are like focused prayers. If casting for someone else, it helps to have their permission and allow their own belief in the spell to add power to yours, but if they are not able to be asked, you can cast the spell for the highest and best outcome for that person. You can spell cast for healing the body, mind, and spirit and for an added boost of energy and vitality to get you through difficult challenges.

Body Scan Spell: Take a rose quartz and charge it with an anointing oil or favorite essential oil. Cast a sacred circle with sea salt. Stand in the center of the circle, and, starting from your navel area, scan the quartz up the length of your body to your head, then back down to your navel. Scan down from your navel to your toes, then back up to the navel. Do this with the back of your body as best you can. As you scan, envision the quartz dissipating all diseased cells, tissues, organs, blood, and bone. Imagine the quartz empowering your body as it moves over it with vibrant good health and perfect functioning. You can do this spell in silence to help you focus on visualizing, or you can chant something easy over and over such as, "Out with disease, in with good health." Keep the chant simple because this spell is more about seeing and feeling a cleansing occurring as the rose quartz scans the body. When you are done, step out of the circle, and place your rose quartz on your altar, or carry it with you to remind you to reaffirm your good health.

Healing Another Person Spell: First, get the person's permission unless they are so ill as to be incapacitated. Then, you must intuit whether casting a spell for their healing is the right thing to do. Because we cannot know the bigger picture of life, we must not assume that

Rose quartz is used in this beauty product as a roller that one can run over the skin, not only helping with surface issues but also deeper tissue health.

healing is a part of someone's greater destiny, but if you feel strongly, then try this spell. Take a white candle and a piece of paper. Write the name of the person on the piece of paper. Light the candle, and burn the paper saying, "As this paper is reduced to ashes, so, too, is the disease within my friend's body reduced to nothing. As the flame consumes this paper, so, too, does the light consume my friend with healing energy. So mote it be." Burn the candle for a few minutes, then blow it out, thinking positive thoughts of your friend as whole, healthy, and healed. Repeat this spell once a day as often as needed.

Simple White Candle Spell: Light a white candle for purity and cleansing. Say the words, "Sacred flame, cleanse from me all disease. Sacred flame, purify my body and restore me to perfect health. Sacred flame, remove any illness and replace it with vitality, love, and joy. So mote it be." Feel the flame within clean out all dark energies, illness, and disease. Envision being surrounded by a white, loving light that cocoons you and protects you. Let the candle burn down as you go about your day, envisioning yourself healed and healthy.

Guidance and Direction Spell: Take a handful of soil, a handful of grass, a handful of bark or tree leaves, and a handful of seeds. Place the objects onto your altar and cover them with the palms of your hands. Repeat three times:

Earth, grass, leaves, seeds
Reveal the path to suit my needs.
Show the signs to lead my way,

Sun Energy Spell

Healing often means a little time out under the warm rays of the sun. Here is an energizing spell for yourself when you're feeling sluggish and tired. Cast a circle of sea salt or stones outdoors where you can be directly under the sun. Do this spell at noon, when the sun is high above and its warm rays are strong. Dress lightly or go skyclad if you have a private place to do this. Close your eyes and hold your arms up and out as if taking in the sun's rays. Turn your face up to the sun. Repeat three times:

Sun light, sun light, infuse in me a spirit bright.
Warm rays, warm rays, energize me in all ways.

Lower your head, so you are not facing the sun now. Stand for at least 10 minutes, soaking up the sun. This is the least amount of time needed for the body to absorb vitamin D from the sun's rays, so 15 minutes is even better. End with "And so it is." Leave the circle and go about your day. A variation is to do the above spell in the morning sun while doing sun salutations or overhead stretches.

Guide me toward my path today.
So mote it be.

You need to be open to signs, synchronicities, and symbols that arise each time you do this spell, for they are markers and guideposts, showing you which way to go. Trust them and trust your intuition.

Bad Habits Be Gone Spell: Take a piece of white paper, a marker, a candle, a glass of water, and a match or lighter. Write the habit you wish to banish on the piece of paper. Light the candle and burn the paper over it. Repeat three times:

Bad habits block my way,
Clear my bad habits today.
Bad patterns burn away,
Good habits come my way.
So mote it be.

Now pour the water over the candle and ash to banish your bad habits forever.

✧°✧**✲ ✳ ✳ SPELLS FOR PROTECTION ✧°✧✲ ✳ ✳ ✳

Make a home protection spray using one cup of moon water, one teaspoon salt, and three drops of rosemary essential oil. Mix it together and put it into a spray bottle. Spray the corners of your home in a clockwise direction, saying, "Bless this house and all who dwell within. Let no negative spirits cross the threshold or penetrate these walls."

Protection magic shields you from negative energy, entities, and people. Salt absorbs bad energy. Sprinkle some salt on the various doorsteps and windowsills to keep out bad vibes. Keep black tourmaline, quartz, or obsidian in different rooms to protect against negative influences. Smoke cleanse or sage your home regularly to clean out evil and negativity.

Protective Circle Spell: During the next full moon, try the protective circle spell to protect your entire home from negative energies. Go outside at dusk with sea salt and move in a clockwise motion from the front door around the house as you sprinkle salt. Do not pour too much on plants or flowers and stay close to the foundation of the house. As you spread the salt, state your intention out loud: "This salt protects my home and all who live and visit here. This salt keeps harm away. This house is now surrounded in a circle of protection. So mote it be." Imagine an aura of white, protective light around your home until you are back where you started at the front door.

Protection Jar: Get a small jar, and put inside bits of vervain, honeysuckle, and peppermint leaves. Add a garnet stone and a piece of black paper with a spell written in silver pen: "Let no evil

You can cast a protection or healing spell on the world in general. This spell can focus on justice, peace, or a deeper respect for the natural world.

pass this boundary. Let no negative forces pass through the protective aura to harm anyone here. And so it is." Put the jar in your home, or bury it right outside the front door to cast a "glimmer" around the house and on all who live inside. A glimmer is like a glow or aura that you surround yourself or another with to keep them safe from harm. You can perform glimmer spells on just about anything by visualizing a circle of powerful, white light around them and writing and speaking that intention. Some people call it a "shimmer." Use whichever term tickles your fancy as long as you believe it works.

Spell for a Just World: You can cast a protection or healing spell on the world in general. This spell can focus on justice, peace, or a deeper respect for the natural world. Any type of justice you seek, personally or as part of the collective, can be used here. Just change the wording of the spell accordingly, and use herbs, candles, or stones that speak to a particular issue such as crime, abuse, injustice, poverty, or putting an end to war. These spells should really come from the heart and soul. Don't think they won't count in the greater scheme of things. Little pebbles can create a big ripple in a pond, remember? You might use a blue or purple candle for justice,

protection, and good will for all. A white candle could be used to cleanse the world of negativity. A green candle represents growth and prosperity for all. Yellow stands for an increase of joy, happiness, and sunny days ahead. Make a sacred space or circle at your altar or go stand outside under a full moon. Light the candle and hold it up to the sky. Call upon your god, goddess, or the universal forces. As you turn to each of the four directions, say:

> Divine justice melts all hatred.
> Divine justice burns all negativity.
> Divine justice consumes all greed.
> Divine justice destroys all evil.

Once you have turned to all four directions and said all four statements, say:

> Divine light shines on all darkness.

Let the candle burn for a few minutes as you envision a more peaceful, loving world. Then, blow out the candle, and end the spell. Do this every day or night during a crisis or whenever you feel like casting goodness out into the aether for the planet. Some might ask if a spell like this can heal a broken planet, but those who work with the magic of nature know that the real work is done first in the individual. Heal the person first, and the planet is sure to follow.

✿ ✦ ★ ★ ★ SPELLS FOR PROSPERITY ✿ ✦ ★ ★ ★

No shame exists in wanting money. Money is not the root of all evil; it's just paper that represents an exchange of energy. How you use money can be good or evil, not the money itself. Prospering financially allows us to not only help ourselves but help others. No spiritual preference comes to the poor, so why not cast out for abundance of money as long as you intend it to come in the

highest and best ways possible and to no one's harm or detriment? Here are some candle spells for money increase and prosperity.

Money Come Quick Spell: This spell attracts money into your life. You will need one green candle; one large, shiny coin; and a cinnamon essential oil (or you can make your own with a carrier oil and a few drops of cinnamon). Also, include one giant bay leaf, which attracts success and good fortune. Bless and consecrate all your tools. At your altar or other quiet place, put the coin underneath the candle. Anoint the green candle with your cinnamon oil while speaking the intention out loud in the present tense: "I cast this spell for financial increase in the highest and best ways and to no one's harm." Now write out the spell. Words spoken and written double the power. Some people write on the bay leaf itself, so keep your intention short. Light the candle and hold the bay leaf over the flame. Let the candle burn down completely, but do not leave it unattended or overnight. When it is down to the base and cool to the touch, take the coin and carry it on you for good fortune to find you.

Easy Candle Spell: Find a candle the color of what you wish to manifest: red or pink for romance, blue for purpose or success, white for truth, light blue for better health, silver for insight and intuition, black for strength, green for money, etc.

A green candle, a coin, a bay leaf, and a good spell may be just what you need to increase your good fortunes with a money spell.

Also, find a piece of colored paper the same color as your candle. Write your intent on the paper and fold it up. As you do this, visualize what you desire, and feel it as if it already exists. Light the candle and let the paper burn. You can put the paper in a nonflammable dish if you are worried about burning your fingertips! As your intention burns, say out loud the words you wrote on the paper. Put feeling and emotion behind them. Add an incantation such as "Flame and fire, bring my desire." Get as specific as you want, and no, you don't have to rhyme, but it makes remembering the incantation a lot easier. Repeat this three times, then let the candle burn down completely. Once it does, get rid of the candle and the ashes. You can bury the remains outside, knowing that as you do, your desire is already on its way to you. Other incantations for candle spells include:

Fire, fire, it's love I desire.
Money comes to me today, as this candle burns away.

As you visualize and feel the effects of your spell working, remember to also wish that it comes in the highest and best way possible and for the good of all concerned. This assures that you only want your intentions to work without harm to self or others.

Money Incantation: Speaking of money, you can speak your way to money as you drink a delightful tea. This kitchen witch spell is adapted from a spell online on a free spell site and combines the pleasures of making and drinking tea with a powerful money incantation. Take a pinch of ground cinnamon, a pinch of minced fresh ginger, a pinch of nutmeg, and a pinch of ground flax and add to a cup of boiled water. Let it steep for 10 minutes. As it steeps, close your eyes, and visualize the intention of the spell.

Money, love, success, health—in this case, it's prosperity in the form of more money. Imagine and feel how great life would be with more financial abundance. Chant this three times:

Money, money, come to me,
Extra money set me free.
Bring me increase, bring me wealth,
Let me enjoy financial health.

Then, strain the tea into a cup, and toss the herbs or add them to your compost pile. Drink the tea and know that a money increase is on the way.

Money Candle Spell: Take a green candle and carve a dollar sign into the wax. Fit as many as you can around the candle. Write your money intention on a piece of green paper, and light the candle. Read the intention out loud as you burn the paper in the flame. Envision money coming to you in all ways, expected and unexpected, to the good of all involved and the harm of none. Feel yourself as a wealthy person, happy and free of money problems, able to share and help others. Visualize for five minutes, then blow out the candle. Repeat this spell for three days in a row. If you want, you can add a chant that draws money to you. Just keep it short, keep it present moment, and put the force of your belief behind it. You can do the above spell before going to a casino or buying a new stock for your portfolio, as it can attract moneymaking decisions and opportunities. The above spell can be used before applying for a desired job but end the spell with "This or something better, so mote it be" to keep yourself open to even better job offers. Job

Money Luck Jar Spell

Find a small jar and put in bits of honeysuckle and four-leaf clovers. Add green agate, jade stones, and a green piece of construction paper. Write upon the paper: "Money comes into my life from all directions and from all sources. I welcome money now in the highest and best way and to no one's harm. So mote it be." Place the jar in your home, or bury it for thirty days by the light of a full or waxing moon. You can leave it buried or dig it up under the next full or waxing moon, redoing the spell if needed. Be patient and be open to not just actual money but also to new opportunities to make money.

A dollar here, a dollar there,
I find more money everywhere.

spells are best done during waxing moon phases and on Sundays or Wednesdays.

Prosperity Spell: You will need a decorative bowl, a green sachet or charm bag, three silver coins, cinnamon, cedar oil, and sandalwood incense. Light the incense. Set the bowl upon your altar or magical workspace. Put the cinnamon powder and cedar oil into the bowl and mix it. Surround the bowl with the three silver coins. Take your dominant hand, and touch each coin, saying:

Silver coin that honors the moon,
Bring to me a financial boon.
Draw more coins to come my way,
And shower me with wealth today.

Repeat this three times as you touch each coin. Then, take the coins, put them into the bowl, stir three times with the finger of your dominant hand, then place into the sachet or charm bag. Place it under your pillow or carry on you for thirty days. You can start this spell on the night of a full moon and keep it near you until the next full moon.

Circle Money Spell: Take a piece of white paper and draw a circle in green ink. Inside the circle, write an amount of money you would love to make quickly, say, for a seminar or class or a vacation. Put a plus sign after the amount to invite even more than what you are asking for. Fold the paper, and light a green or gold candle. Light the paper, and, as it burns, envision holding a check or cash for the amount intended in your hands. See yourself on vacation or attending the seminar. Say three times: "As I intend, so let it be. Money and more comes now to me." Visualize for a few moments and then blow out the candle, saying, "This or something better, for the good of all involved, to no one's harm. So mote it be." You can also end the spell with "As I wish, it will be."

Financially Free Spell: During a full moon, place a green or gold candle under the light, and light the wick. Gently brush the smoke from the flame toward you with your cupped hands. Speak your intention three times: "I am financially free to spend, save, spare, and share as I please." Close your eyes, and envision yourself as stress free with no money worries. Imagine the home you will own, the car you will drive, the clothes you will wear, as if they are happening NOW. Smile, laugh, or jump for joy. Then, open your eyes, and say, "This or even more is on its way to me in the highest and best way possible. So mote it be." Be open to money and opportunities but also to meeting new people who may have a direct line to a higher-salary job or moneymaking venture. Another variation of the above is to take your last bank statement and burn it over the flame while saying, "Money flows in, lack flows out. My income increases, my bank account increases, my wealth increases. Thanks be to the god/goddess for setting me financially free. And so it is."

Fast Money Spell: You need a bottle or jar with a cap. Find five small coins, five medium-sized coins, and five large coins. Put them into the bottle or jar along with five tablespoons wheat flour, a pinch of sesame seeds, five cloves or cinnamon sticks, five cloves of Jamaican pepper, and five whole pecans. If you can find four-leaf clovers, add five to the jar or bottle. Wait for a full moon and go outside. Shake the ingredients together and cover the jar or bottle. Repeat five times: "Silver, copper, gold, and herbs, bring me wealth." Put the jar or bottle in the southwest corner of your yard or in the house if you have no yard, preferably the kitchen, to bring money and abundance your way. Be sure to end the spell with the usual "in the highest and best way and to no one's harm, so mote it be."

Business Success Spell: Sometimes, running your own business can be quite a challenge. Things don't always

Money Mojo Spell

Find a small, green mojo bag or a green tin or tube. Grind two pinches of each of these into a powder and put inside the bag, tin, or tube: pine leaves, cedar, cinnamon, allspice, and ginger. Carry the bag, tin, or tube with you to a job interview, meeting, bank, or just to give you more financial confidence. You can take it to work and sprinkle the powder around your office or cubicle to bring a higher salary, promotion, or better opportunity.

go as planned, and factors beyond your control influence the flow of money, opportunities,

and clients. Try this spell to boost business success and clear away blocks from other people who may be in opposition to your goals and desires. Take a handful of bay leaves, a green ribbon, a green candle, three gold coins, and a piece of paper that is pliable in your hands like parchment. Take the gold coins and bay leaves and put them in the center of the parchment paper. Cover them by folding the four sides over. Tie your green ribbon around the parchment package, and light the candle. Hold your parchment package while looking into the flame. Then, close your eyes and meditate for a few moments, visualizing your business as a huge success, with no problems or blocks and everyone involved happy and on board with your goals. Really feel how it would be to have your business going so well. Say: "As the candle burns, my income turns. As the flame increases, my difficulty ceases. Let these coins bring my business luck and wealth. Let the candle's flame burn away any blocks to success. And so it is." Now open your eyes, take the parchment package, and put it in your briefcase, laptop case, or office where you do business. Put it somewhere only you can see it. Let the candle burn down.

Success in My Career Spell: Take one blue candle, one green candle, and matches or a lighter. Light the candles and close your eyes. Visualize your dream career. Feel yourself happy and fulfilled. See your large paycheck and imagine the wonderful things it buys you. Really feel this, then open your eyes and say:

Blue for success and confidence,
    green for prosperity and
    wealth,
Bring to me the perfect combina-
    tion in my dream career.

You can repeat it three times and end with the usual "So mote it be." Let the candles burn out, or if you must leave them unattended, blow them out first. Do this spell as needed until your dream job manifests.

Attract Business Success: Here's a similar spell to bring in new business and customers/clients. You will need an object that represents your business such as a business card or something with your logo on it. It can be an object that symbolized your field such as a type-writer charm for a writer or a tire from a toy car for a tire company. Take this object along with a green candle, a red rib-bon, three gold coins, and a piece of parchment paper. Wrap the gold coins and the business card/item in the paper and tie it with the ribbon. Light the can-dle, and hold the parchment package while repeating:

Let this spell bring to me,
Brand new opportunity.
Let the candle burn away,
Obstacles that come my way.
Help my business thrive and grow,
As this flame burns, let it be so.

Put the parchment items into the jar, seal the jar, and keep it at your work-place (hidden if you don't want to be asked questions!). Blow out the candle.

Wealthy Bath: This herbal bath serves to relax you while creating a mag-ical potion to take with you into meetings and potential job interviews. Add three drops each of cinnamon essential oil, pine oil, basil oil, and patchouli oil into a warm bath. Add a handful of Epsom salt or sea salt to the bath. Soak for 15 min-utes while envisioning the positive out-come of the interview or meeting. Before you drain the bath, get a small vial or tube and fill it with the bathwater. Take the vial or tube with you to your interview or meeting and expect success!

Welcome Wealth Spell: Here's a fun spell to attract wealth into your home. Place a four-leaf clover, dried basil

Paper Bag Spell

Get a small, brown paper bag like the kind for a school lunch. Write an amount of money you would like to have on a piece of green paper (with a plus sign to keep the door open for more) and why you want it. Fold the paper in half and put it in the bag along with a fresh one-dollar bill. Bury the bag outside under the moonlight and chant "money grows, money flows, from one to many more" three to ten times, ending with your usual sign off. As you chant, envision your dollar bill taking root in the earth and growing into a huge money tree you can pick from anytime you want. Then, leave the bag buried, and expect money or moneymaking circumstances to unfold before the next full moon.

leaves, a silver coin, and a sprinkle of patchouli oil or dried herb under your welcome mat outside your front door. Stand on the mat and face north, saying three times: "Welcome wealth into my home. Welcome prosperity to all who dwell within." You can also sprinkle the ingredients into potted plants kept near the front door for extra wealth attraction.

Magic Moola Spell: Take a green candle and anoint it with a scented oil of choice. Place the candle on a saucer or small platform. Around the platform or saucer, place money, including coins and bills as if making a wreath. Put some aside for the chant. Light the candle, and repeat this chant three times while gazing upon the money wreath and adding another coin or bill to the wreath:

> As this candle is surrounded by
> money, I am surrounded by
> wealth.
> As this flame decreases, my wealth
> increases.

When you have placed all the coins and bills around the candle, let it burn for 5 or 10 minutes as you contemplate how you will feel with prosperity and wealth. End the spell with "So mote it be, money comes to me, in the highest and best way, for the good of all concerned."

Employment Spell: Get a thick, green candle and Bergamot or bay leaf incense. Charge or anoint your candle, and either cast your sacred circle or stand at your altar. Carve your name on the candle. Light the candle and the incense. Focus on the candle flame as you visualize yourself in the job or career of your dreams. See it, feel it, hear it. Now repeat three times: "I call upon the forces of the universe to bring to me the perfect job or career in the highest and best way possible. I ask the god/goddess to fit this career to my talents, loves, and gifts so that I make a great salary and feel fulfilled. Let this career be my dream career and let me be surrounded by loving and supportive colleagues. So mote it be." Once you have repeated this three times, blow out the candle, and let the incense burn down.

★★★ SIMPLE VERSUS ELABORATE ★★★

Spells can be quick and simple or intricate and time consuming. Never feel as though you must do a shorter spell if you are the kind of person who enjoys really getting into the ritual preparation and spell-casting details. The reverse also holds true; never believe that because you cast short and sweet spells, they won't work. The spell has to fit the spell caster to really work its magic. Being authentic in your magical practice means you are much more likely to take it seriously and stick to it.

Moon Magic

The moon is a powerful symbol in spell casting, as you can see from many spells in this book and elsewhere. Performing spells and incantations by the light of the moon empowers and enchants on a deeper level. Witches are often associated with the moon, which represents the Divine goddess, the feminine night as opposed to the masculine day and the realm of the sun. The moon affects the tides and the menstrual cycles of women as well as mood … and magic.

When it comes to spell casting, the phases of the moon are of critical importance. From new moon to full moon, each phase is associated with different intentions, influences, and effects, all of which are involved in the success of spell work. This belief system is similar to astrology in that it focuses on heavenly bodies having a direct influence on our bodies. As above, so below. The phases of the moon can either help or hinder your spell casting. A good example would be casting a spell for something new during a new moon, a time of all possibility and a clean slate, and doing a letting-go spell during the waning moon, which represents the ending of something.

✴ ✴ ✴ ✴ ✴ PHASES OF THE MOON ✴ ✴ ✴ ✴ ✴

As the moon goes through its cycles, as visible from Earth, those who believe in the energies and magic of the nightly beacon work different kinds of spells.

• Dark Moon—When no moon is visible in the sky, it means the sun is not reflecting light off of it for us to see. We call this a new moon, and it is a powerful time of renewal, rejuvenation, new beginnings, putting new ideas into practice, and anything else that involves an ending that opens new doors of opportunity whether in love, health, wealth, or success. Rest up during this phase, for big things are coming! Also, focus on mindfulness, going within, and preparing the body, mind, and spirit for the ascending energies to come. Get centered, get grounded, and focus on the authentic part of you.

· Waxing Crescent Moon—When the moon is a crescent coming back into view from a new moon, we can cast spells and work magic for the energy and resources we need to take our new ideas and bring them closer to fruition. Waxing crescent is also a great time to work on discipline and the will, which will be needed to follow through on the new plans we made during a dark or new moon. It's an exciting moon phase because it represents the beginning of a comeback!

· Waxing Gibbous Moon—Consider the moon three-quarters full and bursting with opportunities. This is a great time to finally conquer those bad habits and triumph over challenges and obstacles that popped up in our path to our chosen goals and dreams. Spells at this time are potent, indeed, and you feel as though big things are on the verge of finally happening.

· Full Moon—The most powerful moon phase, when the moon is full and bright. Full moon magic is, well, simply *magical*. Our spells are charged with so much extra energy, and our desires carry with them the fullness of expression and manifestation just like the moon itself.

This is a great time to banish all that no longer works for our new plans we made during the new moon and only focus on the things we truly want. Full moon magic is a huge boost toward the next steps or the fulfillment of the spells we cast earlier. It is a time for important spells involving the things that carry the most weight in our lives and a time for developing our intuition, psychic abilities, dreams, and the powers of divination. Because the moon is associated with the goddess and the Divine feminine, we may feel a draw inward, even as the sight of a full moon brings out external wildness and expression.

Beware, though, of the full moon hangover due to the intense energies that make it harder for people to relax or sleep well. Symptoms include desiring to be alone, poor focus and concentration, decreased energy, mood swings, tension headaches, muscle aches and pains, a sense of vibration throughout the body, enhanced intuition, vivid dreams and nightmares, and a general sense of restlessness and irritability.

Try a full moon ritual bath. Use a sachet or cloth sac, and put in some sea salt or Epsom salt, rose petals, lavender buds, and an amethyst crystal. Put the sachet in the hot water as you bathe. The sea salt helps you neutralize negative energy and restore mineral balance. The rose petals make you feel beautiful and goddesslike. The lavender calms the mind and purifies the water. The amethyst increases your

The Moon plays a bigger part in our everyday lives than most people realize, and a specific part of that deals with its phases and how they are an important part of spell casting.

intuition and divination skills. You can try any combination of herbs and tools for a full moon ritual bath but put them into a sachet or sac to avoid a messy cleanup afterward.

• Waning Gibbous Moon—Back to three-quarters full, but now, we are moving toward a dark sky again. This is a time to repel negative things, including people, and review what did not work for us before, making sure we banish it for good. It's a good time for decluttering and for cleansing and charging our altar items and spell casting crystals and stones. Spells to end things can be cast during this time and continued until the dark or new moon.

• Waning Crescent Moon—The moon is saying goodbye for now, so say goodbye along with it to all that does not serve you. The waning phases of the moon are said to be "baneful" by pagans. The focus is on elimination and banishment, but it's also a time to make more room for what is to come. Cast spells for insight into new guidance and direction. Work on smoothing out the rough edges that came up during other phases. This is a very powerful time for ridding your body of toxins, your home of what is no longer used, your life of toxic people and situations, and your spirit of negative energies.

• Half-Moon Phases—These are also wonderful times for casting appropriate spells. Some people love to spell cast during the half-moon phases rather than crescent or gibbous. It's a personal thing. Just remember that spells should be cast for empowerment; new ideas, projects, and opportunities; increased energies; and more spiritual and intuitive power on the moon's approach to full. The moon's approach to new or dark would mean performing half-moon magic that is more focused on removing things; decluttering the body, mind, and spirit; and getting rid of habits and behaviors that didn't serve you well on the upswing. Moon magic is never an exact science and is open to the interpretation and input of the practitioner, which directly affects the intentions cast and their ability to manifest in the proper way.

Moon Magic

Moon magic is all about waxing and waning, going dark and blazing at full light along with the moon itself, and aligning with the energies available at the time. Our ancestors tracked the passage of time by the phases of the moon. Each year, twelve or thirteen full moons occur, which averages out to one every 28¼ days. The moon phases were associated with growing and reaping times for crops as well as marking celebrations and passages of time before calendars were created. Many cultures even named particular moon phases as a way of describing the living conditions they were experiencing at the time.

These names usually included a plant or animal name that was symbolic of the time period, such as:

Moon Deities

Every culture has one or more deities, gods and goddesses both, associated with the moon.

- Inuit—The god of the moon, Alignak, is also the god of weather. His domains are the tides and eclipses and even earthquakes and tectonic activity. His job in Inuit myth is to take the souls of the dead to Earth, where they are reborn, like the moon is in every cycle. Alignak became the moon god when he was banished from Earth for having an incestuous relationship with his sister, who became the goddess of the sun.

- Celtic—The goddess Cerridwen is the keeper of all knowledge as the one who watches over the cauldron of wisdom. She is associated with the moon and the feminine power of intuition. Her symbol is a white sow to represent fertility and motherhood. Cerridwen is the goddess of the Lower World in Celtic mythology.

- Aztec—In a reverse of the Inuit myth, where the moon is represented by a god and the sun a goddess, Aztec myth speaks of Coyolxauhqui, the sister of a powerful sun god named Huitzilopochtli, who killed his siblings upon their births and tossed Coyolxauhqui's head to the sky, where it became fixed as the moon. Her name means "golden bells," and she is often depicted as a beautiful woman wearing delicate bells.

- Roman—Diana, the huntress, is a popular mythological moon deity, although she started out as the goddess of the hunt. She is Jupiter's daughter and a sister to her twin brother, Apollo. She represents the sacred and Divine feminine and evolved into an actual moon goddess in later traditional tellings of Roman myths. She is called a light-bearing goddess and is often depicted with a bow, arrow, lantern, and stag.

- Greek—Diana's Greek counterpart is Artemis, the Greek goddess of the hunt. She shares most traits of Diana as well and also became associated with the moon in post-Classical writings. Hecate, the Greek mother goddess, was later elevated to the goddess of the spirit world, and, as a dark goddess, she became associated as well with the moon. She is associated with childbirth, ghosts, magic, and the dark moon and was the only child of a star goddess named Asteria, the aunt of both Apollo and Artemis. Hecate was born during a new moon period associated with another lunar goddess, Phoebe. Selene, the sister of the Greek sun god Helios, is associated with all aspects of the moon. She was originally Phoebe, the moon goddess, and is also called Luna, then later was more often associated with Artemis, the goddess of the hunt. The story is that Selene descended from the sky every night to sleep beside her beloved shepherd prince, Endymion, who was doomed to eternal slumber. She had famous parentage, too. She was the daughter of the Titans Hyperion and Thea.

- Polynesian—Sina lives inside the moon and protects night travelers. The myth states that she lived on Earth but got tired of the bad treatment she endured at the hands of her husband and family, so she went to go live on the moon. She is called Hina in Tahiti and was said to have been so curious about the moon, she paddled there on a magical canoe!

- Egyptian—Egyptian myth has many a moon god. Thoth, Osiris, Min, Duau, and Khons (the sun of Amen and his consort, Mut) are all moon gods. Egypt never worshipped goddesses associated with the moon.

- Storm Moon for January, a winter month when many dealt with winds and rains.
- Snow Moon or Hunger Moon for February, a time of sparse food and ice-cold weather.
- Worm Moon for March, a time when warmer weather brought out the earthworms and the return of the birds. Native tribes often called it the Crow Moon to mark the return of the crows at the end of the winter.
- Hare Moon marked the month of April and the association with Easter, fertility, and the rabbit as a symbol of procreation and full spring.
- Flower Moon meant it was May because April showers would bring May flowers to bloom.
- Strawberry Moon marked the coming of June, which meant the strawberry crops were ripe for the picking.
- Buck Moon meant it was July, the time for deer to grow their antlers.
- Sturgeon Moon in August marked the return of these fish to large bodies of water. Another name for August's moon was Green Corn Moon.
- Harvest Moon meant September had arrived, and it's the closest full moon to the Autumn Equinox. Yes, it's time to harvest the crops and prepare for the coming chill.
- Blood Moon symbolized October; it was also sometimes called Harvest Moon and Hunter's Moon. This month was the time to stock up on meat and

other foodstuffs for the winter months ahead.

- Beaver Moon signified November, the time for trapping beavers for their furs, a necessity for those about to survive a cold, harsh winter.
- Long Night Moon or Cold Moon was December, when the temperatures plunged. December was also called Long Night Moon because the nights were now the longest they would be.

The moon fascinates us and creates a sense of wonder, awe, and even longing. The moon is featured in many a fairy tale and throughout mythology and folklore, almost as an actual character in the stories. Pagans believed the moon was "full" for a period of three days and performed rituals and magical workings during this potent time, recognizing that the sensations the moon affected on them were to be taken seriously and revered as sacred.

Lovers and romantics can attest to the power of a beautiful, bright full moon overhead, and animals also behave and respond in accordance to the phases of the moon. Many a song has been written about the light of the moon and the love it inspires. Seems that we, like the ocean tides, wax and wane and grow dark and light, so it's only natural that we work with the moon for magical intentions and manifestations. The connection between us is as old as our existence here on Earth.

Moon spells can utilize stones, crystals, herbs, and any other objects associated with the particular phases and desires of the spell caster. Having a variety of items available to use during each phase is a spell caster's goal. Learning to create spells or use those already available is really about tuning in to the symbolic influences that match best with our desired goals.

Going from new to full is a time of growth, expansion, and "brightening" up our lives. Out of the dark of the mind and imagination, we bring forth thoughts, ideas, goals, and dreams. We then empower ourselves with the tools needed to make them come true.

Going from full to new is a time of going within, receding our energies, and casting off and away what we don't want to bring back with us. We banish. We turn down the light and dim the energies. We renew, refresh, and prepare to be reborn. It's really that simple.

As above, so below.

MAKING MOON WATER

A full moon is a great time to make moon water to drink or use for spell casting. To make moon water, you need water from a natural source and a clean, transparent jar. If you plan to drink the moon water, be sure to choose the best quality water you can find. Cleanse the jar to avoid any attached negative energies. During the height of the full moon, place a jar of water directly under the moonlight. Retrieve the jar just before sunrise. Store moon water in the fridge until you plan to drink or use it. Keep it away from sunlight. Moon water can be used to water plants; cleanse crystals and stones; wash your hands and face; mix special potions; add to bathwater; fill a dark, colored bowl; and learn to scry. Any moon magic and spell casting done during the full moon phase will be amplified in a positive manner when using moon water as a foundation.

Another use for moon water is scrying, a form of divination that requires achieving a trancelike state and staring into a medium like water, oil, or a mirror to look for symbols, signs, and images that can predict the future. Water scrying is one of the most popular forms of divination in Earth-based traditions and is easy to learn.

You'll need some moon water, a nice bowl (you can decorate your own bowl with symbols and sigils important to you), a silver candle and a white candle (or, if you can find one, a silver-and-white single candle), something to light the candles with, a rose quartz crystal, and a smudge stick or sandalwood or patchouli incense.

First, purify the area where you plan to scry. This can be a table or an altar or outside under the light of the moon. Use the smudge stick or incense to clear the air. Place some of the moon water into your bowl. You can use rainwater if you haven't made moon water or purified water from the store. Place the crystal into the bowl of water. Light the candles, and stare at the flames to help you enter a slightly altered state of consciousness. This can also be achieved by meditation, chanting, or via incense. Also, speak your intention at this time for what you hope the scrying will reveal.

Now stare into the water. You should feel a sense of clarity, focus, and calm. Look into the water and try to focus on the crystal. Be patient and relax. Scrying can take some time. With your intention in mind, soften your eyes, and relax the muscles of your face. Keep focused on the water and crystal. Breathe deeply and take note of any images and intuitions that come into your mind. Let

them come and go like the breeze. If you try to hold on to an image, it will break your focus. Be an observer, and let things come and go across the movie screen in your mind. If your mind wanders, gently bring it back to focus. You may begin to see words or images in greater detail, or they may repeat themselves. This is important. Ask them what they are trying to tell you. What do they want you to know?

When the images start to fade, you can take in a deep breath and end the scrying, bringing your mind fully back to the present moment. Write down any images, words, phrases, or intuitions that came to you, knowing that even if they don't make sense in the moment, they will at a later time, sometimes days or weeks later. Messages don't come with a time frame.

Some tips:

Moon water is made during any full moon and creates a water that has a higher positive manner when used as a foundation for spell casting.

- Leave the moon water out overnight to absorb the light and then scry the next night.

- If you live near a pond or lake, you can even scry off the body of water.

- Messages you receive might be for someone else, so stay open to that possibility and signs as to who it might be for.

- Find a beautiful, symbolic, decorative bowl, so it has more meaning.

- Make scrying part of a regular moon ritual practice to become sharp at divination.

- Once you're done scrying, pour the water on your herbs and plants.

The Power of Plants and Herbs

Plants are a big part of our everyday lives. We know what a plant looks like and are surrounded by them in nature, our food, textiles, clothing, and other items we use on a regular basis. They use sunlight and the act of photosynthesis to produce sugars, oxygen, and other substances; root; and grow just about everywhere. They take in carbon dioxide and release oxygen into the air. They cannot move of their own accord but are living things that grow on land and in water. They include species of mosses, ferns, herbaceous plants, trees, bushes, vines, woody plants, flowering plants, and those that produce vegetables. The two main types of plants are flowering and nonflowering. Other plants produce spores, cones, and fungi and cones used for reproduction. Plants are used as food and medicine and as ingredients in many products we consume every day. Many plants have woody stems, which differentiate them from herbs, and the wood is used to make everything from a guitar to a birdhouse.

If the plant is the whole organism, then herbs are the parts of the whole. Herbs are usually defined as soft plants with no lignin, which is the chemical substance that makes woody stems. Herbs are the parts of the plants used in teas, foods, and medicine such as the root, leaves, flowers, fruit, resin, root bark, and seeds. They are called "herbaceous plants" in botany, and, in general, herbs and plants are often used to describe the same organisms. Herbs have a shorter life span and are used in cooking and medicines thanks to their tastes, odors, and healing properties. Herbs are also widely used in beauty treatments, balms, lotions, creams, and cosmetics; for cooking and cleaning; and as disinfectants. Herbs are divided into annuals, which are planted at the start of each growing season and don't normally survive winter frost; perennials, which are planted once and survive the winter to rebloom each spring; and biennials, which are planted in the late spring and

---

complete their life cycle in two growing seasons.

Herbs are grouped as defined by the ancient Greek philosopher Theophrastus, who divided the entire plant kingdom into trees, shrubs, and herbs. Pot herbs include the onion; sweet herbs include spices such as thyme; and salad herbs include things like wild celery. In the seventeenth century, pot herbs became known as vegetables and could be grown outside of just a large pot. Yes, it gets confusing, and you can always refer to all of it simply as plants or greenery!

The use of medicinal herbs goes back to as early as 5000 B.C.E., when Sumerians utilized a variety of them in medicines. Cuneiforms showing herbs have been discovered by archaeological excavations and in ancient texts. The first herbal concoctions may have been formulated in 162 C.E. by the great physi-

cian Galen. Ancient Chinese traditional medicine has always included herbs for thousands of years, as has the Ayurvedic tradition of India. The ancient Greeks were the first of the Western cultures to use herbs in their medicines and healing agents followed by the Romans, Persians, and every other culture on Earth, including the Native and indigenous peoples of Africa, Australia, and the Americas, who always knew of the power of Mother Earth to heal.

Religious traditions all over the world recognized the sacred nature of particular herbs such as the frankincense and myrrh brought to the stable where Christ was born in the New Testament; the tulsi of Hinduism, also called "holy basil"; the sage of Wicca; and the cannabis of the Rastafari. Some herbs, when burned, created a sense of calm and relaxation and became favorites of practitioners of yoga. Patchouli, lavender, and vanilla are

Herbs are not only used as a flavoring agent in cooking; they are often helpful for different spells. As with the culinary arts, spell casting can benefit from a little of just the right herb.

soothing scents often associated with meditation. Native Americans considered the aromatic smoke from white sage and cedar to be sacred plants, and shamans from all over the world were familiar with which plants and types of mushrooms created hallucinations and an altered state of consciousness, including peyote and salvia plants. Mistletoe was sacred to European pagans, and the ancient Greek myths featured Viscum album, calling it the "golden bough" of Aeneis, who went on after the fall of Troy to help found Rome.

Today, we are seeing a revival of natural and alternative medicines and the use of herbs and plants as a result of increased rates of a host of diseases despite "modern miracle" pills courtesy of a massive pharmaceutical industry. The understanding that old-timey medicine wasn't the stuff of ignorant "grannies" cooking up remedies in their kitchens but wise and experienced people who worked with natural elements to cure and heal without adding more symptoms and side effects is part of a reemergence behind new scientific research into the properties and compounds of herbs and plants and a growing body of evidence that they do indeed work just like Granny told us they would.

✻ ✦ ✦ ✦ ROOTS ✦ ✦ ✦ ✦

In Voodoo and conjuring, the root of the plant is the most important part. Whether used in its whole form or ground into a fine powder, the use of roots in magical practices is called rootworking. Roots are also used in kitchen witchery and pagan practices. Ginger is a root that is kept whole, sliced, or ground depending on the type of spell and how it will be presented. Roots are usually foraged and are more difficult to acquire than plants and flowers, but they pack a potent punch for spells and, in many cases, as medicines.

Some common roots for rootwork include:

• Angelica Root—A sprinkle of this ground root in the four corners of your home protects you from evil. You can also use it on entryways, windows, and any opening to the outside of the house. Putting some of the powdered root into an herbal bath removes hexes and curses.

• Bloodroot—If you carry a piece of this root in a red bag, it will protect you against hexes, curses, and evil. Burning bloodroot incense is said to stop a wayward lover, but if you carry a piece of the root on you, it will attract a new lover your way.

• Calamus Root—This root is all about power and control. It is used to bring and increase power in hexing or spell

Roots are a powerful part of nature and used in the practices of voodoo. There is a belief ginger has properties such as good health and luck.

casting when burned as incense. If you place some in the corners of your kitchen, it dispels hunger and attracts abundance. It also binds spells and makes them more powerful when they do manifest.

• Devil's Shoestring—This root protects you from harm and attracts good luck and fortune. It can help you land a great job or get you a promotion if you carry a piece into interviews and meetings, or you can use it to charm the opposite sex.

• Galangal—This is another root that can remove a hex or curse. If you chew on a piece while thinking of something you desire, then spit it out, it will manifest. Carry a piece for protection and to attract good luck and good health. If you have to go to court, bring a piece with you or burn it in incense form for two weeks up until the court date for a favorable decision.

• Ginger Root—Seeking a little adventure? Carry ginger root or make ginger root tea to draw exciting, new adventures into your life. It also brings prosperity, success, confidence, and sexual attraction. Put some ground ginger root into a locket, amulet, or mojo bag to bring you good health and protect you from harm. If you ever find a ginger root that looks like a human shape, keep it for some extra-powerful magic.

• High John the Conqueror—This is the most widely used root in Voodoo and Hoodoo because it removes obstacles and helps you conquer challenges if you keep a piece on you. Carry some in a red mojo bag for luck in love or in a green mojo bag for luck in money and success. You can turn the root chips or ground powder into sachet powders, incense, and floor washes.

• Licorice Root—This is another power root that can help you gain power and advantage over others. You can use licorice root in spell work to change someone's mind or influence their decisions but be careful when doing this. What comes around goes around!

• Lucky Hand Root—This is the root of a rare wild orchid that looks like a hand with fingers. It helps gamblers win big, and musicians claim it helps with fingering instruments.

• Orris Root—This attracts men to you if you're a woman looking for love and is used in spell casting for love, desire, attraction, and finding the perfect mate. In Voodoo, it is called the love drawing powder and can be put into sachets or mojo bags or sprinkled on sheets or in herbal baths to attract a lover or two.

✦✦✦ SPICES ✦✦✦

Let's not forget spices. They are a part of kitchen witchery, spell casting, and medicinal healing, too. Magical spices can be found in the cabinets and cupboards of every kitchen, each with their own particular power, but how does a spice differ from an herb? Spices are seeds, fruits, roots, barks, or other plant substances that are used to color, flavor, or add preservatives to food. They are not made from flowers, leaves, or stems as herbs are. Many spices possess antimicrobial properties and are used to fight infectious diseases in warm parts of the world. This also helps preserve meat from spoiling, too.

Spices are usually ground down to a fine powder, especially for cooking, and

Why Bring Frankincense and Myrrh?

Those familiar with the New Testament story of the Three Wise Men bringing gifts to Bethlehem know that three important items were given to the Christ child in the stable that night: gold, frankincense, and myrrh. Gold is the obvious choice for a great baby gift, but why two gum resins that were extracted from shrublike trees grown in the dry climates of Asia, Africa, India, Saudi Arabia, Ethiopia, and Yemen?

Frankincense is a whitish resin from the Boswellia tree and is a popular ingredient in essential oil blends. It has healing benefits and also allows the body to properly absorb nutrients. Among its properties, it is a powerful antiseptic and disinfectant that boosts the immune system against disease and infections. Topically, it helps cuts and scrapes heal, prevents infection, and reduces acne breakouts and scarring. The smoke of the burned plant is used in cleansing rituals, and the oil assists relaxation and meditation because it reduces blood pressure and cleans out airways. Those who use a few drops of the essential oil in a diffuser can attest to its calming effects. Frankincense was used by ancient Egyptians to prepare the dead for burial, and it also had a big hand in regulating the menstrual cycles of women and relieving cramping.

Myrrh is a reddish resin from the Commiphora tree and is a wonderful essential oil for its sedative ability and topical use as a disinfectant. Like frankincense, it fades scars, aids digestion and respiratory issues, and benefits skin ailments. It has antifungal properties to help get rid of athlete's foot and ringworm. Myrrh softens dry, chapped skin and helps blood flow throughout the body, aiding in detoxes by increasing sweat. Therapeutic-grade myrrh is best to avoid chemical treatments. Do not consume myrrh unless it is indicated as food-grade, and even then, talk to your doctor or nutritionist first. Neither frankincense nor myrrh should be used by pregnant women, as the essential oils are potent, but women who have given birth can use the oils on stretch marks.

Aside from all the amazing properties of frankincense and myrrh, they are highly symbolic resins. Gold, the "other" gift, is said to represent Jesus as a king of kings; frankincense is a symbol of the priestly role Jesus took on; and myrrh represents his upcoming death and use in embalming, so it only makes sense that someone bringing a special gift to a very special birthplace would choose those with incredible value, healing power, and symbolism.

were considered a hot commodity in many cultures that used them to trade and barter for goods. During the Middle Ages, for example, pepper and cinnamon were in high demand and brought in a good price. As spices became used for medicinal purposes, their value rose, and the demand went up for imported spices from other parts of the world. Saffron was one of the most expensive and desired spices during the late Middle Ages. The discovery of the New World introduced allspice, chocolate, vanilla, and chili peppers into the global market, allowing the Americas to compete with much older cultures and their signature spices. Spices can be worked with alone or blended in mixtures. Each has its own signature odor, taste, and color and are not expensive to purchase from the local market.

DOMESTIC MAGIC

Practical magic. Kitchen witchery. Green magic. Hedge magic. Domestic magic. Everyday magic. It goes by many names, but it all describes someone who works magic at home with what they have around the house. Whether from the kitchen cupboard, spice rack, local forest, or outdoor garden, the idea is that we can all use herbs, plants, and other materials for magic and spell casting without having to travel far and wide and spend a lot of money. Even cooking and preparing meals is a part of this type of magic because the foods we consume carry with them not just nutritional value but the intention of the one who makes the meal. Using intention and spell casting over meals can be the only altar kitchen witches need to put out good energy and hopefully influence and help those they love.

Herbs and plants grown at home or in gardens bring a personal touch to spell casting and healing because they are purposely planted and tended to. Kitchen witches know that an herb like basil not only makes for a great pasta sauce, but it also brings good luck. When kitchen witches aren't cooking, they are spell casting and mixing brews, potions, and medicines based on the items they have handy and their knowledge of what does what.

Many of the ingredients needed for kitchen witchery are available to you in the kitchen, the herb garden, or any one of a dozen local sources, and most come at little or no cost.

Knives, stirring spoons, brooms, and ladles all become charmed items to assist in the practical magic of bringing love, money, success, health, and happiness into the home. The stew pot becomes a magical cauldron, and the teapot brews a mix for every occasion. Even the heat of a stove can become part of a spell to heat up a love relationship, or ice can be used to freeze something you wish to be stopped. Everything has a symbolic use, and it's all fair game to those who practice this ancient, ritualistic form of magic that dates back to when women mixed up spells and cures right in their kitchens to benefit everyone in their village.

Mackenzie Sage Wright, a witch for over twenty-five years, writes in "Types of Witches: How to Be a Kitchen Witch" for *exemplore.com* that "kitchen Witchcraft, also known as Cottage Witchcraft, combines hearth and home with magic and enchantment. The lines between the magic and the mundane are blurred as the witch brings magic into everyday life and everyday chores. It's not very ceremonial in nature; it's about putting that spark of magic into everything as you go about your domestic duties." It's easy to see how anyone can, and perhaps already is, a kitchen witch when they create meals with love and the intention to bring happiness and health to others.

You don't even have to be an actual witch to do kitchen witchery. Every religious tradition has its home and hearth beliefs and rituals, many involving cooking and preparing meals with reverence and intent. You can do your own thing in your own kitchen and garden and make the practice what you want it to be according to your existing beliefs and traditions. If you have ever thrown salt over one shoulder to ward off evil or made a salve of garden plants or herbs to help heal your child's cuts, you have engaged

in this practical magic. Nor do you have to live in the middle of an enchanted forest, for those in urban areas, apartments, and condos can be kitchen witches, too. Anyone can grow a few plants or an herb garden, even with minimal space. You can grow them in planters, window boxes, or even large cans! Find a sunny spot, or, if you have a balcony, place them where they will receive adequate sunlight.

Think magically about every step involved with not only cooking but gardening, cleaning the house and yard, and hosting family and friends for get-togethers that are themselves a kind of ritual. Those who celebrate Thanksgiving start the meal with a prayer of thanks and gratitude. This is like setting an intention or casting a beautiful "spell" on the meal and those partaking.

Though it is best to grow organic plants and herbs, you can also buy them at the store or a nearby farmer's market. Just be sure to charge them when you get them home to prepare them for positive use and banish any negative attachments they may have brought into the kitchen. You may gain a whole new reverence for food and begin being more aware of waste. Start recycling or composting as a way to reuse the gifts nature provides.

Kitchen witches know that even the icky chores like doing the dishes or picking up dog poop from the yard can all become little magical practices when you have the right attitude. Even making

> Think magically about every step involved with not only cooking but gardening, cleaning the house and yard, and hosting family and friends for get-togethers that are themselves a kind of ritual.

lasagna can turn into something incredibly special when it's accompanied by a spell. Vacuuming the rug becomes a banishment ritual, and even taking your morning shower is a cleansing ritual to prepare you for your day.

The only thing required is a good education on herbal remedies, which plants are beneficial and which to avoid, and maybe how to cook, although even that can be improved with practice! Maybe your grandmother or aunt knows of some wonderful spells or remedies she used. Find out if your own family heritage includes some domestic magical practices you can carry on and then pass on to your children. It is also fun to use the plants and herbs indigenous to your area and is a great opportunity to learn about the natural environment right outside your door.

Learning about plants and herbs may sound intimidating; so many are out there, and some are not conducive to cooking or spell casting, but thanks to the abundance of information out there in the form of books like this one, classes, social networking groups, and the Internet, it doesn't have to be scary or overwhelming.

✧ ✧✧ ✧ ✧✶✶✶ PLANTS AND HERBS ✧ ✧✧ ✧ ✧✶✶✶

The following is a list of plants, roots, flowers, and herbs and their properties. The word "botanicals" is a great umbrella term for all the different choices you have when using nature's gifts in healing and spell casting or in religious and spiritual rituals. If something cannot be eaten or consumed or is toxic, it will be indicated as such. Because of allergies, always test out what you plan to use beforehand on a patch of skin, preferably just inside the elbow, then cover with a loose bandage for at least a half an hour.

There is a large resource out in the world that our ancestors discovered is not only tasty but has desirable bodily effects for us. Botanicals are found easily and can be used in many ways.

These botanicals can be used in many ways: as ingredients in potions, infusions, teas, or oils; sprinkled about in dried or flower form; worn in amulets and necklace bottles; kept in the house and grown outdoors; used in cooking; made into salves and balms; or placed into sachets and mojo bags. Heck, throw some into your morning smoothie! The magic of green magic, kitchen witchery, herbal magic, practical magic, or whatever name you choose to call it is this— anything goes! Ideally, keep them on hand in a dried form so they can be used for a much longer time period. Do all of your chopping, cutting, and grinding into a powdered form before you spell cast, so they are ready when needed, or buy them from a reputable source already prepared. Use the leaves, stems, and flowers because even dried, they will maintain their power and scent (for essential oils and lotions). Be aware that you must label everything because dried roots have no distinct aroma that distinguishes one from the other, like flower petals do.

Before consuming, ingesting, or exposing the skin to any herbs and plants, you may want to check with your doctor and assure that no contraindications exist with any medicines you may be taking. Many of these herbs/plants listed are innocuous, but some have hormonal properties or astringent properties that may cause adverse reactions. Be smart about your herbal magic, and get to know the natural world before diving in.

This list in no way covers every possible herb, plant, flower, or root on the planet but serves as a fairly comprehensive guide to the most popular items used in both herb/kitchen witchery, spell casting, folk magic, and medicine.

· Acacia—Used in spell casting, acacia provides protection and attracts love and money. It can also increase psychic abilities. It is used in holy oil to anoint altars and magical working places. You can also use it to anoint candles and other items used for spell casting. It also heals wounds and provides relief for a sore and raw throat.

· Acorn—These wonderful little seeds can be used in charms and spells for protection, good luck, money, popularity, strength, courage, and personal power. The acorn tree was sacred to the Druids and is associated with personal and spiritual growth. Put an acorn in your pocket or bag or grind it for spell casting. Place acorns on your altar to promote wisdom, abundance, financial fortune, and luck, but be careful; having acorns around is known to attract fairies!

· Adder's Tongue—An herb for stopping gossip and slander, it is also called serpent's tongue and is considered sacred to deities that were associated

Types of Herbs by Taste

• Salty—High in minerals and sometimes diuretic, these herbs can affect the fluid balance in our bodies. Plantain is a salty herb.

• Pungent—Strong in odor and flavor, warming and spicy, these herbs make you sweat. Think cayenne pepper.

• Sour—These herbs stimulate the digestive system and are full of healthy antioxidants. Elderberries are an example of a sour herb.

• Bitter—Bitter in taste such as the Oregon grape root or oregano, these herbs stimulate the digestive system and lower inflammation.

• Sweet—Try astragalus in a tea for an example of a sweet herb, one that restores energy and strengthens the immune system.

with snakes and serpents. The American adder's tongue is used to make medicines but differs widely from the English plant version. It looks like a small fern with a spore-bearing stalk that resembles a snake's tongue. It was once a popular treatment for tuberculosis.

· Agrimony—This herb is great for protection spells and induces sleep. It works great in dream pillows and even stronger as a sleep aid if you mix it with mugwort. The oil is used for cleansing and ritual healing, including cleansing someone's aura. It is also a great counterhex/curse herb to use to break a curse put on you and send it back to the person, to boot! In the Middle Ages, agrimony was placed on wounds during battle to help heal and stop the bleeding.

· Alder—Another flowering plant and tree that is sacred to the Druids, alder is used for protection and divination. It

A succulent plant long revered for all of its healing properties, aloe vera is used in many compounds to relieve pain and soothe the skin.

is associated with the weather and weather magic. The alder tree is a member of the birch family.

· Alfalfa—A plant used for spells involving money, prosperity, and stopping hunger. A great herb for avoiding financial disasters and misfortune. Consuming the juice can aid in regrowing lost hair, especially if used in a mix with carrots.

· Allspice—Comes from a tree in the myrtle family grown in Central and South America. It is called allspice because it has the scents of many species, including nutmeg, cinnamon, cloves, pepper, and juniper berries. Considered a "power spice" because of its strong masculine energy thanks to its association with the planet Mars, allspice is a powerful aid in business success and restoring mental acuity. The dried berries of the allspice tree can be made into sachets or a fragrant oil or incense, used in spells to uplift, empower, and attract money and good luck. Its antiseptic properties make it useful for fighting infections and can even treat depression when used in aromatherapy. Allspice also helps stop indigestion.

· Almond—Use the nuts whole or ground in spells for money and abundance of good things. You can burn it in incense form to attract prosperous opportunities. The almond also promotes wisdom and is one of the healthiest foods to consume, containing protein and plenty of vitamin E to help hair and skin look healthy and fresh. Try to find organic almonds if possible.

· Aloe Vera—Loaded with seventy-five active compounds, this plant has been used for thousands of years as medicine but also for its nutritional benefits. The sap contains anti-inflammatory and pain-relieving compounds. It's a natural remedy for diabetes and is clinically proven to lower blood sugar and triglycerides. Aloe vera sap applied directly to the skin helps with the healing of cuts, burns (especially sunburn), and wounds and is a potent digestive system detoxifier when taken internally. Aloe vera gel mixed with a few drops of almond oil rubbed into the scalp and left overnight (wash out with shampoo) helps hair growth. It is a great laxative, aiding constipation, and has even been shown to work much better than a placebo in a study of chronic psoriasis. In spell casting, use it for protection and to attract good luck.

- Ambergris—A popular protection plant that also arouses curiosity, vitality, and interest and opens the doorways of the heart to receive love. It's a stimulant and can boost energy in tonics and blends.

- Angelica—This European plant is now grown in the United States for its many medicinal purposes. It can reduce coughs, colds, bloating, menstrual pain, nerve pain, arthritis, stomachaches, and motion sickness. Use the dried roots and seeds in syrups and infusions, but do not give to pregnant women or diabetics because of its ability to raise blood sugar levels.

- Angelica Root/Dong Quai—This enhances feminine power and sexuality, protects children from evil, and gives women magical abilities. This item is often included in a conjure or mojo bag in Voodoo practices along with exorcisms to rid evil entities. Sprinkle the ground root outside your home to protect from criminals and negative energy. The dried root can cause visions and prophetic dreams and helps to elevate energy levels.

- Anise (Star Anise)—The seed of anise can help prevent nightmares when used in a sleep pillow. As incense, it is a potent protection and purification herb and is often used during an invocation of Mercury or Apollo. Anise wards off the evil eye and protects against the curses of others.

- Apple—The food of the gods, apples can be utilized in spells for fertility and fruitful endeavors. Apple wood makes a great wand, and apple cider can be used to symbolize wine or blood in rituals. If you cut an apple in half, you can see a "natural pentacle": a five-pointed star. Apples are used for protection, and an apple branch wand brings love and luck but also attracts faeries. As for the fruit itself, apples are powerhouses for physical well-being; just be sure to buy organic or grow them yourself. If you buy them, wash them well with a scrubber to remove any pesticides, as they are one of the most widely sprayed fruits.

- Apricot—The fruit is not only good for you, but in a love spell, it will bind two people together as passionate lovers. Apricots help keep fevers under control and are wonderful for eye, stomach, liver, heart, and nerve health thanks to an abundance of vitamins and minerals. Dry them for a tasty snack in between spells! Apricot oil is wonderful for treating skin ailments and as a carrier oil for infusions, balms, and salves.

- Arnica—A healing herb great for use in salves and balms. Apply to bruises and sprains, and the pain and inflammation will vanish. Arnica not only reduces swelling and trauma to skin and tissue but also stops the pain associated with overused muscles from hiking or walking without the nasty side effects of pharmaceuticals. It has been used for

these properties as far back as the twelfth century in European countries. The most common type, arnica montana, is part of the daisy family, which includes chamomile, yarrow, echinacea, and calendula.

· Aster—Make an oil for calm and relaxation, or use the flowers in a smudge to chase off negative spirits. The whole plant can be steamed or smudged to quiet crazy energies. Chinese herbologists use aster for many things, including controlling bleeding, curing hepatitis, and treating snakebites.

· Avocado—The fruit and seed bring happiness, health, and a long life. Avocado paste soothes skin disorders, and avocadoes in general are a superfood and one of the healthiest fats you can eat. Make a wand from the growth of the pit of an avocado, and it will come in handy for all types of spell casting. Avocado oil is one of the most widely used oils in herbal salves and

Everyone is familiar with the common banana, but did you know it can help with intestinal issues, can treat arthritis and burns, and can even be an aphrodisiac?

balms, as discussed later, as a carrier or binding oil.

· Baby's Breath—A lovely flowering plant for happiness, true love, and a pure heart. A favorite for weddings and springtime parties, this lovely, little, pink flower grows in clusters that look like gentle, cloudlike blooms.

· Bamboo—Used for protection, luck, breaking hexes and curses, and fulfilling wishes. The stalk makes a great magic wand, and the leaves are a stimulant and aphrodisiac. Bamboo leaves also stop blood flow.

· Banana—Bananas work wonders on intestinal issues and heal impotency. The scent of a banana is considered an aphrodisiac. Bananas offer plenty of potassium and help treat anemia and arthritis. A banana poultice heals burns and wounds.

· Barley Grass—Works to protect from negative energy and attract love and healing.

· Basil—Sprinkling this dried herb around your home will banish evil. Give the gift of basil to a new homeowner to bring them good luck and protection. Basil is used in exorcisms to banish demons and can bring love when used in a love potion. This is a sacred herb for money and success and drives away the evil eye. It is the one of the most widely used herbs in spell casting and kitchen witchery.

· Bay Leaves/Bay Laurel—Use them for protection and to ward off hexes and jinxes. Sacred to the god Apollo, bay leaves bring good fortune, healing, strength, and the power of divination. Place bay leaves under your pillow to increase prophetic and lucid dreams. Put the whole leaves in a sachet or pouch, or place one leaf in every corner of your home to keep all those within safe. Bay leaves are often used to consecrate things such as musical instruments and objects on the spell casting altar. Burned in incense form, it assists in prophetic visions. As a medicine, bay is taken orally for infections, congestion, allergies, asthma, anxiety, and even psychosis.

- Bayberry—This perennial shrub brings good luck, good fortune, and relief from pain and stress. The root is particularly useful in spell casting but be sure to only take a small part and leave the rest to grow on.

- Bee Balm—The pretty flowers of this plant give a hot and spicy flavor to foods that help flush the sinuses and clear stuffy noses. The thymol found in bee balm is a potent antibacterial, antifungal, antiviral ingredient that fights off infections, allergies, and illnesses of the respiratory system. Bees love the flowers, thus the plant's name!

- Belladonna—*Toxic! Do not consume!* This powerful herb is poisonous and should not be treated lightly. Handle with care, as it can be absorbed through the skin. In spell casting, it is used to assist astral projection and divination and is often made into a flying ointment used with witches to achieve an altered state of consciousness. Again, this is a very toxic and dangerous herb and should only be used by the most knowledgeable practitioner.

- Benzoin—In incense form, benzoin is used for purifying and cleansing. It helps with focus and concentration and draws prosperity and the ability to astral travel. The oil can calm and soothe anxiety and is often used as a scented vapor to soothe the mind from exhaustion and stress.

- Bergamot—Used to attract money and prosperity in charms and spell casting.

Also promotes good sleep habits. It heals cuts, bruises, scrapes, and acne when used externally.

- Black Cohosh—Well known for its properties that relieve symptoms of menopause, this perennial plant, topped by a long plume of white flowers, is native to North America and part of the buttercup family. It has been studied extensively for reducing hot flashes, cramping, and other "female" maladies, especially during premenopause and menopause, especially for women who were not able to take estrogen. This plant offers protection, love, courage, and power, and, in supplement form, it also enhances energy.

- Black Pepper—This spice can be used to banish negative spirits and energy. It is often used in exorcisms to protect against evil and demonic energies. The spice boosts metabolism and increases serotonin production.

Also known as "nightshade," belladonna is easily distinguished by its dark-purple berries. The berries were once used to make women's pupils larger, which was considered beautiful during Renaissance Italy (*bella donna* in Italian means "pretty lady").

- Black Walnut—Use the nuts and the hull to detoxify the body, especially the intestines. The hull can fight fungal infections. Make green hull juice by mixing greens with ground hulls; this is known to destroy intestinal parasites.

- Blackberry Leaves—Dry and grind to use in spells for healing, protection, and attracting prosperity. Apply it to charms and candles to increase their spell casting power. Dry the fruit and grind into a powder to put into healing potions. Considered a superfood, blackberries are powerful, anti-inflammatory antioxidants, and chewing the leaves heals sore throats and mouth sores.

- Bladderwack—This plant, along with Irish sea moss, is great for reducing mucus and congestion because it has antiviral and antimicrobial properties. It also reduces inflammation, aids in weight loss, and promotes a healthy digestive system. Bladderwack also helps with eye and heart health and can reduce the effects of radiation. It also helps detox heavy metals out of the system.

- Bloodroot—A perennial herb that has special roots that give off rhizomes, useful in medicines. The rhizomes are also found in the leaves, which should be dried before use.

- Bluebells—Bluebells are called "fairy flowers" because legend has it that if you trample them, you will be cursed by fairy folk. Grow them to keep the fairies on your side, and plant them on graves to comfort those who come to mourn and bring peace to the dead. If you want to stop nightmares, hang bluebells above your bed. If you can turn a bluebell inside out without breaking the flower, legend says that you will find your true love.

- Boneset—This herb is used in exorcisms by rubbing the leaves on the possessed person's body, then the leaves are burned outdoors to rid them of demons. Sprinkle a boneset infusion around the house to keep out evil.

- Buckeye—*Toxic! Do not consume!* The nutlike seed of several trees of the same family is known to aid divination and bring money, wealth, and good fortune when used in charms and spells. The seed and plant are toxic, so use for spell casting only.

- Broom—Used in spells for protection, working with the wind, and assisting divination. It is often made into handfasting or ritual brooms. Grind into a powder, and sprinkle in and around the house for extra safety and to rid evil demons. The stem oil stops toothaches. Because of its potential to cause hallucinations in large doses, it has become associated with the method of witch travel, the famous flying broomsticks, but may be more symbolic than literal!

- Burdock—A biennial plant with roots that can be dried and used in cooking and spell casting, especially in tinctures, burdock is considered an antioxidant superpower when it comes to natural healing. Be aware that the roots are oily and go rancid fast, so

Black Walnut

Use the nuts and the hull to detoxify the body, especially the intestines. The hull can fight fungal infections. Make green hull juice by mixing greens with ground hulls; this is known to destroy intestinal parasites.

be sure to clean and dry them quickly. The leaves remove negativity and purify the body's tissues. The root is used for protection spells and love spells since it is considered an aphrodisiac and for general healing. Burdock has some diuretic properties. In traditional healing, it has been used to remove toxins from the blood and slow the growth of cancers. Can be used in tea form or small amounts of fresh or dried root. It is a diuretic, so if taking internally, drink plenty of water.

- Butterbur—An herb that rivals any over-the-counter allergy drug. Studies show that it treats allergy symptoms as well as the leading ingredient in Zyrtec, cetirizine, without the drowsy side effects.

- Cactus—The plant and its flowers are used in banishing and protection spells, especially the needles. Cacti grow well in the home and are great for kitchen witches. Place small cacti on your altar or in your kitchen to protect your home. Try to place them in the four directions of the house for best protection.

- Calendula/Marigold—Calendula is a perennial plant that is a close relative of the marigold plant. It has yellow flowers that look like daisies because they are a part of the daisy family. Calendula is a powerful antiviral, anti-inflammatory herb that is often used in salves and infusions. Use it in spells to honor the sun and sun gods. The oil from the plant can consecrate altar tools and remove negative energies and attachments, and the petals can be included in incense for divination. Put it in sacred baths to honor the sun and hang calendula garlands around the house for protection. Calendula salve, cream, and balm heals cuts,

wounds, scratches, scrapes, and rashes and treats skin diseases such as psoriasis, eczema, and skin ulcers.

- California Poppy—A sedating plant that reduces anxiety and stress and can help alleviate insomnia without groggy side effects or the threat of dependency. The roots and aboveground parts of the flower work best in a tincture, with just a few drops providing relief, but you can also make a tea. This plant could cause uterine contraction in pregnant women and is best avoided. Do not give to children under the age of six because of sedating properties.

- Camellia—Attracts riches, luxury, and the admiration and respect of others. Pink camellia is used to gain love or mesmerize another person. Red camellia works to draw love, affection, and happiness.

- Camphor—*Toxic; do not consume!* Use the leaves for promoting divination and prophetic dreams. Assists in easing spasms, breathing issues, and pain when camphor oil is used in vaporizers

A perennial flowering plant that has elements good for many uses, calendula is used in healing salves for the skin.

and aromatherapy. It can also treat wounds and skin disorders.

- Caraway—The plant and seed can attract lust, mental acuity, health, and protection. The seeds calm and soothe, and they also assist in meditation. Bake the seeds into bread, muffins, cookies, etc., and you may induce lust and infatuation from those who consume them! The seeds made into tea form stop colic and digestive disorders.

- Carnation—These colorful, flowering plants offer healing, energy, strength, and protection and create affection in spells for love. The pink flower is used for love and friendship. The red flower brings admiration and respect. The purple flower assists with spells for making changes. The white flower promotes innocent and pure love.

- Catnip—This plant and its associated herb are effective in any ritual or spell involving feline deities. Mixed with other herbs, it aids in love spells and, if grown outside the house, attracts positive spirits and energy. Put a little catnip in a charm or mojo bag for good luck all day, but don't be surprised to see a line of cats following you wherever you go.

- Cedar—A powerful smoke or incense for cleansing and purifying. Used in spells, cedar promotes courage, power, strength, healing, and protection. A favorite of Native Americans and indigenous tribes. The oil makes a natural insecticide and, as medicine, stops breathing issues, congestion, infections, bronchitis, and acne and other skin disorders.

- Celery—Use the stalk and leaves for spells to bring love or lust, enhance psychic abilities, and strengthen the mind. It lowers blood pressure and stops cancer when the stalk is eaten, and the entire stalk, leaves, and celery heart contain a ton of fiber, vitamins, and minerals. Juice those to get the benefit or include all parts of celery in salads. Celery is anti-inflammatory and helps manage diabetes and blood sugar, promotes liver health, boosts the immune system, acts as a diuretic to rid the body of excess water, protects the heart, and aids in a healthy digestion system and weight loss. It contains no fat and makes a great and filling snack.

- Chamomile—This is the "lucky" herb and is used in spells for love, money, and wealth. When worn in a charm or mojo bag, it can create sexual lust in others. It is a gambler's favorite flower! Use chamomile in spells for uncrossing a hex, cleansing the spirit, and washing off negative energies from the body when used in a rinse or lotion form. The tea is soothing for an upset stomach and aids sleep with its calming properties. The incense form rids the body and mind of stress and anxiety. Sprinkle it around the house inside and out to ward off bad energies.

- Chaste Tree—Not used much in magical work but another strong plant for relieving PMS symptoms in women when taken in herb form with minimal side effects. You can grow chaste trees at home in your garden for the lovely clusters of blue/purple flowers, or take an organic chaste tree supplement for the medicinal benefits.

- Cherry and Cherry Bark/Wood—Burn the bark in incense to increase its powers of divination. Creates lust in others for you when used in spell casting. The actual cherries are an aphrodisiac and also work better than most pain relievers thanks to their anti-inflammatory properties.

- Chia—The tiny, black seeds of the Salvia hispanica plant are potent antioxidants, and just two tablespoons gives you more potassium than a banana, more than five times the calcium of milk, and more than three times the iron of spinach. High in magnesium, fiber, healthy fats, and omega-3 fatty acids, the seeds of the chia plant can be eaten whole, sprinkled onto salads and meals, or ground and included in juices and sauces. Chia seeds have been considered an important plant by ancient Mayan and Aztec healing traditions. The word "chia" means "strength" in the ancient Mayan language. Today, chia seeds are considered a superfood because of the abundance of vitamins and minerals packed into the tiny, little seeds.

- Chickweed—This common plant found throughout North America attracts love and increases fertility. Use in a poultice or make into a salve, balm, or ointment to help relieve dry and inflamed skin with its cooling effect. It is also called starweed because of its little, star-shaped flowers. It has been used as a folk remedy for hundreds of years to cure asthma, constipation, blood disorders, skin ailments like psoriasis and eczema, and obesity. High in vitamin C, important trace minerals, and potassium, it prevents infection and inflammation. You can eat the young shoots in salads, too, or infuse it with apple cider vinegar. Be aware that reports have been made of paralysis caused by using large amounts of the plant in infusions. Use in small doses.

- Chicory—A biennial plant that has a wonderful root for many uses, even making a tasty coffee brew! In spell casting, it removes blocks and obstacles and attracts the good favor of others. It makes a great digestive tonic.

- Chili Peppers—Use sparingly to heat up a relationship, bring love and fidelity, break a curse, or cast out negative energies. Chili peppers are part of the *Capsicum* genus and nightshade family; the capsaicin charges up the body's metabolism and improves red blood cell formation, cognitive function, and clears out sinus and nasal congestion. It also lowers blood pressure and acts as a natural pain reliever.

- Chives—This grassy plant can be used in spells and charms to aid weight loss and protect the home and body. You can pick chives right out of the ground, rinse them off, and put them in a salad for their oniony taste.

- Chocolate/Cocoa—The cocoa tree is considered sacred, and the oil from the beans is a great love attractor. Dark chocolate is an aphrodisiac and also a superfood that, consumed in moderation, lowers blood pressure and reduces free radicals. Never give chocolate to your dogs or cats. It can be ground into a powder or melted to use in spell casting concoctions.

Often referred to as a "superfood," chia seeds have been eaten by man as far back as the ancient civilizations in Mexico and South America.

- Chokecherry—Native American tribes use this as an all-purpose medicinal treatment. The berries are pitted, dried, and crushed into a tea or a poultice to treat a variety of ailments such as coughs, colds, the flu, nausea, inflammation, and diarrhea. As a salve or poultice, it treats burns and wounds. The pit of the chokecherry is poisonous in high concentrations, so remove the pits before using.

- Chrysanthemum—A protection flower that also brings cheerfulness to the mind and spirit. Red flowers are used for love spells. White are used to draw out honesty and truth and to protect against negative spirits.

- Cilantro—A popular herb that helps expel heavy metal toxins from the body. Contains chelating agents that attach themselves to the toxins and are released through the excretory channels.

- Cinnamon—A great spice to use in prosperity spells. Sprinkle some around

A very popular spice with a great array of properties from being an aphrodisiac to helping digestion to lifting one's spirits, cinnamon can be used in love spells and assists with psychic abilities.

the altar to promote healing, raise spiritual energies, bring success, increase energy, and foster good luck. Wear some in a charm, eat or drink with foods to aid digestion, or burn in an incense form to increase wealth and lift the spirit. In an incense, cinnamon is used to bless a room or house. This spice is also considered an aphrodisiac. Wear a bit of cinnamon in a locket or charm when going out on a date or being with the one you want to commit to you. It works great in erotic love spells and sexual spells to increase libido. The tea form not only helps with digestive issues and headaches but aids in the development of psychic abilities and clairvoyance.

- Citronella—When burned in candle or incense form, it wards off bugs and mosquitoes while cleansing the aura. It encourages greater creativity and imagination and clears the mind of clutter while boosting psychic powers. Used on the skin, it can aid irritations and improve the look of wrinkles. Rub it on your feet to stop excessive sweating.

- Clover—A good-luck plant that also promotes success and wealth. Clover banishes negative spirits from the home and is often used in rituals to consecrate tools on the altar. Four-leaf clovers bring amazing good luck. White clover grows everywhere and is known for medicinal benefits. Because of its anti-inflammatory properties, it boosts the immune system when used as an infusion or strong tea. Wash it well before using if you pick it yourself to get rid of possible pesticides. Red clover is a highly sought-after weed for herbal medicines because of its high mineral, vitamin, and amino acid content. It has a gentle detoxifying effect on the body and helps deliver nutrients to the vital organs while ridding the body of metabolic waste. Red clover contains phytosterols, the building blocks of hormones, and helps balance hormonal issues. It can prevent hormone-related breast and prostate cancer. Red clover treats respiratory infections, boosts the immune system, and detoxifies the liver. It makes bones stronger and contributes to heart health. Drink it in a tea, or include the dried herbs in foods and juices. Red clover salves, balms, and ointments are a popular natural topical medicine.

- Cloves—Not only do they smell strong, they bring good fortune, love, and protection from evil spirits when used in charms and spells. Cloves are wonderful for attracting new friendships and have a masculine, protective quality, too. Cloves possess antibacterial, antiviral, antifungal, antimicrobial, and antiparasitic properties that dissolve the eggs of parasites and worms in the intestinal system.

- Coconut—The tree that gives us coconuts should be commended for providing us with one of the healthiest foods on the planet in the form of coconut oil. Over 1,500 studies have been published showing the positive benefits of coconut oil, and it is considered a healthy fat that promotes weight loss, lowers cholesterol levels, and improves skin and hair. Coconut oil contains about 62 percent medium chain triglycerides, known as MCTs, which are burned by the body as fat and also promote the burning of the body's own fat stores. Coconut oil is the best oil for cooking because it has a high heat stability of 350 degrees Fahrenheit.

- Coffee—The drink is a stimulant and is used in many rituals. Coffee added into the bath has a healing effect. Coffee is known for boosting energy, mood, and clarity, but space it out to avoid overstimulation from caffeine.

- Columbine—Attracts love and increases courage and self-esteem. The pretty, tall stalks of flowers are known to attract butterflies.

- Comfrey—Use for magical healing and money spells and to assist in the good outcome of real estate deals. Rub comfrey on your wallet to draw money to you, and sprinkle some comfrey tea on your luggage to assure safety when traveling. As a medicine, in small doses, it can aid digestion, ulcers, and bronchitis. Not meant to be consumed in excess.

- Coriander—An herb to fight off evil spirits and attract love, health, and good fortune.

- Cornflower—Considered the patron herb of herbalists and botanists, this flowering plant brings psychic abilities.

- Cotton—Brings luck, protection, and rain when needed. Used by fishermen for good catches and safe waters.

Not only are cucumbers edible and good for you, they can even be sliced and used to cover one's eyes to rejuvenate the skin beneath. You probably know that, but did you know they assist with astral travel as well?

- Cowslip—A healing plant that can also help you find lost treasure.
- Cucumber—The plant and actual cucumber can calm someone who is overexcited when rubbed on their skin, and it also cools and soothes sunburn. Slice thinly and place on the eyes during meditation to assist in astral traveling. Cucumber slices also heal undereye bags and circles. Hold a slice of cucumber on the roof of your mouth for 90 seconds. The photochemicals found in cucumber kill bacteria that causes bad breath.
- Cumin—The spice is used for protection, fidelity, and preventing theft. Mix it with some salt, and sprinkle around the perimeter of the home to ward off bad juju. It can be used in love spells and promotes loyalty and monogamy. Roasted cumin seeds heal mouth sores. You can boil a teaspoon in water to make a tea that soothes urinary tract issues and promotes a healthy bladder and kidneys. Cumin tea is a natural sleep aid.

Most people consider dandelions just weeds, but the flower, stem, and roots can all be used in spellcasting.

- Cypress—The wood can be burned in incense form to aid in divination and lessen grief and sorrow. This tree was sacred to Apollo. Hang a branch in the home for protection and carry a charm to calm a stormy mind. Cypress has the power to even give luck to the deceased and can be used in death and funeral ceremonies and rites.
- Daffodil—This bright, yellow flower brings love, fertility, luck, and positive vibes when grown in the home or garden. Put it on the altar to banish negative spirits. Daffodils signify springtime and are a great way to honor the goddesses of spring and fertility like Ostara and Brigid.
- Daisy—A sweet flower used in spells for love, fertility, lust, luck, and healthy babies. It is used in Wiccan baby blessings and, when grown in a baby's room, adds extra protection. Wear daisies to attract love to you.
- Damiana—The leaves of this plant can bring a new lover to you or draw back the intense passion you once had with an old lover. Use carefully because you might get what you wish for.
- Dandelion—We think of them as weeds, but dandelions are powerful for calling in spirits to assist you. As children, we all loved to blow on the seeds and make a wish, and, as adults, we can use them in spells to increase divination skills, bring prophetic dreams, and protect us while sleeping. Both the flowering part, the stalk, and the root are used in spell casting. Dandelion has long been used to fight bile and liver problems. Consuming them in plant form on salads or in tea form helps heal urinary infections, inflammation, eczema, psoriasis, digestion problems, cancer, diabetes, high blood pressure, irritable bowel syndrome, and a host of

other issues. Who knew that the most widely recognizable weed packed so much healing power? Pick them, clean them, eat them, or dry the leaves and roots to make dandelion tea.

- Dates—The date is considered an aphrodisiac in spell casting and is used in a dried form. If consumed, it has antioxidants that boost the immune system and compounds that lower blood pressure, balance blood sugar levels, and help prevent Alzheimer's. Just a handful of dates provides the body with magnesium, which dilates blood vessels for better circulation. They also contain potassium and help women who have gone through menopause maintain bone mass by reducing the amount of calcium excreted via the kidneys.

- Dill—Use the herb for protection, drawing luck and money to you and inciting lust in yourself or others. Dill is a popular condiment spice that is part of the celery family with many health benefits. Dill relieves digestion problems like gas and bloating and prevents diarrhea. It reduces the severity of menstrual cramps in women, and its flavonoids and B vitamins can help you get a good night's sleep. Have a bad case of the hiccups? Consuming dill can stop them in their tracks by dissolving trapped gas in the esophagus.

- Dogbane—The tall and poisonous plant is used in spell casting, especially in love spells. It is not meant to be consumed. The word "bane" refers to death and indicates a plant that is not meant for internal use.

- Dogwood—These flowers bring protection, grant wishes, and keep secrets secret, especially if they are in writing. If you rub the leaves on doorknobs, nothing bad can enter the room. The bark of the tree is an astringent and stimulant, so use carefully.

- Dragon's Blood—This plant protects and purifies. It adds extra potency to magic and spells and is used to banish demonic energies in exorcisms. Put a stick under your pillow to cure impotency. Burning the wood resin can bring back a stray lover. As a medicine, it stops pain.

- Echinacea—A healing perennial plant and bitter herb that adds more power to a charm or spell and is offered as a gift to spirits to gain their favor. The root can be harvested right after the first frost and before the first snow. The herb boosts a weak immune system and is both antibacterial and antiviral. Topically, it heals stings, wounds, bites, and skin infections, even poisonous bites from snakes and spiders. It also heals toothaches, sore throats, respiratory infections, colds, the flu, herpes, skin ulcers, and swelling of the

A plant known for its tasty berries that can also be used to make a healthy syrup, elderberry is known as a popular herbal remedy.

lymph nodes. Drink it in tea form or in a tincture.

- Elder Black Bark—Used in exorcisms and protection spells. Brings peace, prosperity, and overall healing. Elder black fruit promotes monogamy, popularity, and success in business and life.

- Elder Flower—The sacred plant of the Elder Mother, who lives inside of trees. The frothy flowers fight the signs of aging when infused in oils and is used as a serum on the skin to prevent fine wrinkles and age spots.

- Elderberry—Elderberry is a potent superhealer rich in minerals and vitamins, including vitamins A, B, and C. Used in teas, tinctures, syrups, or extracts, the berries and flowers help heal colds, flu bugs, respiratory infections, fevers, stomachaches, constipation, and viral infections. Elderberry, which is part of the honeysuckle family, is one of the best herbal remedies for boosting the immune system. Because of its pleasant taste, it is a favorite herbal remedy for children when made into a syrup form. The elderberry bush blooms in late spring with its pretty cluster of white- and cream-colored flowers and bursts of small, black, blue-black, or red berries.

- Elecampane Root—This nutrient-rich root works well as an expectorant to alleviate coughs, chronic cough, bronchitis, colds, and the flu.

- Elm Slippery Bark—Use the inner layer of the bark of this tree, found in central and eastern United States, for spells to bring love and understanding and promote divination abilities. It is also called slippery bark elm and has a host of properties that help fight sore throats (slippery elm is a common ingredient in throat lozenges), possibly increase bowel movements, and, in small studies, prevent constipation and bloating.

- Endive—A love spell plant that also incites lust. This bitter, leafy vegetable is loaded with vitamins and minerals and is sometimes referred to as common chicory.

- Eucalyptus—A potent protection and purification aid. The leaves of the tree are anti-inflammatory and great for healing and ridding the body of disease, especially arthritis and muscular pain.

- Eyebright—Helps develop psychic powers and mental acuity. Allows you to see through lies and cast spells for a clear mind. Eyebright is an anti-inflammatory with the ability to stop a cough or sore throat. It also soothes tired eyes and has a cooling effect on the skin.

- Fennel—The seeds are put into charms and amulets for protection, healing, and purification.

- Fenugreek—This bitter herb brings renewed life to flowers and plants when sprinkled in soil. As a medicine, it helps milk flow in breastfeeding women, lowers fever, reduces blood sugar levels, and has both a laxative and diuretic effect. It has antitumor and antiparasitic properties, and the sprouts promote hair growth. Men can use it to increase libido and prevent premature ejaculation.

- Fern—The leaves of the fern plant can be used to bring about mental and emotional clarity and cleanse and purify a room or space in your home or office. Ferns are also used in spells to bring rain and draw riches to you.

- Feverfew—A powerful protection plant, especially for those traveling. Use in spells for inner strength and fortitude.

Feverfew tea can help stop migraine headaches, menstrual cramps, arthritis pain, and muscle spasms.

- Fig Leaves—The entire fig plant, which is part of the mulberry family, is useful in different ways. The fruit aids divination and prophetic dreams and is considered an aphrodisiac. The leaves are potent for love and fertility spells. Fig plants were sacred in the Middle East, and, if you recall, it was a fig leaf that stood between Adam and Eve and complete nakedness in the Old Testament's Garden of Eden. Figs contain phytochemicals and polyphenols similar to garlic. The milky sap of the fig plant was used in Mediterranean folk medicine to soften calluses and warts so they could be removed and to ward off parasites. Research has shown that figs can lower blood pressure, rid the body of dangerous free radicals, and protect against cancer, diabetes, and infections. Fresh or dried figs contain vitamins A, E, K, and B-complex along with minerals. Word of warning—fig leaves and unripe figs release a form of white latex that can cause irritation and allergic reactions when it comes in contact with skin.

- Five Finger Grass—This herb can bring success and influence others to help you achieve success. It is put into a bath to relieve a curse or hex. Take a bath with the herb for nine days to get rid of pesky, troublesome bad luck streaks, or carry some in a green mojo bag to bring money and prosperity.

- Flaxseed—Used to bring money, love, protection, and healing in spell casting. Aids in developing psychic powers. When consumed, flaxseeds are one of the best superfoods for the body and immune system. Flax is one of the first domesticated crops known to man, related to the wild form of pale flax, and is also called linseed. Textiles made from flax are called linens, and the oil is referred to as linseed oil, although we now have flaxseed oil, which contains properties for healing menstrual and menopausal discomfort and relieving hot flashes.

- Forget-Me-Not—A lovely flower that brings true love and preserves wonderful memories. Sharpens the mind and memory.

- Foxglove—A great plant for protecting the home when planted outdoors. Also potent in any spells or rituals that involve contacting spirits. Foxglove contains digoxin and helps with heart ailments. It should never be taken without supervision of a doctor.

- Gardenia—The fragrant and lovely ornamental flower is used in dried form to bring about peace, healing, and comfort to the ill. Potted flowers around a room can create a sanctuary for meditation, although gardenias are finicky, high-maintenance plants.

A bitter herb, fenugreek can lower a fever, reduce blood sugar, serve as a laxative and diuretic, and even assist breastfeeding women.

- Garlic—This herb and spice can invoke the goddess Hecate if you wish, or use it for healing, protection, purification, and banishment of evil spirits and hexes. Garlic is a potent protector against demons (remember all those vampire movies?). Growing garlic in and around your home protects you from evil and attracts good fortune. You can place one clove of garlic in the four corners of a room, office, or house to keep ghosts, demons, and negative energy away. The bulb can be harvested when the leaves start to die but do so before they turn brown completely. Garlic is antibacterial and lowers fever, reduces blood pressure and cholesterol levels, lowers blood sugar levels, and detoxes the body. It is considered a broad-spectrum antibiotic without the side effects of pharmaceutical antibiotics. As an antiviral, it helps fight bad colds, strep infections, and the flu and fights cancers of the stomach and colon. It is considered one of the most healing and beneficial superfoods around. It is also antifungal and can destroy parasites, fungal infections, fleas, ticks, and mosquitoes. Black garlic has twice the antioxidant levels of regular garlic.

- Geranium—A flowering plant that increases fertility and brings love, health, and protection. Geranium is an astringent that can minimize wrinkles on the skin. It is also a potent anti-inflammatory that works wonders to heal wounds. The fragrance is soothing and relaxing and helps relieve anxiety and nerve pain when used in an essential oil massage or bath.

- Ginger—A great perennial herb and root for healing stomach issues, which also promotes protection and general good health in charm form. When ground and mixed with other herbs, it intensifies the beneficial outcome of any spell or charm. Asian healing traditions consider ginger a longevity herb for its internal and external properties. When used as a salve or balm, it heals wounds and skin ailments. Ginger is one of the best medicinal anti-inflammatory plants for stopping nausea, healing morning sickness, controlling spasms and pain, improving circulation and heart health, and aiding digestion. Ginger can be taken in supplement form or brewed into a tea with two teaspoons of freshly grated ginger root per cup of water. Ginger chews are now a popular way to deal with motion sickness while traveling.

Famous for increasing mental acuity and increasing blood flow, the leaves from the gingko rate high on the list of useful medicinal plants.

- Gingko—Sharpens the mind and increases clarity. This tree is sacred to gods and goddesses and is the oldest living plant in the world, considered a "living fossil" because it dates back some 270 million years. It is used as a medicine for improving memory, focus, energy levels, and attention. As gingko biloba in herb form or supplement form, it aids circulation, dilates blood vessels and bronchial tubes, and even treats impotence in men. The tree is so resilient and hardy, it survived the 1945 Hiroshima blast without major deformations.

- Ginseng—A plant used in spells for love, beauty, healing, lust, and protection. Can increase psychic abilities and bring about wisdom and enlightenment. If you cannot find mandrake, use ginseng for spell casting. Ginseng soothes anxiety and enhances sexual vigor. It improves physical stamina and helps the body fight disease. A powerful aphrodisiac, ginseng rejuvenates the body, mind, and spirit. According to WebMD, American ginseng studies have shown some sugar-lowering effects in fasting and after-meal blood sugar levels along with A1C levels in diabetics.

- Goldenrod—Use in money spells. Aids divination skills. As a medicine, it is bitter and astringent but reduces inflammation, stimulates liver and kidney function, and has antifungal properties. Many people use it to treat kidney stones.

- Goldenseal—A wonderful aid in healing rituals and spells for money, prosperity, and financial increase. When used with other ingredients, it amplifies the effects of a spell or charm. The herb is bitter and has blood-purifying effects. It helps with stomach and digestive issues, reduces inflammation and bleeding, and even works as a decongestant for stuffy noses.

- Grape—The fruit and leaves are used for fertility spells and in garden magic to bring money and mental strength.

Red and purple grapes are aphrodisiacs. Grapes, especially the red and purple kind, promote heart health, improve cholesterol levels, aid digestion, support balanced blood sugar levels, and strengthen bones and eyesight. The resveratrols in red and purple grapes and in wine are a known potent antioxidant.

- Grass—This simple plant is abundantly found and used for protection spells and to increase psychic abilities.

- Gum Arabic—Used for psychic and spiritual development, opening the Third Eye, and in meditation. Burn as part of an incense mix to achieve deeper spiritual states and consecrate ritual tools.

- Hawthorn—Use the leaves for drawing happiness, fertility, and good fortune. Used to bring luck to fishermen. Hawthorn tea made of the leaves and flowers helps lower blood pressure and improve blood circulation. It also calms and aids in treating sleeplessness. Hawthorn berries are used to make tea because it increases blood flow to the heart and is even known to help mend a broken heart. Hawthorn tea with rose is a warming drink for cold nights.

- Hazel—Use to attract luck, increase fertility, and protect from lightning strikes. Hazel is a name given to trees and shrubs natural to the temperate parts of the Northern Hemisphere, and witch hazel is specifically a favorite natural, topical medicine for treating insect bites and sunburn and as a refreshing facial spritzer or aftershave lotion.

- Heather—A light, pretty, purple-and-mauve flowering shrub used for spells of protection, love, and luck. Lavender heather brings admiration and respect.

Pink attracts luck and protection. White draws good luck and helps wishes to come true. Heather treats arthritis and prevents kidney stones. It has been used to treat tuberculosis in the past.

- Heliotrope—A powerful aid to bringing about invisibility and increasing prophetic dreams and visions. Used in exorcisms to rid evil spirits.

- Hemlock—*Toxic! Do not consume!* Hemlock aids in astral projection and prophetic dreams. It protects against negative spirits and energies and purifies anything the juice is rubbed on. It was used for flying ointments in medieval times due to its ability to alter consciousness slightly. It has no known medicinal value.

- Hemp—Use during meditation for drawing love, visions, and overall well-being. In medical marijuana form, it has many healing benefits and may effectively treat pain, cancerous tumors, glaucoma, and Alzheimer's. THC, an ingredient in hemp, has tumor-destroying properties. Hemp is such an all-purpose plant, it can be made into dozens of products like paper, clothing, fuel, pasta, foodstuffs, bedding, and containers that won't fill landfills and destroy the environment. The root of the hemp plant can remove radiation from soil through the process of phytoremediation, where the natural growth process of the plant absorbs harmful chemicals in the soil while putting back in beneficial nutrients. This process makes the soil fertile again for future growth.

- Hibiscus—This flowering plant is used to attract love and lust, aid with divination, and promote more vivid and lucid dreams. Tea made from hibiscus can lower blood pressure and fever and provides a great source of vitamin C.

- Hickory—Use in spells for love, protection, and aiding in legal challenges.

- High John the Conqueror—A popular root in Voodoo, often worn inside an amulet. It brings good luck and mastery of skills, and men can use it to boost libido.

- Holly—*Toxic! Do not consume!* A favorite plant at Yule, the berries and leaves can be ground or left as is for spells involving love, stable marriages, good luck, blessings, and happy dreams. If planted or hung outside, it protects the home from bad luck and energy. Carry holly berries to inspire your beloved to worship and adore you. Holly has no real medicinal value.

- Hollyhock—Increases luck, love, money, and wealth and brings success to anyone who lives in the home when planted nearby.

- Honeysuckle—*Toxic! Do not consume!* Draws money and success and brings material wealth. Used in love spells, it binds two people together. Increases psychic powers, especially when rubbed on the temples. Burned as incense, it can aid in magical practices.

- Hops—This plant, which beer is made with, helps with sleep issues. Fill up a sachet with hops and put it under your pillow at night. Hops treats anxiety and has hormonal and antibacterial properties. It's a bitter herb and a diuretic. It relieves pain and muscle spasms but is believed to put a damper on sexual energy.

- Horse Chestnut—Used in money and healing spells.

- Horseradish—The leaves and roots of this perennial herb can be used both for purification and protection from evil and negative spirits, and a part of the root can be replanted to grow for the next year. Though it is best known as a condiment, the plant roots are used in medicines to treat coughs, colic, gout, intestinal disorders, swollen joints, nerve pain, spasms, and bacterial infections. When applied directly to the skin, it eases the pain of inflamed tissues and minor muscle aches.

- Huckleberry—Brings luck and protection and breaks curses and hexes. Put some under your pillow in a sachet to aid in dream magic and prophetic dreams. The huckleberry is the state fruit of Idaho and has been used in Native American traditional medicine for hundreds of years. The small, round berries are similar to blueberries, but they are more tart in taste. Medicines using huckleberry treat pain, infections, and heart ailments.

- Hydrangea—A lovely flower used for breaking a hex or curse. Also attracts love and loyalty and binds two hearts together in love spells.

- Hyssop—This is a purification herb used to cleanse your body and clear your home from negative energy. It works great to remove bad jinxes, hexes, and negative juju energy. Use it to consecrate ritual tools. Steep it in water and clean your altar with it for extra protection. You can also take a ritual bath with it. This bitter and astringent herb can be used as an expectorant, to aid digestion, and lower fever in a tonic form. It is an anti-inflammatory. The actual mold that penicillin is made from grows on the leaves.

- Iris—Use in spells for love, hope, wisdom, and cleansing. The colorful and showy flower itself is named after the Greek word for rainbow and the Greek goddess of rainbows herself, Iris.

- Irish Moss—A potent plant to draw money, luck, and good fortune. It is not a moss at all but a species of red algae that grows along the rocky parts of the Atlantic coast in North America and Europe.

- Ivy—Ivy hung in the entrance of your home will ward off negative spirits and energies. It also discourages unwanted guests. Door-to-door salespeople, beware! Ivy also increases fidelity in love magic.

- Jasmine—This sweet-scented flowering plant is often used to assist sleep and promote prophetic dreams. You can put the flowers in a sachet or under your pillow or burn the flowers in a ritual to attract financial abundance and inspire new ideas. Jasmine is a potent astringent, antibacterial, and antiviral herb. It can cool a fever or sunburned skin. It is considered an aphrodisiac but also has calming effects. Studies show that jasmine has a soothing effect and relieves anxiety and stress. You can keep a jasmine

Besides being the first name of a famous Mark Twain character, huckleberries are rich in antioxidants and are useful in fighting infections.

plant in your bedroom or use essential oils to get the calming benefits of the GABA receptor modulator found in jasmine, which aids sleep and relieves aggression. Researchers have found jasmine aromatherapy to be more effective than anti-anxiety medications, sleeping pills, and sedatives.

- Jimson Weed—Use to attract luck, desires, and wishes in spell casting in its dried form. Also called Devil's Snare, it is part of the nightshade family and is considered a hallucinogen. It's been used in treating addictions and drug abuse, but mainly, it is taken for its deliriant effects of intense visions. Too much of this plant is severely toxic.

- Juniper—Use various parts to burn as incense for protection and to banish ill health. Carry the berries as a charm to attract love. Juniper plants outside the home, especially on your doorstep, will keep out thieves and attract positive energy. The herb is strongly aromatic and bitter. It is both an antiseptic and a diuretic, which improves digestion and reduces inflammation. It makes a wonderful aromatherapy oil.

- Kava-Kava—Brings good luck and protection and increases visions and psychic abilities. The herbal remedy is made from the roots of the Piper methysticum plant that is native to the islands of the Pacific Ocean, especially Polynesia, and is used in rituals and ceremonies to promote calm and relaxation.

- Kudzu—A weed that has been used in ancient Chinese medicine for thousands of years. The roots and flowers are nutritious and alleviate vomiting, nausea, fever, and diarrhea. It also eases menstrual cramps, hot flashes, migraine headaches, and psoriasis. Best used as a tea.

- Lamb's Quarters—This common garden weed is found all over North America and is filled with amazing medicinal properties. It includes the same amount of protein as spinach and plenty of vitamin A, vitamin C, iron, minerals, calcium, and phosphorous. It has properties that improve blood flow, treat rheumatism and arthritis, heal insect bites and stings, lessen the effects of tooth decay, and relieve constipation. The leaves, flowers, and shoots can be eaten in salads or meals juiced or steamed. The seeds are not meant to be eaten in large quantities.

- Larkspur—Brings health and protection from negative energies. Larkspur is part of the buttercup family and ranges from white to purple and blue flowers.

- Laurel—A favorite for brides to wear on their heads, as it brings love, happy marriages, and protection. Ancient Egyptians made crowns of this evergreen tree with small, yellow flowers to put on the victors of the Pythian Games.

- Lavender—The flowers make for a sweet-smelling essential oil, lotion, or potion, and they bring passion, romance, friendship, and harmony. Lavender is also used for protection, purification, bringing peace of mind, and aiding in a good night's sleep when used in dried form in a sleep pillow, a few spritzes of essential oil on your pillow, or in the bathtub to relax and calm before bedtime. Because of its association with Mercury, the messenger, lavender is said to also increase telepathic communication and psychic ability. Lavender oil calms and soothes bug bites and stings. It has a relaxing effect and helps relieve headaches and ear infections.

- Lemon—Grind the rind and use in spells for friendship and love, especially long-lasting love. You can also use the fruit for purification and cleansing spells and rituals. The sour, herbal form can soothe and cool skin and has diuretic, anti-inflammatory properties. It also soothes bites and insect stings and reduces the effects of eczema. Lemon in water helps stop sore throats, and a little lemon juice in the hair lightens and brightens highlights.

- Lemon Balm—Once used by the ancient Romans and Greeks, lemon balm brings love, healing, and success in spells due to its association with the god Jupiter and the element of water, which aids in emotional strength. This perennial herb, a garden favorite for its fast and prolific growth, is part of the mint family from the *Melissa* genus and is also called dropsy plant, honey plant, and cure-all. Lemon balm treats digestive problems, gas, bloating, vomiting, headaches, menstrual pain, and toothaches and has a calming effect that lowers anxiety and stress, yet also uplifts the spirit. It has been used as a part of aromatherapy for treating Alzheimer's, autoimmune diseases, Graves' disease, ADHD, and thyroid issues and also lowers blood pressure, fights off tumors, and, when applied to the skin, treats bites, stings, and wounds. Lemon balm extraction and oil are favorite herbal remedy ingredients our ancestors used for hundreds of years. The delicate lemon flavor makes it a wonderful addition to salads and meals and as a soothing tea or tincture. Dried leaves can be made into an essential oil or a soothing salve, balm, or ointment for the skin. Lemon balm tea is a safe remedy for children to calm restlessness and aid in sleep. It can stop teething pain in babies when rubbed on the gums.

- Lemon Verbena—Use to draw love and to purify and cleanse evil energies.

- Lemongrass—Repels snakes and draws psychic abilities. Soothes the nerves and has antimicrobial, antifungal, analgesic, and antioxidant properties. Used in aromatherapy, it restores energy and fights jetlag.

- Lettuce—Use the leaves to bring love, purification, protection, better sleep, and divination powers.

- Licorice—The root is a powerful agent for controlling others and gaining power over them. It can help change someone's mind but use carefully and only for the benefit of another, or it can come back to haunt you. Licorice tea fights laryngitis and is also a mild laxative. Use internally with caution, though, because it does contain natural estrogen.

- Lilac—Brings wisdom, luck, protection, and love. The flowers are used to treat kidney issues, but it has no other known medicinal values.

- Lily—Used for fertility and marriage rituals to bring good luck and happiness.

A cure for many ailments, lemon balm has a very nice fragrance and is used in aromatherapy; drinking tea made with it can help you sleep, too.

Also great for prosperity spells. You can use lily in spells to break someone else's hold on you. Lily can only be used externally as a medicine. It helps heal irritated, dry skin and treats burns and scalds.

- Lily of the Valley—*Toxic! Do not consume!* Use in rituals and spells to stop bullies and end harassment. Also works in spells for a happy and long marriage and for happiness in general.

- Lime—Used like the lemon for healing, love, and protection. Drops of lime used in incense or rubbed on candles are said to keep someone from cheating. The juice of the lime is great for stopping diarrhea, and the essential oil is energizing and mood boosting. Lime oil is antiseptic, antiviral, and astringent and can be used as a disinfectant.

Lily of the Valley

Toxic! Do not consume! Use in rituals and spells to stop bullies and end harassment. Also works in spells for a happy and long marriage and for happiness in general.

- Lotus—The flower is used in spells for love and protection and also in spells to open something that is locked.

- Lucky Hand Root—A wild orchid that looks like a hand with fingers. It's great for gamblers or those wanting to attract luck, especially with money concerns.

- Mandrake—*Toxic! Do not consume!* A favorite for protection from evil. It can be used in charms and spells to attract money and increase fertility. Put it in a charm to wear and attract love. It also increases visions and the ability to prophecy, as it has hallucinatory properties. All of the plant is toxic and has no medicinal use.

- Maple—The seeds can be used for love and luck magic.

- Marigold—The orange flower petals work to help legal matters, aid in prophecy and divination, attract love, and, when planted around the house, banish negative energy from every room. It is often used in rituals revolving around death and the dead. The oil of the petals is used to consecrate objects and altar tools. No medicinal uses are known.

- Marjoram—A powerful cleansing and purification plant that gets rid of all negative spirits and energies. When used in a sleep pillow or sachet, it can attract pleasant dreams. The leaves can be burned to bring good luck to a new business. Place leaves in the corners of your house for protection or use marjoram in money spells to make them work even better.

- Marshmallow and Root—Burn the root in incense form to protect the home and increase your psychic abilities. Use on the altar during rituals, as it attracts positive spirits to aid your spell casting. The herbal part of the plant brings love and protection and is used to purify objects before a ritual. The herb controls bacterial infections and can boost cellular immunity.

- Milk Thistle—Brings protection, breaks hexes, and heals the body and spirit. This bitter herb is a diuretic that helps restore a healthy liver. It stops a hangover when used in a tonic. It can reduce the negative effects of chemotherapy.

- Mint—An energy herb that brings vitality to the body, mind, and spirit. Use on the altar to attract positive spirits. Plant mint in a pot, though, because if planted outside in the ground, it has a tendency to spread quickly. Mint is used to reduce fever and as an antibiotic.

- Mistletoe—*Toxic! Do not consume!* This plant brings fertility and love in spell casting and also protects from curses and hexes. It's a great charm to attract love, too.

- Morning Glory—*Toxic! Do not consume!* This beautiful, climbing flowering plant is used in spells for binding things and can ward off nightmares. The essence of the flower can help with anxiety and also aids in divination and astral travel.

- Motherwort—A weed that can improve heart health and lower stress. It relaxes blood vessels and lowers blood pressure to improve circulation. Because of its relaxing properties, it relieves anxiety in teas, tonics, and infusions.

- Mullein—A powerful biennial plant that can banish nightmares and negative spirits. It can be dried as an herb, or the root can be used in sachet pillows or in charms worn on the body to attract a lover. As an infusion in tea or added to a salad, this plant has been used by Native Americans to treat inflammation, coughs, congestion, and general lung afflictions. It is quite common and may be growing in your own backyard.

- Mustard—The seed brings opportunity, good fortune, and positive changes. Mustard poultices have long been used to help stop respiratory issues and stimulate the immune system. Mustard packs can also relieve pain and sore muscles.

- Myrtle—Attracts love and true friendships and promotes youth, peace, and wealth. Myrtle was sacred to the goddess Aphrodite/Venus and is said to aid in interpreting dreams. Keep some in a sachet under your pillow. The oil heals sinus infections.

- Nettle—Nettle can stop a hex or curse and turn it back on the person who cast it if you stuff the herb into a Voodoo doll or poppet. Sprinkle the dried form around the perimeter of your home to ward off negative spirits. Nettle was sacred to the thunder god, Thor, and was tossed into fires during storms for protection. The leaves can help stop heavy bleeding, hemorrhoids, gout, and allergies. The roots

A perfect herbal plant for teas that will relax the consumer by easing pressure in the blood vessels, motherwort can be used in teas, tonics, and infusions.

stop allergies and reduce prostate cancer. Nettle is a known treatment for eczema when used on the skin as a topical remedy. It can also be turned into a pesto sauce and be eaten in cakes and soups.

• Nutmeg—A spice for attracting money and luck but can also break a curse and banish negative spirits. Nutmeg is a masculine plant that you should keep on you when playing games of chance. Taken internally, it stops diarrhea and vomiting, bloating, gas, indigestion, and colic. Too much nutmeg smoked or taken internally can produce hallucinations and is considered very dangerous in large doses, so be warned.

• Olive—Use in spells for peace, love, fertility, healing, potency, power, and purity. The oil is a superfood and is sacred to the gods. The eternal flame of the original Olympic games burned olive oil, and those who won competitions were adorned in olive leaves. The herbal form is astringent and antiseptic and works well on lowering blood pressure and fevers and reducing stress and anxiety.

• Oregano—This potent-smelling herb protects against tiredness by giving an added boost to energy and vitality levels. It also assists in astral projection. Oregano oil is chock full of phenols and has antibiotic, antimicrobial, antiviral, and antiparasitic properties that can kill viruses and parasites. The oil has been a favorite medicine all the way back to ancient Greece, where it was used to heal wounds, bites, digestive issues, respiratory infections, and fungal infections. Today, it is used to restore the gut's microbial balance and fight stomach flus, ringworm, sinus infections, acne, warts, allergies,

and eczema. Because it is a strong oil, it should be diluted with a carrier oil before placing on the skin.

• Orris Root—Use it in spells to attract a love partner. In Voodoo, it is considered love-drawing powder when the root is ground up. In its cut form, it can be put into a bath for protection, and the root powder can also be used at bath time for attracting love. It also protects against evil entities. Hang the leaves of the plant around the house for extra protection. As a tea, the orris root can be diuretic. It has little medicinal value but is great for cooking and making perfumes.

• Painted Daisies—Painted daisies contain pyrethrum, a natural insecticide. Plant the colorful flowers in and around gardens as a natural alternative to toxic insecticides.

• Parsley—This popular plant can be used as a fresh or dried herb in cooking and for drawing money and financial prosperity in spell work. It protects your home, and the leaves can be used in spell casting to rid stress and confusion or bring you added strength and vitality after an illness. It is also useful in medicinal remedies. Eat parsley to draw a lover to you, and mix it with jasmine and put it in your sock or shoe to attract others.

• Parsnip—Best for men to use during sex magic and for attracting lust and love.

• Passionflower—Like its name, it brings love, sexual flirtation, friendship, peace, and even better sleep at night. Passionflower has a long history of treating a variety of health conditions. It reduces anxiety and calms chaotic situations. It is bitter, has sedative properties, and, taken internally, can alleviate irritability, insomnia, and even withdrawal from drugs like Valium. It lowers blood pressure and stops muscle aches and spasms. Drink passionflower tea right before bed to calm the mind and help you fall asleep faster. Word of warning: side effects are possible, including vomiting, rapid heartbeat, drowsiness, and dizziness, so talk to your doctor first. Pregnant women, nursing women, children, and people with kidney or liver disease should avoid passionflower.

- Patchouli—A distinctly scented plant that brings love and money and increases fertility. In incense form, it calms, soothes, and attracts success. Smells great in sachets, mixtures, essential oils, and perfumes worn on the skin. Patchouli is used in meditation and yoga studios to assist with relaxation. As an oil used on the skin, it balances emotions and stimulates the growth of new skin cells.

- Peony—The flower protects against curses and brings good luck. Plant in the home for protection, and it even might attract faerie folk into your house! The flower petals are used in charms and spells, but the seed, or jumby bean, can be used in spells to heal conflict.

- Peppermint—Peppermint is a cross between watermint and spearmint. It's a multifaceted plant and a source of menthol. One of the oldest medicinal herbs known, in spell casting, it is used for protection spells and charms, to assist in legal battles, and even attracts money and abundance. If you burn peppermint incense, you can attract love into your life, and if you grow it in your home or garden, it is sure to raise good vibrations and also keep flies and mosquitoes at bay. Peppermint incense can assure that the neg-

ative energies of former homeowners are banished when you buy a new home. Peppermint essential oil, balms, and salves relieve pain, itching, muscle aches, and nausea. Peppermint tea boosts energy and aids in relieving irritable bowel syndrome.

- Periwinkle—*Toxic! Do not consume!* This is the patron herb of Wiccans. It brings love, lust, money, and protection. Use the dried flowers to make a magic mixture more powerful. Periwinkle should not be taken orally, as it has hallucinogenic effects and is toxic.

- Pine—The needles and cones can be used in healing, protection, fertility, and money spells. The scent of pine oil fights fatigue and relieves tension.

- Plantain—A perennial ground cover (broadleaf plantain) that is easy to cultivate in any type of soil with sunshine. Native Americans called it "life medicine," as it has many healing properties and has been used for healing all the way back to ancient times. The powdered root could ward off snakes

A multifaceted plant useful as a fragrance as much as for medicines, patchouli has properties of being a grounding, soothing, and peace-inducing scent on the skin.

and heal snakebites and was said to heal leprosy, dog bites, and epilepsy. It is anti-inflammatory, antiseptic, diuretic, expectorant, ophthalmic, cardiac, and antitussive, and it also is a great alternative medicine for respiratory and breathing problems. The plant extract is antibacterial and effectively stops excess bleeding and repairs wounds and damaged tissue. Poultices with ground or hot leaves stop inflammation, heal cuts and wounds, and even draw out thorns and splinters. Plantain packs a punch when it comes to vitamins and nutrients. It is high in vitamin K, calcium, and other minerals that have a detoxifying effect on the body, and, on top of that, it serves as food for important caterpillars to become butterflies. The young leaves are edible in salads and contain plenty of vitamin B1 and riboflavin. To top it all off, a plantain decoction made of the roots can stop smoking, as it causes an aversion to tobacco. It can be made into a tea, salve, balm, or poultice and is found in many backyards in North America. (The larger species of plantain offers bananalike fruit.)

- Pomegranate—The seeds of this lush fruit, sacred to the love goddess Aphrodite, are used in spells for love, romance, sexual vitality, and fertility. The fruit itself is a potent antioxidant and can be eaten as is or in juices and smoothies.

- Poppy—Brings love, prosperity, fertility, and love. The seeds are used to bring luck and, used in a sleep pillow, can help you fall asleep more easily. The poppy is used in baking and cooking, but the opium poppy is a potent plant that is now protected by monitoring agencies.

- Primrose—If you want to know the truth, cast a truth spell with primrose. It reveals the truth and honesty. The dainty flowers can be put into herbal baths, and the evening primrose oil is a powerful medicine.

- Purslane—The leaves are filled with healthy fiber, omega-3 fatty acids, vitamin A, vitamin B, vitamin C, iron, calcium, magnesium, copper, and potassium. The plant is a powerful medicine used for hundreds of years because of its antibacterial and detoxifying properties that treat high cholesterol, skin conditions, digestive problems, and cancer. Purslane can improve vision, aid weight loss, strengthen bones, reduce fevers, and rid the body of excess water as a diuretic. Plus, it gets rid of inflammation and headaches and can be included in herbal remedies for coughs and colds. The greens can be eaten in salads or juiced.

- Raspberry—The leaves are used in love, protection, and money spells.

Raspberries are another super food. Rich in vitamins and minerals, their leaves can also help with digestive issues.

Raspberry leaves provide respite from diarrhea and intestinal issues and, when made into a mouth rinse, can stop sore throats. Raspberry leaf tea can be put on the skin to soothe irritation and even tighten loose skin. The raspberry itself is one of nature's best superfoods and is full of vitamins and antioxidants.

- Rose—The gorgeous petals bring love, happiness, divination, luck, healing, and intuitive abilities. Rose water is widely used in love spells and potions. The petals can be put in sachets for attracting love and affection and even bring about a good night's sleep. As a medicine, the lovely rose is astringent and aromatic and controls bacterial infections. Rosehips treat colds, flus, scurvy, and digestive problems.

- Rose Petals—Great in spells or worn on the body in charms and lockets for attracting true love. Rose petals and rosebuds are powerful nervines, medicines for healing the nerves, relieving sadness, grief, and depression. The petals are anti-infective and anti-inflammatory and are an effective remedy for wounds, burns, sore muscles, and fatigue.

- Rosemary—An herb that brings love and desire. Used in a poppet or charm, it promotes a sharp memory, good health, and healing. Put it in an herbal bath for extra purification or burn for positive energy. Grow rosemary in your garden or in a pot inside your home, then turn it into a great essential oil for harmony, healing, protection, stress relief, and physical and emotional strength. Rosemary also protects women from harm because it is considered a masculine plant associated with the sun and the element of fire. Aside from being a favorite cooking

herb, rosemary relieves spasms, stimulates the liver and gallbladder, improves digestion and circulation, and has antibacterial, antifungal, antiviral, anti-inflammatory, antioxidant, analgesic, and other properties that make it a potent, all-purpose healing herb.

- Ruda—A magical herb that can ward off evil. Leave a pinch at your front door or carry it in a mojo bag for protection. You can make ruda tea and sprinkle it around the home for protection or use in herbal baths to either set or break a love spell.

- Saffron—A delicious spice used in spells for love, happiness, lust, and healing. It is an aphrodisiac. Use it when working weather magic, or place in sachets in drawers around the house to bring good vibes. Saffron reduces depression, and studies have shown it helps lessen the effects of Alzheimer's disease.

- Sage—A variety of dried leaves can be burned for the smoke used in smudging and cleansing an area of negative energies and spirits. Make your own sage by loosely bundling dried leaves and lighting them at one end. White sage is a favorite purifier. Sage can relieve muscle spasms and tension, stop excessive sweating, improve digestion, and even has antidepressant properties as well as being anti-inflammatory. Oil applied to the skin heals sores, acne, dermatitis, and skin ulcers.

- Saltpeter—A popular but highly flammable herb used in Voodoo and spell casting to keep lovers faithful, especially male lovers. Often used in exorcisms and purification rites to banish evil spirits.

- Sandalwood—Sprinkle it anywhere you want to keep bad luck and energy from entering your home. A little on your altar protects you during spell casting from evil spirits. Use the wood to make a wand or burn it as incense during yoga or meditation.

- Sea Salt—A quality salt is wonderful for cleansing, purification, and grounding rituals. Use it to cast a magic circle before you spell cast. It is also much healthier to consume than your average table salt, but make sure it's organic and doesn't contain any added chemicals or ingredients.

- Skullcap—Use the American skullcap. Though the name sounds creepy, it refers to the little caps of purple and blue flowers at the end of each branch. In incense, it binds lovers and keeps oaths from being broken. In a sleep pillow, it protects from nightmares and brings peaceful slumber. Burn it to diffuse conflicts and negative energy. Skullcap contains a flavonoid that has been shown to protect neurons in the brain after a traumatic brain injury and also has additional healing properties

Sea salt is recommended over ordinary table salt for spell casting because it is free of added potassium iodide and anticaking agents.

for heart health. It can be taken as a powdered extract or in liquid form. *Do not mix this up with the toxic deadly autumn skullcap mushroom!*

- Snake Plant—Snake plant releases nighttime oxygen. Grow the whole plant in a pot and keep in your bedroom to help you breathe better.

- Spearmint—This herb brings healing, love, and financial abundance. The oil is soothing to the skin, and the herb brings aid to digestive problems, gas, hiccups, fever, and upper respiratory tract issues.

- Spider Plant—One of the best indoor plants for purifying the air. Removes the toxins benzene and xylene, known toxins.

- St. John's Wort –An herb that relieves anxiety and prevents colds and fevers. It protects from dark magic and evil spirits. Burn it to drive away demons! Wearing the herb can protect you in war or battle. As a supplement or tea, it helps lessen depression and treats insomnia, menopause symptoms, PMS, shingles pain, sciatica, and inflammation of the stomach and intestinal walls from parasites.

- Stinging Nettle—This plant, when burned, banishes negative energies and spirits. It is associated with the powerful Mars and the element of fire and is a powerful protection plant when carried in a charm bag or sachet. Grind it up and use it in spells to break curses and get rid of bad mojo. Brooms made of stinging nettle sweep away evil from your home. Named for its slight sting to the skin in fresh form when acid is released from the needles, stinging nettle tea helps fight chronic fatigue and illness. The leaves have anti-allergy and anti-inflammatory properties and help lower blood pressure, boost the immune system, lessen allergy symptoms, reduce dandruff, thicken hair, rid the body of excess water, and treat prostate issues in men. It can be boiled and used in salads or baked into chips with a touch of salt or seasoning. The roots are edible when cooked or made into tea. It can have a slight sedative effect that reduces stress. If you harvest it yourself in the wild, use gloves to avoid skin contact with the needles.

- Strawberry Leaves—The leaves of the strawberry plant have medicinal properties that help reduce upset stomach and bloating. Rich in vitamin C, they are great for hair growth and healthy skin, and they also can relieve painful arthritis. The antifungal and antibacterial properties promote healing of the skin. Try drying some organically grown leaves as a tea to aid the digestive system.

- Sunflowers—This bright and happy flower is a symbol of good luck. It is associated with the sun and masculine energies and, in an essential oil form, can boost your confidence and self-esteem. Grow them in your garden for good luck, protection, and good energy, and if you stick one under your pillow at night, it will bring you truths revealed upon awakening. Sunflower seeds are a healthy snack, too.

- Sweetgrass—*Toxic! Do not consume!* This sacred herb can call spirits and guides to your aid. Use in smudging after a sage cleansing to bring in positive and good energies and spirits. Braid it and use as a smudge stick by lighting the tip. It has no medicinal benefits and can even be toxic if consumed.

- Tarragon—Use to being self-confidence and when working with dragon energy in spell casting. The oil can stimulate a sluggish digestive system and stop indigestion, hiccups, and menstrual pains.

- Thyme—This herb/spice attracts love, affection, and loyalty. Burn it as an incense to purify a room or banish bad vibes. Grow it in the home to attract good health. In a sleep pillow, thyme aids in peaceful slumber and happy dreams. Use the herb in a poultice or a tea for improving psychic abilities and purifying the body, mind, and spirit. Thyme is considered a feminine herb associated with the element of fire and can protect your money from thieves and saboteurs. It has the power to stimulate the thymus gland and boost immunity, and thyme oil destroys parasites in the intestines. It can be consumed dry or fresh.

- Valerian—In an herbal bath, it not only relaxes but protects and purifies the body. Used in spells, it creates a sacred space where directed and attracts love. It has sweetly scented, pink-and-white flowers that can be used in a charm bag when dried. Valerian is noted for promoting sleep and relaxation and makes a wonderful and soothing evening tea. In herb form, it lowers blood pressure and improves digestion. Valerian is one of the few plants prescribed by doctors for sleep and anxiety issues and for generalized anxiety disorders thanks to research studies showing its effectiveness as equal to that of drugs like Valium. It does take a few weeks to begin working as a sleep and anxiety aid as it builds up in the system and does have mild side effects of headache, upset stomach, palpitations, and dizziness. Because of its sedative effects, it should never be taken with alcohol or other sedating medications.

- Vanilla—The bean/pod, when used in spells, brings love, lust, and comfort. Use in a floor wash to bring protection and happiness to the home. Vanilla attracts luck and money. It makes a nice remedy for a fever and acts as an aphrodisiac.
- Vervain—This plant has a variety of spell uses. It brings protection, money, healing, good sleep, and, in the form of herbal baths, cleansing of the mind and spirit. A favorite herb of witches, it purifies, brings a youthful energy, enhances dream interpretation, empowers all spells, and is one of the most widely used plants in spell casting.
- White Willow Bark— This plant guards you from negative people and energy. It's used for healing spells and works wonders on a bad headache. White willow bark is a natural pain reliever and fever reducer once used by Native Americans. Aspirin is made with similar ingredients, proving that Mother Nature always does it first and best.
- Willow—The branches make great magical wands, and the leaves are used for protection, divination, and inspiration of new ideas. They also attract love, fertility, and healing and promote intuition.
- Witch Hazel Bark—Use for protection and to keep your lover chaste and honest. Carry the bark to help a broken heart heal or lessen desire for a toxic person. It can also ward off evil. As a topical treatment, witch hazel is well known to heal skin issues.

Vanilla

The bean/pod, when used in spells, brings love, lust, and comfort. Use in a floor wash to bring protection and happiness to the home. Vanilla attracts luck and money. It makes a nice remedy for a fever and acts as an aphrodisiac.

- Wolfsbane—*Toxic! Do not consume! Also toxic to the skin.* This powerful plant is used in Voodoo and rituals such as exorcisms to banish demons and evil spirits. Grind the dried root into a powder for spell casting, but be careful to keep it from coming into contact with your skin, as it can cause rashes and allergic reactions.
- Wormwood—*Potentially toxic.* Remove anger and stop violence with this powerful plant that is part of the *Artemisia* genus along with mugwort. It is used to make absinthe, a toxic, addictive, and hallucinogenic beverage. When burned, it helps promote divination and psychic abilities and facilitates visions and clairvoyance. Though the wormwood plant is indeed a medicine that can be taken internally, the risk for overconsumption on the compound thujone, used to make absinthe, could lead to gastric distress and should be avoided unless you really know what you are doing. Minus the thujone or in smaller doses, wormwood has been used since biblical times to rid the body of parasites and relieve the symptoms of parasitic infections, including fever, diarrhea, cramping, aches, nausea, and bloating. It also has a history of destroying the parasites that get into the bloodstream from infected mosquitoes that cause malaria. Another active ingredient, artemisinin, has been shown in research studies to break down cancer cells and kill them.
- Yarrow—The little, white flowers and feathery leaves of this fast-growing,

wild plant are used for healing rituals and promote divination. In handfasting and weddings, yarrow draws love and peace into relationships. A body of scientific research indicates that this common perennial herb, found growing wild in fields, pastures, and roadsides, is an antiseptic, anti-inflammatory, antispasmodic, astringent medicine for fighting off colds and flus, healing stomach ulcers, reducing fevers, treating urinary tract infections, reducing high blood pressure, and stopping abdominal cramping, and externally, yarrow oil treats wounds and stops excessive blood flow when used in a salve or poultice form. Yarrow has a slight sedative effect, so drink the tea form at night before bedtime. It is a common ingredient in many shampoos, but too much of it can make skin more sensitive to sunlight. You can consume the fresh leaves in salads and meals or dry the leaves to use as an herb.

- Yellow Dock—A weed that promotes the flow of bile to keep the liver clear and aids in digesting fats. It is bitter to the taste but can normalize bowel function in the intestinal tract when consumed.
- Yerba Mate—A South American herb that boosts energy like coffee and gives you more stamina without the caffeine jitters. It also aids weight loss by preventing excess fat accumulation in the body. The polyphenols in this herb are anti-inflammatory and fight allergy symptoms, reduce bad cholesterol, and may reduce the progression of arteriosclerosis. You can drink it in hot or cold teas, coffee-style drinks, or in any of the energy drinks the herb is found in, but keep consumption of energy drinks with caffeine low, as they have been linked to heart attacks and strokes in younger people.

- Yew—*Toxic! Do not consume.* These coniferous trees and shrubs are said to break curses, raise the dead, and protect from demons. The plant parts are not edible but can be used in spell casting without harm. Use yew to contact the dead and communicate with spirits in the ancestral realm. In ancient Celtic times, yew was planted in cemeteries to aid the living in contacting the dead. Yew is extremely toxic to humans and not meant for internal consumption.
- Ylang Ylang—This flower is considered an aphrodisiac and is used in spells for love, sex, self-confidence, romance, and protection. It can help you overcome sexual fears and body insecurities and calms anger and feelings of jealousy in relationships. It's a libido booster, and the oil is known as a powerful tool for connecting to the Divine feminine energy within. Try using it in an essential oil for a sensual massage.
- Yucca—Use this cactus in spells for purification, cleansing, and protection. Parts of the plant can be rubbed on

Yerba mate is a popular herbal drink in South America. It gives you a boost without the jitters that coffee's caffeine often does. It has many medicinal benefits as well.

Natural Pain Relievers

Put away the aspirin, and try one of these natural herbs and plants for pain relief:

- Apple Cider Vinegar—heartburn
- Blueberries—bladder/urinary infections
- Cherries—headaches and joint aches
- Cloves—toothaches and swollen gums
- Garlic—earaches
- Ginger—muscle pain, cramping
- Horseradish—sinus pain
- Menthol—sore throat
- Peppermint—sore muscles and joints, sore throat
- Pineapple—stomach pain, gas
- Turmeric—chronic overall pain

THE NEW WAY TO DRINK WATER

For those who don't like sodas, teas, or other liquids, try functional infused waters. Let these infuse for about fifteen minutes in a jar or glass before drinking either at room temperature or with ice.

- Fill a jar of water with sliced oranges or other citrus fruit plus strawberries for a beauty boost.
- Fill a jar of water with cooling cucumber, mint leaves, and a handful of grapes to relieve stress.
- Fill a jar of water with sliced lemon and lime for an energy quicker picker upper.
- Fill a jar with sliced grapefruit or other citrus fruit plus some shaved ginger for a boost to the immune system.

NATURAL OILS

Natural oils work great for smoother, softer, ageless skin:

- Rosehip Oil—Reduces wrinkles, protects from UV sun rays, evens out skin tone, and fights acne and rosacea
- Jojoba Oil—Moisturizes, cleanses skin, and removes makeup for all skin types
- Neem Oil—Treats insect bites and stings; reduces acne, eczema, and psoriasis; and destroys bacteria and fungus

- Argan Oil—Softens skin and hair, treats acne breakouts, and moisturizes
- Buckthorn Oil—Eliminates acne, reduces scars and wrinkles, regenerates skin cell growth, heals wounds, and evens out skin tone
- Tea Tree Oil—Heals burns, cuts, wounds, acne, and skin inflammation and kills fungus
- Coconut Oil—Softens and moisturizes skin, reduces wrinkles, and softens chapped lips

NATURAL SLEEP AIDS

Plants can help you sleep better. Keep these in the bedrooms of your home.

- Aloe—cleanses air
- Lavender—calms the nerves and aids in falling asleep
- Jasmine—reduces anxiety
- English Ivy—cleans the air of allergens and pollutants
- Snake Plant—takes in carbon dioxide in the day, releases oxygen at night to aid sleep
- Boston Fern—Purifies the air and filters out xylene, formaldehyde, and toluene toxins
- Weeping Fig—Purifies the air and removes benzene and formaldehyde
- Peace Lily—Detoxes and purifies the air
- Areca Palm—Detoxes and purifies the air of major toxins

the skin to treat wounds and other skin issues. Yucca is a medicine, and the fruits, seeds, and flowers are all edible for their high antioxidant properties and vitamin C to boost the immune system and stimulate the production of white blood cells, which fight diseases and infections.

BACH AND HIS FLOWERS

One of the pioneers of working with flower power and healing is the late English homeopath Edward Bach. In the 1930s, Bach made the claim that the dew found on various flower petals contained healing properties. He began work-

Teas and Medicine

Herbal teas are the easiest way to enjoy your medicine, providing a refreshing pick-me-up during the day or a soothing, before-bedtime relaxer.

- Tools: All you need is a nice teapot with a tight-fitting lid, preferably not aluminum, a strainer, and your herbs and teacups.

- Average Dose: If taking for a specific ailment, you can drink two to four cups daily. If for pleasure, enjoy as desired, but be aware of the possible oversedating effects of some herbs and plants.

- Sweeteners: Use raw, organic honey or a natural sweetener if you need it such as stevia. Try a bit of cinnamon, nutmeg, or cloves.

- Brewing: Aim for two cups water to one ounce of dried herbs. This equals one to two tablespoons of dried leaves or flowers. For a single cup, use one teaspoon per cup of water. When infusing fresh herbs, use two to three times the dried herbs, as fresh herbs take up more space. Depending on the

We have all witnessed the beauty of our planet, and Earth magic, or the worship of nature, requires a healthy respect for Mother Earth and the recognition of the gifts she brings us.

ing with various solutions that came to be known as the Bach flower remedies, which were tinctures made of brandy and water. The water contained the dilutions of the flower petal dew and materials. He then packaged and sold these remedies as homeopathic cures, even though no clinical studies ever proved they worked any better than placebos.

Bach and those who swore by his products claimed each of the specific flower remedies contained energetic or vibrational magic that influenced the user. This concept of vibrational medicine is not new, with many new modalities utilizing the body's electromagnetic fields and vibratory states to align with the healing fields of a machine or device. In the case of the Bach remedies, though, no scientific evidence existed that the immune system was in any way influenced and claims to be able to cure cancer and other diseases were considered pseudoscience.

herb, use hot to boiling water. Pour the hot water over the herbs in a closed container and leave it to steep between 5 and 20 minutes, depending on how strong you want the tea. Longer brewing times extract more medicinal properties from the plant parts.

• Straining: You can strain out the herbs and plant parts or let them sit at the bottom of the pot or your cup for increased flavor. If you have a compost pile, throw the plant parts on the pile.

• Storage: Refrigerate teas in a clean jar with a lid. Some herbal teas are quite tasty cold with a few ice cubes. Drink within three days for best results.

For those who claimed it worked, the concept of aligning the proper flower remedy or mix of flower remedies with the illness to be cured was simply another form of green magic, kitchen witchery, or herbal magic. Bach suggested the flower petals captured morning sunlight in the dew, which was then extracted to create the "mother tincture" when mixed with brandy. Was it the flower essence that made people feel better … or the brandy? Bach also believed that the method he used was powerful because it combined the influences of the elements of earth, water, air, and fire to bring back balance and healing to the body, mind, and spirit.

He is quoted as saying, "Nature patiently waits and we have only to turn back to her to find relief from our suffering." His thirty-eight Bach flower remedies are still sold today, and people continue to claim that they bring them greater well-being. Bach died in 1936 but left behind the original flower remedy recipes and the system of use so that it would continue on long after he was gone. "Disease of the body itself is nothing but the result of the disharmony between soul and mind. Remove the disharmony, and we regain harmony between soul and mind, and the body is once more perfect in all its parts," Bach stated, reiterating the foundation of herbal medicine and Earth magic as a way of using the gifts of nature to bring back inner and outer balance.

Japanese scholar Okakura Kakuzō, author of *The Book of Tea*, the seminal examination of how tea has been a critical part of Japan's history and culture, said that "tea began as a medicine, and grew into a beverage." Herbal teas bridge that gap and allow us to enjoy a nice, hot cup of tea while benefiting from the amazing array of healing agents in the ingredients.

Herbal teas are not just tasty; they have healing properties based upon the herbs used. It's easy to make herbal teas, which usually involves dried herbs or flowers steeped in boiling water for 10 to 20 minutes, but they can also be fresh as long as you plan to strain out the plant parts. The longer you let the tea steep, the stronger the taste and the beneficial compounds. You can put the herbs in a tea bag or use a strainer to let the plant parts steep for easy removal. Toss the used plant parts into a compost pile if you have one. If you buy tea bags to fill yourself, look for those that are made of organic materials that can go straight to the compost pile afterward.

Do you want to try making your own chamomile tea? Put the dried chamomile into a tea bag or use fresh chamomile flowers. Use about two tablespoons to one eight-ounce cup of water. Place the chamomile into a cup of boiling water, and let it steep for about 15 minutes, longer if you want it stronger. Then remove the plant parts and sweeten the tea to taste with honey or a sweetener. Add a little whole milk or cream if you want. You can also add a teaspoon of peppermint leaves or lavender for a different twist. You can't go wrong with herbal teas. If it tastes awful, toss it, and start over!

Sweeten to taste using a natural sweetener such as raw honey. When buying already prepared teas, make sure to look for any additives and pesticides and avoid the cheaper brands of teas, as they are weaker in beneficial compounds.

You can buy stainless steel mesh strainer tea balls that can be filled with the herbs or plant parts, immersed into the boiling water to steep, then emptied and cleaned for further use. This keeps the herbs and the water separate. Cup-sized strainers work, too, by putting the herbs or plant parts in the strainer and placing it onto the top of the cup of boiling water, then removing the strainer after 15 minutes, or try silicone reusable tea bags, which are an affordable option. You simply rinse out the bag with running water and let it dry, and it can be used again. You can buy these items online or in stores, and different-colored strainer balls or bags can be filled ahead of time with different tea blends to grab and go. Here are some wonderful options:

- Chamomile Tea—Treats sleep problems, soothes anxiety, and brings a sense of calm and well-being. It also aids digestion and stops minor muscle spasms.
- Earl Grey Tea—This is a citrus bergamot tea that can help activate autophagy. Autophagy is the process by which the body rids itself of dead and diseased cells and replaces them with new cells. It also gives you energy without the caffeine jitters.
- English Breakfast Tea—A prebiotic supporter, which also keeps blood sugar levels healthy while providing an energy boost.
- Ginger Tea—Known for its anti-inflammatory properties, ginger tea also

soothes the stomach, relieves nausea, and aids microbiome health. Ginger tea is known to help stop motion sickness.

- Green Tea—The polyphenols in green tea can help heal damage to the intestinal lining, aid in weight loss, and reduce inflammation.

- Hibiscus Mint Tea—Supports kidney function and healthy skin and is a powerful anti-inflammatory.

- Matcha Green Tea—Boosts thermogenesis and suppresses appetite. A great tea to drink while fasting.

- Mint Green Tea—Supports healthy blood sugar levels, suppresses sugar cravings, and is also an appetite suppressant.

- Mint-Honey Tea—Be sure to only let the mint leaves sit in the tea for 3 minutes but adding mint and honey to tea boosts immunity and fights off coughs and congestion. Add some ginger for an even stronger healing boost.

- Peppermint Tea—Treats upset stomach, clears out the sinuses, and aids digestion. Has a slight numbing effect that helps relieve sore and scratchy throats.

- Plantain Tea—Mix one tablespoon of dry or fresh, whole plantain seeds, roots, and leaves to one cup of boiling water and steep for 10 minutes, then strain. You can sweeten if needed. Sip this tea throughout the day to ward off bad colds and flus.

- Rooibos Tea—Another tea that aids microbiome health and has powerful antioxidants to boost the immune system. It helps to starve bad stomach bacteria and promote good bacteria, and it keeps free radicals at bay. Alleviates allergies and promotes healthy skin and hair.

- Rosehip Tea—Just a handful of dried rosehips added to a cup of tea, with a little honey to boost, gives the body an extra dose of vitamin C.

- Sacred Lily Oolong Tea—Supports the malabsorption of fats and protects against free radicals.

- Sencha Tea—This tea acts as a prebiotic and also regulates ghrelin, the hunger hormone. This supports a healthy metabolism by boosting thermogenesis—the rate at which you burn calories.

- White Peony Tea—Supports the immune system and is also great for weight management.

- Yarrow Tea—Just one teaspoon of the dried herb in a cup of boiling water taken at bedtime calms and soothes the nerves.

Green Tea

The polyphenols in green tea can help heal damage to the intestinal lining, aid in weight loss, and reduce inflammation.

Many of the herbs and plants listed in this section make wonderful teas but avoid those that are known to have a bitter taste or are toxic when consumed. When making teas, always remove the water from the heat source to steep unless the recipe specifically states to steep on low heat or simmer. Always cool a bit before drinking to avoid burning your mouth! Any tea recipe becomes a lot easier when you put the herbs in a tea ball or use a strainer, but many people like to put the plant parts directly into the water. If you want to make a whole pot of tea, which averages four to six cups, just multiply the ingredients four to six times except for sweetener; add that to taste.

Healing Herbal Ginger Tea: To show how easy it is to make your own tea, try this great recipe for relieving pain and boosting the immune system. Mix ¼ tablespoon ground ginger root into one cup of boiling water. Add a cinnamon stick. Steep for 12 to 15 minutes. Use raw, organic honey or a couple of teaspoons whole, organic milk as desired. Strain the herbs and drink the tea!

Chocolate Mint Herbal Tea: A delicious concoction that can satisfy a sweet tooth. For one cup of tea, take one teaspoon of dried mint or one handful of fresh mint leaves. Add ¼ teaspoon of cacao powder or cacao nibs (a pinch more if you love chocolate). Sweeten with honey if needed or add a slice of orange peel for a little citrus boost. Steep for 5 to 10 minutes. Strain the herbs and enjoy!

Tulsi Healing Tea: This tea is great for cold and flu season. Tulsi is also called holy basil and is a mainstay in India's herbal medicine. For one cup of tea, use one teaspoon of dried tulsi, or you can add in a touch of cinnamon and ginger for extra immune-boosting properties. Strain the herbs, and drink two to three times a day to alleviate a sore throat, fever, and congestion. Sweeten with honey if needed.

Lemon Balm Tea: Lemon balm is known for its medicinal properties and its ability to soothe and calm the nerves, which makes it a great before-bedtime tea. For a more potent tea to help you sleep better, add valerian. The two herbs combined work better than most prescription sleep aids! For one cup of tea, use two teaspoons of fresh lemon balm leaves or one teaspoon of dried lemon balm. Steep for 5 to 10 minutes. Strain the herbs out and sweeten the tea to taste. This tea can be given to kids in popsicle form, too, to help them sleep.

Lavender Soothing Nighttime Tea: You can make this with lavender alone, but for a more calming effect to help you sleep, add valerian or chamomile. For one cup of tea, take one teaspoon of the dried herbs (use 1½ teaspoons if blending herbs) and steep for 5 to 10 minutes. Add honey or sweetener if you need it or a teaspoon of organic, whole milk. Strain and drink before bedtime while the tea is still warm. This blend makes a great popsicle, too, for helping kids calm down before bedtime.

Elderberry Tea: Elderberries make wonderful herbal drinks, hot and cold. You can mix in some cinnamon, mint, or

Holy basil, or tulsi leaves, are helpful brewed in a tea for anyone who feels a head cold coming on.

just about any other herb and will only need to add a touch of honey to sweeten. For one cup of tea, use two teaspoons of dried elderberries or a handful of fresh berries in a cup of water. Add your extra ingredients in and bring water to a boil, then reduce heat. Let the tea steep on simmer for 15 minutes to fully absorb berry extracts. Remove from heat, and cool for a few minutes. Strain out the berries and stir in your sweetener.

Lemon Tea: Lemon is always a favorite ingredient and a great way to get vitamin C. Make a pot of this uplifting tea in the morning that the whole family can enjoy. Mix ¼ cup lemon balm, ¾ cup lemongrass, and 1½ teaspoons of the natural sweetener of your choice well in a glass container with a lid. For every cup of tea you want, add a teaspoon to your tea strainer. Pour in hot water and let the tea steep for up to 10 minutes. Remove the tea strainer, and when the tea is cooled to taste, pour into cups and enjoy. To make a pot of any herbal tea, use the above template and just replace the herbs!

Peppermint Tea: Peppermint is a refreshing, wake-me-up herb that can be enjoyed hot or cold. For each cup of water, use one teaspoon of dried peppermint leaves or a tablespoon of fresh leaves and one teaspoon of honey or sweetener. Place the peppermint into your tea strainer, and pour hot water, not boiling, over it. Steep for 10 minutes. Strain and serve.

Yerba Mate Wake-Up Tea: Yerba Mate is a stimulant that has been linked to weight loss, but don't overdrink it to lose those pounds. Try mixing it with lemon balm or hibiscus for even more flavor. For one cup of tea, use two teaspoons of dried yerba mate or your blended herbs for each cup of water. Use hot, not boiling, water. Pour over the herbs and allow them to steep covered for 15 to 20 minutes. You can serve this tea hot or cold with added sweetener to taste. It will give you an energy boost and could become your go-to morning tea.

You cannot go wrong experimenting with herbal teas. Add more ingredients if you prefer strong tea, or steep longer. Don't use sweetener or milk if you prefer it straight and natural. Experiment with blends, always being aware of the medicinal properties so they don't overamplify or counteract one another. Research ahead of time whether the tea blend is okay for kids or pregnant/nursing women.

✿ ✿✿ ✿✦ ★ ✳ ✦ HOMEMADE ELIXIRS ✿ ✿✿ ✿ ✦ ★ ✳ ✦

Elixirs are sweetened infusions of herbs mixed with alcohol, soda, or sparkling water. They are fresh and summery and meant to be consumed cold. You can use any herb or herb blend you choose. The process is pretty simple, and it only takes about 20 minutes to prep and cook up.

You will need a one-quart jar, 3½ cups of water, two to three cups fresh herbs of choice, and 1¼ cups sugar or honey, stevia, or natural sweetener—be aware that stevia is extremely sweet, so you will use a lot less. Experiment with this. Pack the jar full of your herbs, preferably fresh. Cover the herbs with boiling water. Steep for 20 minutes or more. Strain out the liquid into another container and stir in sweetener until completely dissolved. This mixture should last up to two months refrigerated.

You can also infuse dried herbs in brandy or another alcohol with raw honey to sweeten. In general, use about four to fifteen ounces of herbs in a pint-sized, glass jar. Steep the herbs in a tea bag or strainer right in the brandy. If you decide to use honey, you can mix that in before you add the herbs and stir until completely dissolved. If using brandy or another alcohol, the process takes a bit longer. After you cover your jar of herbs with honey and alcohol, you want to seal the jar when full, and let this mixture brew for at least one month before straining out and bottling or drinking. Shake the jar once daily to keep everything fermenting properly.

Make a cold elixir using the above recipe, but cover the herbs with cold, sparkling water and a touch of honey to sweeten. When choosing your herbs, make sure to include some with sweeter tastes like elderberry, and don't be afraid to add spices like cloves and nutmeg or a handful of cacao nubs. The sun method of making elixirs allows you to use direct sunlight indoors or out. Just put your herbs in a clean jar and pour honey over them. Instead of adding boiling water, seal the jar, and put it in a sunny spot for up to two weeks. Be sure to turn the jar over and shake to redistribute the herbs once a day.

✦ ✧ ✷ ✱ ✳ ✴ HERBAL APHRODISIACS ✦ ✧ ✷ ✱ ✳ ✴

Certain herbs and plants can boost libido, increase energy, increase blood flow to the genitals, and make you feel good and randy all over. The concept of aphrodisiacs is an ancient one, as our ancestors worked with the natural world to find plants and foods that, well … turned them on. When working with herbal teas, potions, elixirs, infusions, and consumables, keep in mind that some herbs

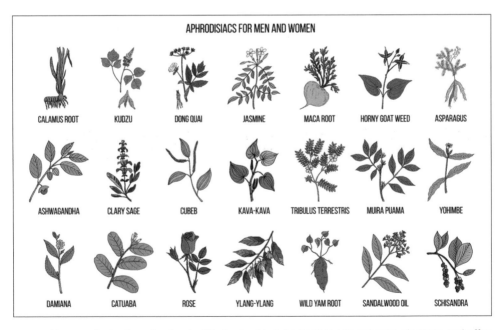

APHRODISIACS FOR MEN AND WOMEN

CALAMUS ROOT   KUDZU   DONG QUAI   JASMINE   MACA ROOT   HORNY GOAT WEED   ASPARAGUS

ASHWAGANDHA   CLARY SAGE   CUBEB   KAVA-KAVA   TRIBULUS TERRESTRIS   MUIRA PUAMA   YOHIMBE

DAMIANA   CATUABA   ROSE   YLANG-YLANG   WILD YAM ROOT   SANDALWOOD OIL   SCHISANDRA

Here are just a few of nature's gifts to mankind, herbs that can enhance pleasure and offer an aphrodisiac effect.

are specifically designed to relieve anxiety, depression, and stress and bring about a feeling of well-being, which is paramount to feeling sexy and attractive.

Herbs that act as stimulants can help boost a sagging sex life. Try the following:

Ashwagandha	Guarana
Astragalus	Licorice
Damiana	Maca
Ginger	
Ginko	Rhodiola
Ginseng	Yohimbe

If you want to indulge the senses, try:

Angelica	Orange Peel
Cacao	Peppermint
Cinnamon	Red Clover
Cloves	Red Raspberry
Coriander	Rose
Dong Quai	Star Anise
Nutmeg	Vanilla Bean

These herbs can be used alone or in blends; add honey for an added aphrodisiac boost. Experiment with which herbs make you feel energetic, vital, and sensual. Make elixirs or potions with a bit of your favorite alcohol.

Damiana Chocolate Love Liqueur (recipe from One Willow Apothecaries): For this recipe, you need one ounce of dried damiana leaves, two cups of vodka or brandy, 1½ cups water, preferably spring water, one cup of honey (or less if you prefer less sweet), vanilla extract, chocolate syrup, rose water, and almond extract. Soak the damiana in the vodka or brandy for five days. Strain and put the liquid into a bottle with a cap. Soak the alcohol-drenched leaves in the water for three days. Strain and reserve the liquid. Over low heat, warm the water extract, and add your honey to taste. Dissolve the honey fully, then remove the pan from the heat. Add in your alcohol extract and stir repeatedly to blend. Pour this into a clean bottle or jar, and add a touch each of vanilla extract, rose water, chocolate syrup, and almond extract to taste. Let this steep in the bottle or jar for one month or longer, as it will taste smoother with age. Use this recipe as a template to switch out herbs and try your own mixes.

Rose Petal Elixir (recipe from Bear Medicine Herbals): For this recipe, you need one pint-sized mason jar, fresh rose petals to fill the jar (clean them off first!), just shy of one pint of brandy or vodka (higher-proof alcohol requires that you dilute it with 50 percent water for best results), and ⅓ pint of raw honey. Fill the jar with rose petals loosely. Add in honey to coat the petals. Pour in your brandy or vodka to the top of the jar. Place a piece of plastic wrap over the jar's mouth to prevent the mix from taking on a metallic taste, then put the lid on tightly. Set in a cool, dark place for three to six weeks before straining and drinking.

✦°✧ ✳ ✶ ✷ MEDICINAL MUSHROOMS ✦°✧ ✶ ✶ ✷

Mushrooms are fungi, not plants, but they, too, have medicinal properties, and many are edible. Mushrooms are, in terms of evolution, closer to humans than they are to plants. Ancient Egyptians ate mushrooms for longevity, and they have been a staple in Chinese medicine for thousands of years. This is not about psilocybins or "magic mushrooms," which are discussed later in the book. Over two thousand species of edible mushrooms exist on the planet, but some of the most commonly used mushrooms for healing are listed below. These varieties of mushrooms can be foraged, depending on where you live, or purchased at a whole-foods store or farmer's market.

Some mushrooms in nature are potentially poisonous, so it behooves you to have an understanding of which are safe and which are not. Fungi can help restore the immune system, aid in better sleep, and cure many physical, emotional, and mental illnesses. These mushrooms can increase the flow of oxygen to the cells in your body and regulate blood sugar, lower stress, and benefit mental acuity; plus, they taste great in salads and meals. All mushrooms contain beta glucans, which are anti-inflammatory and boost the immune system. They also inhibit the presence of aromatase, which produces estrogen, and may protect against breast and ovarian cancers. The lectins in mushrooms stop cancer cells from growing and dividing.

Some mushrooms in nature are potentially poisonous, so it behooves you to have an understanding of which are safe and which are not.

Even the most widely used "button mushroom" contains powerful anti-inflammatory properties and is popular for cooking. Check with your doctor before taking reishi internally in capsule form, and always make sure you are getting the best, most highly recommended natural product. This applies to all the mushrooms listed here. If you forage your own, be sure to clean them thoroughly before drying, cooking, or using in any other form.

Some of the top superstars of the mushroom family are:

• Chaga—Considered the best medicinal mushroom in the world for its ability to treat cancers, stomach issues, and a whole lot more. Its earliest recorded usage goes back to seventeenth-century Russia, where it was a part of folk medicine, and it is considered a miracle for health even today. Chaga contains polysaccharides, which boost lymphocyte production to strengthen the immune system and fight off infections. As an antioxidant, chaga is a superstar, with a single cup of chaga tea packing the same amount as eating thirty carrots, according to the website *Better Nutrition*. It's a lot easier to drink a cup of tea than to eat a bag of carrots, unless you're a horse. Chaga's anti-infection properties fight viruses, knock colds out of the body, and can have long-term health benefits that keep you from getting sick in the first place.

• Cordyceps—If you want to increase your athletic performance or just feel better physically, cordyceps are for you. These long, squiggly mushrooms are a parasitic fungus that support balanced blood sugar levels, increase energy, reduce fatigue, and help lessen the symptoms and severity of bronchitis and breathing issues. Their anti-inflammatory properties contribute to better heart health overall (they lower triglyceride and total cholesterol levels), and the beta-glucans found in cordyceps help oxygen get to the body's cells and boost the amount of ATP, or adenosine triphosphate, in the body, which supplies energy and makes cells function optimally. You can even lower your blood cholesterol levels without having to take drugs with horrible side effects. Cordyceps can increase physical endurance and improve overall stamina by increasing blood flow.

- Lion's Mane—Given this name because of its pom-pom appearance, this mushroom is known to work on the mind, boosting memory, sharpening focus and concentration, and even protecting the nervous system. Widely used in Chinese medicine, it treats stomach and digestive problems and has even been shown to assist in stimulating new neuron growth to help the nervous system work optimally and lessen neurological disorders, even reverse the mental effects of aging on cognitive functioning. Lion's mane compounds stimulate the neurons to regrow and trigger remyelination, which keeps neurons healthy and able to conduct electrical signals properly and efficiently. It is also a mood booster. This wonder mushroom has no known side effects, and it has even been suggested that they can fight cancers. It is an antibacterial, anti-inflammatory, and immunomodulating fungi that provides so many benefits, it's hard to understand how so few people know about it.

- Reishi—Used in traditional Chinese medicine for over two thousand years for healing and prevention of disease, reishi is known as the "spirit plant" that relaxes the body and mind. It is known to boost the immune system and fight off viruses, infections, skin disorders, diabetes, cancer, HIV, hepatitis, sleep disorders, heart and liver diseases, bacteria, and parasites. The collective influences of reishi bring about well-being to the body and the mind and even help hormonal systems operate at their best. Reishi mushrooms regulate various cellular functions and reduce anxiety and depression. They are a bit bitter but can be dried and made into a tea or ground and added into a protein drink if taken internally, or they can be used externally in salves, lotions, and balms to keep the skin youthful and protect against aging and damage. Reishi also has powerful antihistamine properties and, when taken daily, can eliminate allergy symptoms. Reishi fights off free radicals and contains a ton of antioxidants like vitamin C, vitamin A, beta carotene, and selenium. It can be found in the wild and in backyards growing in parts of eastern North America.

- Shiitake—Shiitake mushrooms are valued for their savory taste all over the world. They also contain compounds that boost immunity and heart health and fight cancer. Native to East Asia, they are readily identifiable by their tan to dark brown color and their large caps, which grow to between two and four inches. They are found near decaying hardwood trees and are now grown in Canada, China, Japan, and the United States. In dietary terms, they are low calorie, high nutrient, and high fiber with plenty of vitamins and minerals and the same amount of amino

The shiitake mushroom features several benefits for those who enjoy them, from increasing natural immunities to serving as an anticarcinogen.

acids found in meat. Their anticancer and pro-immune properties come from sterols, lipids, polysaccharides (which trigger the immune system to fight tumors), and terpemoids, which have been widely studied for their medicinal value. The lentinan found in shiitakes can inhibit the growth of leukemia cells. A fungi and not a plant, it is a natural source of vitamin D, essential for overall health—the only plant-type of food that does. They can be consumed fresh, dried, in teas, or in supplement form and have long been used in Japan, Korea, and Russia as medicines. In Chinese medicine, shiitake mushrooms are believed to aid in longevity. They also include compounds that lower cholesterol and reduce the amount of plaque on artery walls, which leads to blockage and heart disease. However, some people can get a rash from eating them raw, and those who use the powdered extract for a long duration can develop rashes, stomach upset, and sensitivity to sunlight.

• Turkey Tail—Named for its fan shape, the colorful turkey tail can knock out a cold or flu and help heal infections. It is a strong immunomodulator that supports the entire immune system to function more optimally. It also contains two beta-glucans, PSK and PSP. PSK may have anticancer properties, and both PSK and PSP can regenerate white blood cells.

Even more popular mushrooms such as button, portobello, and crimini have health-boosting compounds and properties, so enjoy them. Be sure to clean them thoroughly, though, before any use because of possible pesticides and fertilizers.

✿ ₒ ✿✿ ₒ ✿ ✶ ✶ ✶ FORAGING ✿ ₒ ✿✿ ₒ ✿ ✶ ✶ ✶

Become familiar with what grows in your local and regional environment, especially when it comes to plants to avoid. Berries can look like they are edible but be poisonous to humans. In local parks, gardens, out in the woods, or anywhere green things grow, opportunities can be found to find great ingredients for cooking or spell casting. The more knowledgeable you are before you pick and gather, the less you will have to worry about negative side effects and unwanted reactions or picking endangered plants.

Fall is usually the best time to harvest and forage for herbs, roots, berries, flowers, and some plants. Many plants grow better in the cold, while others do well in heat and dry conditions. Roots are especially best harvested in fall months, right after the first frosts. Herbalists say the first couple of frosts help strengthen the roots and make them more powerful for medicinal uses, and undoubtedly, it's the same for spell casting. Once snow and ice set in, getting to the roots will be all but impossible.

If foraging, be aware of the conditions of the soil. To avoid toxins that might be in the soil, look around and see how close the land is to factories, roadways, coal mines, and other potentially hazardous areas. Plants can be overharvested, and it's always better to know ahead of time which plants are somewhat endangered or hard to find. Obviously, taking the entire root out of a perennial plant means that plant is now dead, unless you plan to take part of the root and rebury it where you found it or replant it for your own use, so just take a little for your needs, and leave the plant to continue growing. Learn which plants are perennial and which are annual. Trees and bushes are usually perennial, but they have large enough roots to allow you to take only a small amount while leaving the rest intact below the ground.

Clean the roots and berries, or any other part of the plant you find, by spraying with water or using a vegetable brush to get rid of soil and possible pesticides (critical if the plants are near a farm or found in an agricultural belt). Roots and dried berries should always be stored in a cool, dry place away from direct sunlight.

✿ ✿✿ ✿ ✿ ✶ ✶ ✶ GARDENING ✿ ✿✿ ✿ ✿ ✶ ✶ ✶

Getting out into the warm sun, digging your hands into the fresh soil, smelling the flowers and herbs you grew from seeds, picking the fruits and vegetables that you know are going to taste way better than store bought—all of these things are part of the magic of gardening. It is both a meditation and a form of exercise, creating a deeper connection between you and the earth that provides her gifts. Whether you just like to garden or you plan to make it a part of your magical practice, outdoor gardening can mean planting a yard full of vegetables and fruit trees or just a small patch of basics, preferably with the best organic soil you can find. Organic seeds and certified organic compost are readily available, and you won't need to spray your plants with toxic pesticides.

The knowledge and use of herbs and plants for healing is known as wildcrafting. Growing and cultivating your own garden is itself a craft. You need to know the necessary tools and items required for a beautiful end product. Wildcrafting takes the tools of the natural world (air, water, sun, soil, greenery) and your own unique creative flair and turns it all into a practical supply for cooking, healing, and spell casting, and it can all be done on any budget, in any size space, indoors or outdoors.

Some witches and pagans perform their spell casting and rituals in their own gardens. The circle they stand around might be a tree stump or a special potted herb or flower.

Gardens are wonderful places to commune with the forces of nature. Plant magic is best learned with your hands dirty with soil, immersed in the cycles of sowing the seeds and reaping the harvests of flowers, herbs, and vegetables or fruits. It should be a comfortable place, one that evokes a sense of wonder and connection and a reverence for the birth, life, and death wheel that turns both in the world of greenery and our own human world.

Whether you have a green thumb or one that is slightly brown, gardening can be learned. Books, articles, videos, and tutorials are available online, and any local home-goods store or nursery will be happy to educate you on what you will need to make your garden a success, but most of your education will occur "on the job," being with the plants and learning to treat them with a delicate reverence and respect. These are living things and will grow in accordance with the loving care they are afforded.

Some witches and pagans perform their spell casting and rituals in their own gardens. The circle they stand around might be a tree stump or a special potted herb or flower. The symbolism of the plants adds to the ritual and empowers the spells to be turned into physical manifestations. The magic performed during different phases of the moon is made all the more potent when done outdoors. Different plants grow in different seasons, so rituals and spell casting can be aligned with the time of year, and the garden can be decorated accordingly.

For those who wish to go a bit deeper, buy a current copy of *The Farmer's Almanac*, and it will tell you what to plant where and when, taking a lot of the guesswork out of gardening. You can also ask at your local nursery for plants and herbs that grow well in your area in terms of weather conditions. Don't attempt to grow tropical plants if you live in the desert or vice versa. Work with your environment as much as you can. Even if you do live in the desert, you can create a fantastic garden around a variety of herbs, plants, and flowering cacti.

You can also think of a theme for your garden. Perhaps you want to pay homage to a particular goddess or the magic of the moon. Many people don't know it, but some plants and flowers bloom at night like the sweet-smelling jasmine, the beautiful evening primrose, and a variety of night-blooming cacti. Maybe you like faerie folk and gnomes, or you've always dreamed of a garden with nothing but roses of every color. Do you love the sun? Decorate your garden with symbols of sun deities and hanging items that reflect the bright sunlight. If you are all about the elements, find a way to devote parts of your garden to earth, air, water, fire, and spirit. Personalize the space so that you feel your consciousness lifted each time you enter it.

A healing garden is a wonderful way to work in tandem with Mother Nature and create a setting that is beautiful, soothing, and productive for meditation. Nurturing plants as they grow becomes a spiritual exercise and respite from the busy day. The best healing gardens contain herbs and flowers that appeal to the individual both aesthetically and functionally. Creating a sustainable garden brings an ecological awareness into the connection and deepens conscious awareness of nature, the environment, and the living things we share our planet with. This way, the healing garden not only helps heal the gardener, but Earth, too.

Don't bite off more than you can chew. Start with a small patch, and grow outward from there. Trying to dive into planting an entire backyard garden can be intimidating and exhausting. Take it step by step. Think about doing a special blessing over your garden space before and after you plant to draw in good energies for growth, abundance, and a great harvest to come.

✫°✫°✫°✳**★★★ HERB GARDEN BASICS** ✫°✫°✫°✳★★★

A few simple steps need to be followed to prepare your garden area for growing plants and herbs. The first and most important step is to find the proper location, where the garden can get plenty of sunlight (unless you're planting shade plants; then, you may want two separate growing areas). The location should also be close to the house if you will be harvesting herbs to bring into the kitchen. Look for a spot that gets at least 6 hours of sunlight.

Then, you want to check the soil. You need well-drained soil that is not sandy or clay-based. You should mix in some compost with any soil to increase the nutrients the plant will benefit from. Also, be sure to have a nearby sprinkler head, unless you plan to water yourself manually. If you have hard soil, you will need to loosen it beforehand with a shovel to turn it over. Loosen to a depth of eight to twelve inches and rake the soil to provide proper aeration.

Pick the herbs you will plant based on necessity. Some herbs are perennial, and some are annual, so know the difference. Common herbs that most people are successful growing include basil, mint, oregano, sage, dill, rosemary, chives, and cilantro.

Plant the seeds, or the starter plants if you have those instead, according to packet directions. It is easier to use starter plants, but some people enjoy the patient process of watching a seed take root and grow through the dirt. Don't be afraid to harvest the herbs several times, as this will produce even more of the leaves and flowers to harvest again. If time is a concern and the winter frosts are coming, you can take the plant parts and dry them or freeze them for use over the colder months. Be sure to water them according to the instructions on the packet of seeds or the starter planter, but you can also stick your finger in the soil. If it's bone dry, water them!

Cover the garden with a light mesh if you are concerned about critters such as rabbits, squirrels, gophers, rats, and larger

insects. Look at your neighborhood garden center for natural pesticides, or you can make your own with various ingredients:

- Neem oil spray is a powerful pest deterrent made from a high-quality neem oil. The leaf of the neem plant has long been known as a powerful medicine and deterrent to pests. Perhaps it is the bitter taste and strong odor, although it is not poisonous to birds, animals, plants, or humans. You mix one ounce of the neem oil and half a teaspoon of a mild, organic liquid soap in two quarts of warm water. Put it into a sprayer and use it right away for the best potency. It is best to spray young plants, as it is more effective and longer lasting.

- Spider mites can be kept at bay by mixing two tablespoons of pink Himalayan salt with one gallon of warm water. Spray on the areas needed. Salt sprays work great on outdoor plants and indoor plants alike. Try sprinkling some of the salt directly around the base of the plant, too.

- Have a lot of ants? Try ten drops of citrus essential oil mixed with one tea-

This is an example of a large and well laid out herb garden. Your's should be the size you feel you need. Smaller potted herbs on a windowsill can do the job.

spoon of cayenne pepper in a cup of warm water. Shake it up and put it into a sprayer.

• Eucalyptus oil is a great way to keep flies and wasps away. Just sprinkle a few drops of this particularly strong-smelling oil on your plants.

• Another great, natural pesticide involves mixing three tablespoons of liquid, organic castile soap with one ounce of orange oil in a gallon of warm water. Shake up the mixture, then spray it to keep ants, roaches, and slugs away.

• For a natural tick repellent that you can rub on your skin, try mixing these ingredients, doing a quick allergy test on the inside of the elbow first before applying: one cup of witch hazel, five drops of peppermint oil, five drops of cedarwood oil, four drops of rose geranium oil, three drops of lemongrass, and two drops of lavender.

Eucalyptus oil is a great way to keep flies and wasps away. Just sprinkle a few drops of this particularly strong- smelling oil on your plants.

• Chrysanthemum flower tea is a natural pesticide that works on all sorts of insects and can be stored for up to two months. Boil some of the dried flowers in a pan full of water for 20 minutes. Strain, cool, and put into a spray bottle. You can add a drop or two of neem oil to make it even stronger.

• Rabbits can do plenty of damage to your garden, so plant some geraniums nearby. You can put them around your garden area as an extra deterrent. Geraniums are annuals, but you can harvest the seeds to replant.

• Finally, try mincing a clove of garlic with one medium-sized onion. Add it all to a quart of warm water, and mix. Wait about an hour or two, then add a teaspoon of cayenne pepper and one tablespoon of liquid castile soap. This is a potent spray that can be stored in the refrigerator and has a shelf life of about one week.

HERBS IN CONTAINERS

Without a nice yard space for gardening, you need to get a bit more creative. If all you have is a patio space or a balcony off an apartment or condo, you can plant herbs outdoors in pots or containers of various sizes. Adapt the outdoor potted garden to what space you have and use colorful flowers and pots to make it pleasing to the eye.

Start the potted garden in the spring after the final frosts. Use six- to eight-inch pots to start and fill each one with moist potting soil. Try to fill as high as one inch under the rim of the pot. Dig out the center with your hands and plant the seeds or starter herbs. Pat the dirt around them and water them. Set the pots in a place where they will get at least 6 hours of sunlight, although you may have herbs that prefer shade. Check your seed packet or starter plant label.

Water potted herbs daily or when the top inch of soil is dry. Stop watering when the excess drains from the bottom of the pot. That's it! Protect from birds and pests, and you've got yourself an herb garden even in the smallest of spaces.

Some of the best container herbs include:

- Basil—Loves the direct sun and thrives in pots and window boxes. Make sure the soil is watered and drained properly and harvest the leaves frequently. Trim back to encourage new growth. If using for cooking, pinch off the flower buds as soon as they appear. If they fully flower, your basil leaves lose flavor.
- Chervil—An annual herb that has a flavor similar to anise and parsley. It grows well in moderate sun and cool room temperatures and can be replanted every few weeks to keep a constant supply of young leaves for cooking and medicinal use.
- Chives—This onion-flavored herb is wonderful for cooking and grows best in bright light. It grows fast and can be cut and used frequently.
- Mint—Mint is an aggressive grower and in containers must be cut back often. The sprigs are wonderful in cooking and in spell casting, and you can choose from many types of mint plants. Peppermint and spearmint are popular choices. Mint plants love rich, moist soil.
- Oregano—This flavorful herb grows well in containers, but it grows prolifically and needs to be controlled. Harvest often and enjoy the dried herb in cooking and spell casting.

- Parsley—Another hearty herb that takes well to containers and pots. It is the most-used herb in cooking after basil.
- Rosemary—An aromatic shrub with needlelike foliage, this is a staple of cooking for the amazing flavor it imparts. It can be grown in full sun and then brought into the home once the weather turns colder. Rosemary can grow upward like a small tree, or the cultivars can drape over the pot or container like a fern.
- Thyme—Thyme thrives in containers and pots. It is very drought tolerant and doesn't require too much attention. The tiny leaves spill out over the container and look lush and wonderful. Thyme needs full sun and just enough water to keep the soil moist; it can even be a tiny bit on the dry side. It is a hearty herb that grows well without much fuss.
- Wheatgrass—Grows well in pots indoors and outdoors and is a powerful detoxifier that is high in enzymes. Wheatgrass restores the alkaline levels to blood and purifies and cleanses blood. It increases energy and aids weight loss. Use wheatgrass to build a strong immune system and clear up skin. It even reduces body odor! Considered a superfood, this wonderful plant is anti-inflammatory and may strengthen the body from cancer and aging.

✴✴✴ ATTRACTING POLLINATORS ✴✴✴

If you plant nectar- and pollen-rich flowers, you can fill your garden with butterflies, hummingbirds, and bees. Pollinator gardens should be pesticide free and filled with colorful wildflowers and plants that bloom regularly, so mix up your garden with annuals, perennials, and shrubs. The key is to provide continuous blooms throughout the growing season, so try large areas of native and non-invasive plants.

First, plant dill, milkweed, and fennel in your garden so that butterfly larvae can feed on it. Keep this part of your garden free of any repellents or pesticides that might harm bees, butterflies, or hummingbirds. You can also buy artificial nesting boxes to increase the number of pollinators drawn to your garden, or provide a compost pile, grass cuttings, or a log where they can hide and take care of their young ones. Add a few rocks for sunning and shady spots to serve as windbreaks and places they can get out of extreme heat. You also want to provide additional feeders for hummingbirds and butterflies and some water via a bowl or birdbath.

If you want to attract bees, plant:

Aster	Marjoram
Basil	Mint
Bee Balm	Mullein
Bee Plant	Poppy
Bergamot	Rose
Borage	Rosemary
Cosmos	Sage
Geranium	Sunflower
Goldenrod	
Hyssop	Thyme
Lavender	Verbena
Lupine	Zinnia

You can attract pollinators like bees and butterflies to your garden if you add the right flowering plants.

If you want to attract butterflies, plant:

Alyssum	Hollyhock
Aster	Lavender
Bee Balm	Nasturtium
Butterfly Bush	Oregano
Calendula/Marigold	Sage
Cosmos	Verbena
Daylily	Yarrow
Fennel	Zinnia
Goldenrod	

If you want to attract butterfly larvae/caterpillars, plant:

Borage	Nettle
Fennel	Thistle
Hollyhock	Willow
Milkweed	

If you want to attract hummingbirds, plant:

Bee Balm	Impatiens
Begonia	Iris
Butterfly Weed	Lily
Cardinal	Lupine
Columbine	Nasturtium
Dahlia	Paintbrush
Delphinium	Petunia
Foxglove	Sage
Fuchsia	Salvia
Geranium	Verbena
Gladiolus	Yucca
Hollyhock	Zinnia

You can see from the above lists that many plants attract all three pollinators. Plenty of choices will grow well in your climate and zone. Build your own pollinator habitat, and get the kids involved. They will love to look for colorful butterflies and watch hummingbirds buzz from flower to flower. Do a little research if you want to choose non-native plants to make sure they are not toxic to pollinators. Sometimes, all it takes is walking around your town and noticing what other people have in their gardens that naturally attract pollinators.

When creating your garden, use a variety of host plants and nectar plants. Host plants allow the pollinators to lay their eggs. This is especially important for butterflies to keep their life cycle. Host plants like native milkweed attract monarch butterflies and their caterpillars. Nectar plants provide the food that bees, butterflies, and hummingbirds feed on and carry to other plants. Native wild-

flowers are best; look for flowers that bloom during the spring and summer seasons.

Most native plants require full sun for half the day, so consider a location with adequate sunlight, and make sure your soil is not too acidic or clay based. If it is, consider adding compost or a top-soil to encourage pollinators and keep the flowers growing in abundance. If you are not sure which plants work best in your environment, head over to the nearest nursery or gardening store and ask.

✦ ✦✦ ✦ ✦ ✦★★★ INDOOR GARDENING ✦ ✦✦ ✦ ✦ ✦★★★

An indoor kitchen or sunroom herb garden is a cinch and an easy way to have what you need close at hand, but remember a few important things to be successful; herbs grown indoors luckily don't require a lot of space, but they do require attention.

- Provide a sunny spot
- Keep the temperature indoors between 60 and 70 degrees
- Grow each herb in its own pot unless you purchase a multipot with separators
- Wash pots before planting
- Use the best indoor potting soil you can find
- Make sure the herbs get fresh air
- Water as required on seed packet or starter plant container

Most herbs need approximately 6 hours of sunlight, and some need more. Others thrive in shadier areas, so place them near windows accordingly. East- and west-facing windows get the most morning and afternoon light, but south-facing windows offer the brightest light and most hours of sun during the shorter

and colder winter months. This is especially important if the plants are tropical or semitropical. East-facing windows will remain cooler for most of the day since the light that comes in will be from the

Having an indoor garden is not difficult. You can grow herbs and other plants in pots placed in sunny areas of the house. It's easier to protect plants from insects indoors, too.

rising sun hours. If you don't have windowsills, you can use indoor window boxes or tables. If you don't have much sunlight to speak of, you can purchase a CFL light bulb or a full spectrum grow light and place the light over the plants, or look for an indoor gardening light system at your local home-goods store if you plan to have more than just a windowsill or two in use.

Plants left in direct sunlight do need to be monitored for air temperature. Most homes are cooled/heated within the 60- to 70-degree range, which is ideal. Basil is one herb that can stand a bit higher temperature. If any of your herbs show wilting leaves, consider the temperature! If your plants are too close to the window, it might be a bit too cool, especially if strong breezes often come in through the screen.

Watering should be slow, and you must allow the soil to dry out between watering. Stick your finger down two inches, and if the soil is dry, then it's time to water. Do not pour water all over the plant. Go slow and avoid backing up the drainage holes with an overflow of water. Two or three times a week should be sufficient.

Keep pot and container size in mind once the plant starts to grow. If the pot doesn't have enough room for spreading roots, it's time for a bigger pot! Pots and containers come in all sizes and shapes, but they must have adequate drainage holes. Use a saucer under the pot to catch excess water if it didn't come with one. Decorative trays work nicely, too. You can also make your own, filling it with magical symbols that are important to you. Be sure to empty out the saucer or tray to avoid standing dirty water.

Many household stores carry a variety of planter boxes and sets. Once you bring them home, be sure to rinse the pots off with water before you put in the soil. When purchasing soil (and don't use your own yard soil, it isn't nutrient-rich enough and may contain mites and bugs), make sure it is a potting mix or blend and suitable for indoor gardening. It should assist with drainage and contain an aerator like vermiculite or perilite, the tiny, white stones found in many soil mixes.

If you choose to fertilize, look for an herb fertilizer with seaweed extract or a fish emulsion for extra nitrogen, which helps plants grow bigger, healthier leaves. Fertilizing times can vary, so start with once a month, and see if it is needed more often. Many fertilizers contain micronutrients that your plants need, but they don't need an excess of them.

Last, but not least, talk to your plants! Give them some positive energy, maybe even a blessing, or play lovely music nearby. Plants have been proven to react to emotions and music, so create a growth-inspiring environment for your kitchen garden. When you harvest the leaves to dry and make herbal remedies or use for cooking, be sure to thank the plant for its gifts. Kitchen witches know that gratitude helps growing!

Keep in mind that you can always extend your herb garden by taking some cuttings of the original plants. Basil and mint are two herbs that root in a simple glass of water. Plant them once the roots begin to spread.

For hundreds of years, kitchen witches and healers have used various remedies to ease ailments and conditions modern humans pop a pharmaceutical pill for today. Before a pill existed for every problem, more natural means were used for relieving pain, reducing stress and anxiety, healing wounds, promoting heart health, lowering blood pressure, calming a stomachache, and so much more.

A growing body of evidence shows that alternative treatments using herbs and plants work just as well as pharmaceutical drugs without the nasty side effects and high costs. Herbs have a much lower chance of being overdosed on and are generally safe to use, although it is always good to check with your doctor for any issues with prescription meds you must be taking. Herbal cures don't add on more problems. For example, when you have a respiratory bug, you may take something for the congestion, the pain, the coughing, and to help you sleep. Pharmaceuticals all have side effects that can bring about even more symptoms on top of the ones you already have.

Herbal cures also work to stimulate your own immune system to become stronger and allow the body's innate healing ability to kick in. Our bodies know what they need, and what they need is not a chemical concoction mixed up in a cold laboratory. Nature has provided us with healing plants in abundance. Why not try an old-timey cure for a modern illness?

Many doctors and nurses also incorporate holistic, natural remedies, knowing that our ancestors had a close relationship with Earth and its gifts, which can heal most any ailment. One warning, though: Buying herbs in a grocery store baking aisle may be cheaper, but the quality of the product you end up with is less effective. These dried herbs have been exposed to air, shipping containers, light, moisture, and who knows what else before they got to your store's shelves. If you are going to purchase your herbs and plants, do so at online and brick-and-mortar stores that specialize and know their stuff. When it comes to your health, you don't want to scrimp and compromise.

This list is not comprehensive, but it gives you an idea of how almost any ailment has at least one herb that can help alleviate it. The master list earlier in this book is filled with choices, but here are a few favorites:

- Anxiety—Chamomile, valerian, and lavender are all known to calm and soothe, especially in tea form. Hops treats anxiety, stress, tension, nervousness, and irritability. Passionflower tea is wonderful before bedtime to calm the nerves.

Besides the fact that many pharmaceuticals come from plants, home herbal remedies can aid the body's natural healing powers to act more effectively.

- Bites and Burns—Aloe vera cools and soothes burns and sunburn. Lavender essential oil treats burns and wounds. Witch hazel treats burns and bites and is a mild astringent and antiseptic. Calendula extract treats burns, scrapes, and rashes. Calendula oil heals psoriasis, diaper rash, eczema, acne, and wounds to the skin and is a natural sunscreen in ointment or salve form. Citronella is used to repel bugs (think of those strong-smelling citronella candles burning during backyard barbecues) and can also treat bug bites.

- Boils—Garlic is antimicrobial; it keeps infection down and reduces inflammation of the skin. Ginseng improves immune response and fights infection. Tea tree oil heals boils when applied directly. Echinacea treats infected boils.

- Constipation/Stomach—Chamomile and peppermint both calm stomach pain and ailments such as IBS.

- Digestion—Comfrey in tea form eases digestive problems. Activated charcoal can stop gas, vomiting, and diarrhea. Ginger capsules or teas help stop digestive issues such as nausea, acid reflux, vomiting, and motion sickness. Peppermint essential oil and peppermint tea both treat upset stomachs. Peppermint in any form banishes gas and bloating. Fennel gets rid of gas in the GI tract, and the oils calm stomach cramps and flatulence. Dill also works to calm an upset stomach and relieve gas and cramping. Marshmallow root and chamomile treat digestive issues, and stinging nettle leaves help get rid of water retention.

- Dizziness—Ginger reduces symptoms of vertigo and motion sickness and can help stop dizziness. Gingko leaves increase blood flow to the brain, which stops dizziness, vertigo, and headaches.

- Fatigue—Cocoa, coffee, ginseng, and black and green teas have caffeine to boost energy and lift the spirits.

- High Blood Pressure and Heart Health—Garlic and hawthorn regulate blood pressure levels. Cocoa, the kind found in dark chocolate, contains compounds that reduce cholesterol and high blood pressure. Hawthorn also treats many cardiovascular diseases, including congestive heart failure. Green tea compounds lower cholesterol and can treat symptoms of angina. Like garlic, hawthorn can regulate blood flow.

- Pain—Arnica gel or cream treats sore muscles, bruises, muscle pain, and sprains. Because it is anti-inflammatory, it helps heal more quickly. Feverfew contains a chemical that helps relieve migraine symptoms. Muscle pain can be relieved with creams and ointments containing wintergreen leaves, which also stops nerve pain, headaches, and menstrual cramps. Willow bark contains compounds that act just like aspirin and work on all types of pain, including back pain and cramps.

- PMS and Menopause—Black cohosh is a potent medicine to treat cramps,

Ginger

Ginger reduces symptoms of vertigo and motion sickness and can help stop dizziness. Gingko leaves increase blood flow to the brain, which stops dizziness, vertigo, and headaches.

PMS, acne from menstruation, and all menopause symptoms. It can induce labor in pregnant women, so use with care. Red clover calms hot flashes and breast tenderness from PMS and hormonal changes. Menstrual cramps can be alleviated with kava, red raspberry leaves, and chasteberry.

- Skin—Borage seed oil treats eczema, seborrhea, dermatitis, and inflamed skin. Chamomile soothes inflamed and irritated skin and heals eczema. Tea tree oil treats acne and other skin disorders, including athlete's foot. Aloe vera calms irritated skin and heals acne. Calendula in the form of marigold oil heals wounds and soothes acne flare-ups. Herpes sores can be treated with comfrey, ginseng, garlic, and echinacea, or rub some lemon balm over blisters and sores.

- Sleep—Chamomile in tea form before bed is a wonderful sleep aid. Essential oils containing bergamot, mandarin, sandalwood, and frankincense all have calming properties that promote sleep. Lemon balm leaf aids a good night's sleep and can rid you of restlessness that keeps you from relaxing.

- Throat/Respiratory—Stop a cough with mint, menthol, or eucalyptus oil, which also loosen mucus and help stop congestion. Goldenseal and echinacea treat tonsillitis and help clear up a stuffy nose. Eucalyptus essential oil or vapor can relieve stuffy noses and help clear up sinus infections. Stinging nettle tea treats allergies, hay fever, the flu, and even heart problems. Astragalus, a staple of ancient Chinese herbal medicine, stops the buildup of pus and discharge and heals throat and tonsil infections. Elderberry syrup fights cold and flu symptoms. Licorice root contains natural enzymes that coat the throat and relieve sore throat pain. All hot, herbal teas can help soothe sore throats and cold and flu symptoms, including chamomile. Geranium is known for relieving respiratory illnesses and works twice as hard when combined with echinacea. Asthma can be treated with coffee and green and black teas containing caffeine, which help open the airways and relieve wheezing and coughing. White chamomile reduces inflammation associated with allergies and strengthens the immune system, but if you have a ragweed allergy, do not use this plant!

- Warts—Rubbing aloe on warts for a few weeks can held get rid of them, as can rubbing the inside of a banana peel on them. Use bandages to tape the banana peel in place over the wart and replace it every few days. Within a week or two, the wart will be gone. Milk thistle is another plant known for healing warts when made into a salve and applied directly onto the wart repeatedly until it is gone.

- Yeast infections—Cranberries are noted for helping to clear up yeast infections when consumed whole or as a juice. Garlic is an antifungal and can be used in a suppository for yeast infections. Goldenseal is an antiviral and antiseptic remedy that can be applied as a tincture to genital warts. Taken in supplement form, it stops yeast infections by reducing the presence of candida.

Infusions and concoctions are meant to be consumed in tea form, hot or cold, or frozen as popsicles or ice cubes, but they can also be topical healing agents or an herbal bath or wash. Infusions have been used for thousands of years as healing medicines. A hot infusion of herbs and plant parts draws out the healing properties of flowers, leaves, aromatic roots, and dried herbs. Herbs can be mixed and matched to create any number of infusions in the form of teas or hot drinks. The longer the plant parts or herbs are steeped, the more powerful the flavor and the nutrients.

Water is the usual base for an infusion, but you can use wine, juices, or oils. One note—some infusions containing acidic ingredients may react with metal, so use a glass, enamel, or ceramic container. Avoid mixing and pouring infusions into nonstick containers, aluminum, or pewter, as toxins can leach into the mixture.

Here is how to make a simple hot infusion: Put one to three tablespoons of dried herbs or plant parts (chopped or ground) into a tea strainer. Place the strainer in a teapot or mug. Heat water to boil. Pour hot water over herbs/plant parts to cover them. Cover the teapot or mug to allow the volatile oils to remain trapped. Steep for 15 to 20 minutes, then strain and use. Steep longer for a stronger infusion. Some herbs will be better cold infused such as mucinous herbs like peppermint leaf, rosebuds, marshmallow root, freshly harvested herbs, and lemon balm.

Cold infusions are made by filling a quart jar with cold water. Take approximately one to two ounces of the herb/plant matter and put it on a cheesecloth or inside of a tea or muslin bag. Wet the herbs in the bag quickly, then submerge them into the jar below the waterline. Cover the jar and allow the blend to infuse overnight. Strain herbs the next morning with a mesh screen or clean cheesecloth, pushing down on the herbs with a spatula or spoon. Cold infusions can be made into juice pops for kids, too, with a touch of natural sweetener if needed.

✳✳✳ HERBAL BATHS ✳✳✳

Nothing is more soothing than a hot bath and adding herbs and flowers to the water takes it to a whole new level. Herbal baths combine an already calming environment with additional properties that heal the body, mind, and spirit. The bath can be cleansing and purifying in a literal and spiritual sense, even aiding in doing a little magical work in the tub. Because herbs and plants have magical and botanical healing properties, they can turn a typical bath into something more sacred and meaningful.

Aromatherapy oils in the bath are not only pleasurable but healing. The warm bathwater allows the pores of the skin to absorb the oils into the skin and the vapors to be inhaled. Menthol, peppermint, camphor oil, chamomile, and lavender make wonderful aromatherapy baths that soothe the skin and open up the respiratory tract for easier breathing during colds and sinus infections. Essential oils in the bath can cleanse, purify, detox, soften, uplift, relax, soothe, and energize, but be careful to dilute stronger herbs in a carrier oil or in milk before adding to the bathwater. Chamomile and lavender are not irritating in oil form, but all oils should be swirled into the bathwater to disperse and dilute or mixed with sea salt for the same effect.

Hydrotherapy is the use of hot baths for therapeutic purposes, and it is suggested that bathing in hot water should only be done once a week, according to Sebastian Kneipp, a founder of the Natural Medicine movement and father of hydrotherapy. In an article for *Prevention* magazine, "16 Healing Herbs for the Most Amazing Bath of Your Life," Kneipp states that taking too many hot baths weakens the body's immune system. Never under any circumstances bathe in extremely hot water. He suggests ending every hot bath with a splash of cold water on your extremities and face, then your entire body.

Warning alert: If you have blood pressure issues, ask your doctor first before taking hot baths with cold washes. Hot baths can lower blood pressure, and cold water can spike it temporarily, so avoid hot baths if you have any kind of heart issues. Take a warm bath instead, and skip the cold wash afterward.

Cool-water herbal baths are refreshing during hot weather months. Once you get over the shock of stepping into cool water, the effects are invigorating. Add essential oils to soothe and soften the skin. This makes a great morning wake-up bath to increase energy and vitality for the day ahead.

Herbal baths consist of three types:

· Putting whole flowers or handfuls of herbs directly into the bathwater
· Brewing herbal tea ahead of time and pouring into the bathwater

· Buying commercial herbal tea bags (larger than cup-sized tea bags) and immersing into the bathwater

Some easy herbal baths require very little in the way of ingredients such as the aromatic rose bath, which combines rose petals of every color with peppermint and a touch of parsley or lavender directly to bathwater. The smell of roses and mint calm and yet bring clarity to the mind. If you grow roses outside and parsley indoors, this is an herbal mix you can have at your fingertips.

Because many herbs are antibacterial, antiseptic, antifungal, antiviral, and anti-inflammatory, they can be mixed and matched for whatever ailment you need healing for. Some work better on muscle aches and pains, while others induce calm and relieve stress and anxiety. Review the master list of herbs and plants and see what you may have on hand already to help heal a headache or prepare a busy mind for a good night's sleep.

Try boiling water (not for your bath!) and pouring it over fresh parsley leaves and roots, then letting it sit for a while. Take that infusion and pour it into your

Treat yourself to an herbal bath, and there is nothing better for soothing the nerves.

bathwater to benefit from parsley's healing power.

Lavender is a favorite for herbal baths and can be used in an essential oil form as a soothing "cleansing" bath for body and spirit. Because lavender was sacred to the goddess Hecate, you can also use it as a way to acknowledge her.

A ginger and rosemary bath works wonders to relieve nasal/sinus congestion, relieve sore muscles, and detox the body. You can make a strong tea blend first, then pour it into bathwater, or grind fresh ginger root, and toss a few sprigs of rosemary directly into the water. Essential oils of ginger and rosemary are an alternative. Add four or five drops of each to the bath and relax! This particular blend alleviates menstrual cramps,

but don't ever get into a superhot tub when cramping or when pregnant.

If you have experienced any kind of abuse or violation, a great cleansing bath for the spirit combines sea salt into the bathwater with essential oils of rose, lavender, sandalwood, frankincense, and myrrh. This bath combines aromatics with powerful purification herbs, but you can add or change out any for something that has more of a resonance with your own spirit.

A weekly detox herbal bath can reset the body inside and out. Use a handful of fresh lavender, two teaspoons of juniper berries, one teaspoon of comfrey leaves, and one teaspoon of celery seeds. Steep the herbs ahead of the bath in hot water for 20 minutes, then

Thyme for Healing?

Few people are aware of the amazing benefits of the simple kitchen spice thyme. The herb, whether used directly in cooking or as an infusion oil, can fight off just about any infection of the throat and lungs. Several scientific studies point to the healing properties of thymol, a phenol obtained from thyme oil, which shortens the duration of respiratory illnesses. As an antibacterial, mixing thyme with other potent antibacterials such as oregano, cinnamon, and lemongrass can even significantly relieve strep throat symptoms and cut its duration. Two drops of thyme oil diluted in a mouthful of water is a powerful gargle for sore throats and can get rid of coughs and the shortness of breath that comes with respiratory issues. Combining thyme extract with primrose extract is another superhero against bacterial infections and may work as well as an antibiotic. In a world reeling with superbugs that are antibiotic resistant because of the overuse of those drugs for the last several decades, it is good to know that nature is filled with super cures that do not have the kind of dangerous side effects we hear about in pharmaceutical commercials!

strain the liquid. Set the liquid aside and put the strained herbs into a sachet or bath sac/pouch. Add the liquid to the bathwater and hold the sachet under the faucet as you get into the water. The lavender and juniper oils detox the system and provide a lovely scent to boot.

Although milk is not an herb or plant, bathing in it does wonders for the skin. Add milk, honey, and a few drops of essential oils like lavender or jasmine that smell good and mask the milk odor to the bath and luxuriate just as Cleopatra and other notable and wealthy women of power once did in ancient Egypt. Add about five ounces of milk and a few tablespoons of powdered or liquid coconut milk for extra skin benefits. A touch of honey adds to the healing and beautifying properties, but you will want to warm it up before adding it into the bathwater. Moisturizing oils include avocado, castor, sesame, safflower, calendula, apricot, and jojoba, so do a little experimenting to see what your skin likes best.

Chamomile baths can relieve pains and aches and bring a sense of calm to a busy mind before bedtime. Try a bath with chamomile and lavender flowers or essential oils to get you in a relaxed and sleepy mood, as both have a sedative effect (these two herbs make a wonderfully soothing foot bath, too!). A valerian infusion poured into a hot bath is another herbal sleep aid, or try steeping hops flowers in hot water, straining, then adding the cooled liquid to the bathwater for a tranquilizing effect. You can also put some valerian in dried form into a sachet or bath pouch and let it float in the water as you relax or hang it under the faucet as the water runs.

For a morning bath, add some dandelion flowers to freshen the skin and lift the spirits. Another mood booster is mint, which wakes up the body and mind to face the day. Fight aging with an herbal bath of ½ cup rose petals, ½ cup lavender flowers, ¼ cup green tea (dried), and rose essential oil. You can make an infusion ahead of time or drop the ingredients in fresh or in a sachet or bath pouch. If you choose to infuse, let the ingredients sit in a sealed container or jar for at least 24 hours before using.

Hops is known to relieve insomnia and bring about relaxation, as are lavender, rosemary, and orange blossoms. Jasmine and lavender are wonderful for renewing tired-looking skin. Having trouble breathing? Add eucalyptus oil to the bath to open the nasal passages and clear the lungs. Try stinging nettle to lessen aching joints or meadowsweet to relieve muscle soreness after a good workout.

You can buy or make your own bath salts. Epsom salt baths are good for a variety of ailments, and the salt is found in many natural-food stores. Another healing and relaxing salt is pink Himalayan, which can be a bit pricey, but a little goes a long way. A simple Epsom salt healing bath includes 1 to 1½ cups of the salt mixed with ½ cup of baking soda. You can then add several drops of your favorite essential oil to the mixture. Stir it up well and get rid of clumps and lumps, then use right away. This makes enough for two herbal baths, so you can cut the mix in half for just one. Always be sure to mix your essential oils with a good carrier oil unless you are buying them premade. Carrier oils, as mentioned earlier in this book, prevent skin from overreacting to the main oils and are also good for the skin. Think of apricot, avocado, or almond oil as easy-to-find carrier oils.

Baths using steeped leaves and flowers allow you to mix and combine to find your favorite blends, or just use one herb in particular. You can throw in the flowers as you bathe. Alternatively, if you want to steep them ahead of time, put a handful or two of each herb or flower into a pot filled with water. Heat to boil, put a lid on the pot quickly, then remove from the heat. Let the mixture rest between 20 minutes and 2 hours. Strain the liquid from the mix, and put the liquid into the bathwater.

Peppermint and spearmint leaves boost the mood and spirit even as they cleanse the skin. Rosemary leaf combats fatigue and jet lag. Lemon balm leaves calm the nerves and help bring about a good night's sleep. Try an herbal bath of two teaspoons each of basil, dandelion, and wild cherries placed inside a muslin bag to boost your divination abilities.

Add several drops of patchouli oil, grapeseed oil, olive oil, sandalwood essential oil, and jasmine essential oil into a bath to create a "glamour" that makes you feel and look more attractive to those you come in contact with afterward.

> Baths using steeped leaves and flowers allow you to mix and combine to find your favorite blends, or just use one herb in particular.

Going back over the herb master list in this book, it's easy to see just how many choices can be used for a healing and rejuvenating bath. Some might be more energy boosting, thus better for a morning bath. Others calm and soothe and are better before bedtime or after a hard day's work. The purpose doesn't have to involve any practical magic or kitchen witchery at all to make a bath a time of communing with the self and the gifts of nature. An apple a day may keep the doctor away, but an herbal bath once a week may be just as effective!

Another method involves putting herbs or flowers into a mesh or cloth bag, preferably muslin, then putting that into a tub filled with extremely hot water. Let that steep for enough time to allow the water to cool to a temperature you desire. Do not get into the extremely hot tub! By the time you are ready to bathe, the water will be infused with the herbs or herbal mix. Make several of these bath bags for future use and keep in a cool, dry place. Use soon, or you will have to resort to dried herbs and flowers if you plan to keep them around longer. Many stores today sell prepackaged herbal bath infusions and bath "bombs," which combine aromatics with various natural ingredients that can be tossed into a bath without any work. Just be sure to check the ingredient list for any possible allergens and additives.

Herbal baths, like drinking teas, can be a time of self-care and quiet time, so the purer the ingredients, the better. Ritual bathing is an ancient rite, used in many cultures as communal baths or during particular religious holidays. Even today, many cultures have sacred and ritual bathing practices that are about more than just cleaning off the dirt and sweat from the skin. They are about cleaning the mind and spirit, too.

Sore and tired feet can use their own herbal bath. Foot soaks are easy to make and can not only soothe but make a powerful detox. Try one of these variations.

Combine two cups of baking soda, one cup of Epsom salt, ten drops of lavender essential oil, and the juice of one squeezed lemon; add the mixture to a foot tub filled with warm water; and soak your feet for 30 minutes. You can leave out the lemon and still get a great detox that draws out toxins from the skin, lowers stress, balances the pH levels in your body, improves circulation, and lowers cortisol and other stress-related hormones. The above makes a detox herbal bath for the entire body, too. Just use more Epsom salt (two cups) and only half a cup of baking soda. Sit in the bath of warm water for 20 minutes. Try replacing the lavender oil with coconut oil, comfrey oil, calendula oil, or coconut milk powder for another detox foot soak or bath.

Here's an herbal foot soak that smells good, too. Find a large pot or foot tub and fill it with warm to hot water. Add half a cup of Epsom salt. Grind some orange peel into the water or add the peeled grind. Add some plantain, preferably fresh. Add in a few drops of coconut oil. Then, let your feet soak for 20 minutes. When you take them out of the tub and dry them, rub some remaining coconut oil on them to make skin supple and soft.

✱✱✱ DECOCTIONS ✱✱✱

Infusions and concoctions, as we learned earlier in this book, are mixes and blends that draw out vitamins, enzymes, and aromas from volatile oils. Infusions and concoctions can include flowers, roots, and leaves in their dried or powdered form or as essential oils. Making tea to drink is an act of creating an infusion, and infusions can be refrigerated as a cold drink or frozen into ice pops.

What on Earth is a decoction, though? This is a term you will see used widely in herbal remedies, kitchen witchery, green magic, and so on. A decoction is a tea blend that is made of roots, berries, bark, and seeds. It is simmered to extract the properties of these parts of the plant and is much stronger and more concentrated than an infusion. The dictionary definition of a decoction is "an aqueous preparation of plant parts

Foot soaks are easy to prepare and both relax and detoxify the body.

boiled in water for 15 to 20 minutes until the water volume is halved."

When making a decoction, it helps to grind or crush the roots, bark, or seeds beforehand. You can preheat the plant for half an hour and then use what doesn't evaporate as the foundation of your decoction. Break the plant parts or grind them up and place them into an earthenware container if you have one. Cover the plant parts in water, cover the container, then boil it until the water volume is halved. The preparation is then strained, cooled, and either used right away or refrigerated. It can keep for approximately three days.

If you don't have an earthenware container, place the ground or crushed plant parts into a small saucepan with one quart of cold water. Slowly heat the water to simmer and cover. Simmer be-

tween 20 and 45 minutes. Strain the water into a quart jar. Keep the herbs in the strainer. The water will not fill the jar, so you can add a bit of hot water over the herbs in the strainer until the jar is full.

Once you are ready to use the decoction, usually either as a warm tea or cold drink/ice pops, you can add natural sweeteners such as honey or stevia leaf powder to taste. This kind of decoction can also be used in herbal syrups or added to juices. If you want a stronger decoction, use the woody parts of the plant like the stem or, if a tree, the bark. However, this decoction should be allowed to sit overnight after boiling before you strain out the herbs/plant parts. Also, press the plant parts into the strainer with a spatula or spoon to get as much of the decoction out as possible.

✴✴✴ HERBAL SYRUPS ✴✴✴

It's true that a spoonful of sugar makes the medicine go down, but if you are

An antioxidant, echinacea oil contains a number of helpful substances that are antimicrobial. It is a perfect herb oil to have in any syrup.

avoiding excess amounts of sugar and prefer an all-natural remedy, then an herbal syrup is perfect. These sweet formulas work wonders with children who refuse to take normal medicines because of the awful taste. Many kids refuse to take store-bought medicines because they know it's medicine. Letting kids help make the herbal syrups allows them to sweeten it to their own taste and gives them a sense of accomplishment and self-care.

An herbal syrup is an ancient medicinal method that combines healing herbs with honey or some natural sweetening agent to create a liquid that can be consumed as a drink or even sprinkled on top of a dessert, into tea or a hot liquor drink such as a hot toddy (the use of alcohol makes this a tincture), or put into a juice smoothie. Herbal syrups are decoctions mixed with honey for thickness. Use raw, unfiltered honey for the best and most nutritious results. Honey is a powerful anti-allergenic and overall healing food all by itself, but make sure it is organic and contains no additives.

To make an herbal syrup, follow these basic steps, adding in the particular herbs you wish to use for their healing properties. Get a nonreactive pot or slow cooker, a teaspoon, a tablespoon, a spatula, and a glass jar with a lid for storage. Decide if you are making an infusion, decoction, or tincture first based upon the herbs used. Some of the most commonly used herbs for syrups are elderberry, ginger, rosehips, echinacea, hawthorn, lemon balm, tulsi, fennel, dandelion root, and marshmallow root. If you don't like honey or stevia-type sweeteners, you can sweeten the mix with cloves, cinnamon, or cardamom.

Elderflower and elderberry are both exceptional herbs for reducing cold and flu symptoms. These herbs not only reduce the duration of the illness but strengthen the cell walls to keep the virus from penetrating. Elderberry is a known cure for improving flu symptoms and has been studied scientifically for decades for its ability to drastically cut the effects of the virus down. You can add echinacea, a microbial, or goldenseal, an antibiotic/anti-inflammatory/astringent for an extra boost to the immune system. Because elderberries are edible and taste good, they can be used in a variety of forms—teas, syrups, meads, and sparkling sodas.

Ginger and astragalus also strengthen the immune system and cut the duration of illnesses. Astragalus has been shown in studies to increase white blood cell and antibody productions and fight off infections. Ginger is a known

antiviral/antibiotic/anti-inflammatory that prevents viruses from attaching to the walls of cells. Ginger syrup is a powerhouse medicine to stop menstrual cramps and aid digestion.

Syrups containing elecampane help heal sore throats and clear up respiratory issues, including pesky coughs. This herb also soothes inflamed tissue to allow for clearer breathing. Two tablespoons of elecampane, licorice root, ginger, and elderberries in one quart of cool water plus one to two cups of honey or sweetener makes a potent sore throat remedy. Add ¼ cup of brandy for an adult who wants a little extra healing boost.

Calming herbs such as hawthorn berries, chamomile, lavender, and valerian can be combined with ashwagandha root for a soothing and calming blend. Use three tablespoons of each herb to one quart of cool water (which will simmer to two cups) plus one to two cups of honey/sweetener. If adding alcohol, stick to the ¼ cup of liquor to one cup of syrup rule.

For a strong herbal syrup from a decoction, use one ounce of herb per sixteen ounces of water in a nonreactive pot. Warm the water over a low heat until it simmers. Cover to reduce the liquid to half its volume so that the mixture thickens. When you end up with a cup of liquid, add in about eight ounces of honey, then rewarm the mix until it is combined, stirring constantly. Never let the liquid get too hot. Keep below 110 degrees. Cool completely before pouring into a clean, sterile, glass jar. If you wish to add tinctures, do this now. Cover the jar and label it, so you know what syrup blend it is. The syrup will store in a refrigerator for up to three months, six months if you are using alcohol in an added tincture.

Do you choose dried herbs or fresh herbs? Fresh is usually better because the plants contain volatile oils and more vitamins in their natural form. However, sometimes you can't use the plants right away, so if you decide to go with dried, remember this guideline when looking at syrup recipes: 3 parts fresh = 1 part dried.

When it comes to sweeteners, some herbalists suggest the 2:1 ratio of two parts herbal decoction or infusion to one part honey or sweetener. You would need to start out with four cups of water to simmer it down to two cups, then add a cup of honey or sweetener. The sweetening agent adds to preserving the syrup, so it has a longer shelf life. Other herbalists like the 1:1 ratio. Try them both out and see what is more palatable to you. Honey can be mild or strong in taste, depending on where you get it. Honey is the best choice because of its own many medicinal values and properties, but only if you buy it organic, raw, and unprocessed. Raw honey is probiotic and contains an abundance of vitamins, minerals, and amino acids that aid the immune system and help with digestion, blood clotting, lowering cholesterol, improving skin tone, and balancing hormones. As an anabolic, honey also builds strength and increases stamina and general well-being. Honey alone is used to fight off allergies and seasonal respiratory distress, so combining them with powerful herbs in a syrup gives you a double dose of good medicine.

> Do you choose dried herbs or fresh herbs? Fresh is usually better because the plants contain volatile oils and more vitamins in their natural form.

Honey is also antibacterial, antiseptic, and anti-inflammatory and can heal wounds and sore throats, promote tissue healing, and ease ulcers. Yes, it is not an herb or plant, but using it in conjunction with herbs and plants makes them all the more potent and effective. Honey is the great electuary—medicines that make it easier to take other less palatable medicines!

Sugar is cheap but not a very healthy choice. Stevia is more natural but extremely sweet, so use very little to taste. Glycerin allows flavors to come through and is a strong preservative but is not readily available (try a health-food or whole-foods store). Molasses is cheap but thick and strong in flavor. Be careful with molasses because of the high iron content.

A general dosage is approximately one or two tablespoons for an adult, half or one teaspoon for a child, taken three times a day until the malady disappears (unless otherwise indicated). Always check first with doctors before using, as some children may be allergic to an herb or to honey. Avoid adding alcohol if children will consume the syrup. Note that syrups that contain honey are not suitable for children under the age of one; try another sweetener for babies.

Ginger-Lemon Syrup: Combine one teaspoon of fresh ginger juice with one teaspoon of raw honey. Add a few drops of lemon juice squeezed from a fresh lemon. Take this three to four times a day to aid digestion, help fight flus and bugs, and lower fevers. The antimicrobial and anti-inflammatory properties of all three ingredients make a potent expectorant, too.

Honey Cough Syrup: Pour one quart of filtered, cold water into a medium-sized saucepan. Add ¼ cup each of freshly grated or dried ginger root, chamomile flowers, marshmallow root, and organic lemon juice, plus one cup of raw honey. Bring the mixture to a boil, then reduce to a simmer. Simmer until the water volume is halved. The ideal is to have one cup of liquid once it is strained. Strain the liquid into a clean, sterile, glass jar. You may want to warm the jar up with your hands, so you are not pouring into a cold jar. Seal the jar, and store in the refrigerator for up to two months.

Dandelion Syrup: Combine two cups of clean, pesticide-free dandelion flower petals, three cups of water, and ⅛ of a lemon rind and mix over high heat. Let it boil, then remove from heat. Cover it, and let it sit overnight. In the morning, strain with cheesecloth or strainer, and squeeze out all of the liquid with a spoon or spatula. Now combine in the pan the infusion you just made with 2½ cups organic sugar, half a cup of raw, organic honey, and a pinch of cinnamon to taste. Let this simmer for about an hour and a half, stirring often. Then, when the syrup is the consistency you want, let it cool. You can use right away or store in an airtight jar or container and put it in the refrigerator. If you do not consume sugar, you can experiment with adding more honey or some natural sweetener but be aware that natural sweeteners are often quite potent, and you won't need nearly as much as plain, old sugar. Experiment!

Elderberry-Ginger Syrup: Pour one quart of cold spring or distilled water into a large pot. Add in two cups of dried, organic elderberries, two to three teaspoons of dried ginger root, and one sweet cinnamon stick. Bring the mixture to a boil, then reduce the heat and let simmer for 30–45 minutes. Remove from heat and let it steep for one hour. Use a funnel with a cheesecloth overlaid to strain out the herbs and berries. The liquid may still be hot, so be careful! Press down on the herbs and berries with a spatula to push the liquid through the cloth. Discard the herbs and berries in your compost. Cool the liquid to room temperature and add in one cup of honey or other chosen sweetener (double this amount if you want to increase shelf life). Stir well. Add one cup of brandy or vodka into the herb/honey mixture if desired. Pour into clean, sterilized glass bottles or jars, cover, and store in the refrigerator. During cold and flu season, take one to two teaspoons a day (adults only if alcohol was added).

Elderberry-Plantain Syrup: Combine two cups of cold water with half a cup of

Making elderberry syrup in batches is one way to have it on hand for cold and flu season. With its high antioxidant content, it boosts your immune system.

dried elderberries (or one cup fresh) and ¼ cup of dried plantain leaves (or half a cup fresh) in a medium saucepan. Turn down the heat, and let it simmer for 20 minutes. Strain the herb mix through a mesh or muslin cloth or cheesecloth in a clean, glass jar or bottle. Squeeze down on the herbs with a spatula. Pour the liquid back into the saucepan and add half a cup of honey. Stir over a very low heat until well mixed. Repour the liquid into the glass jar or bottle. You should have about half a cup or a bit more of the syrup. Seal the jar, label it, and refrigerate. Take one teaspoon per hour as needed for children, one tablespoon for adults.

Simple Elderberry Syrup: Combine one cup of dried elderberries (or two cups fresh) and four cups of water in a saucepan and bring it to a boil, then reduce the heat so it gently boils for an hour. Take it off the heat to cool until it's room temperature. Strain the berries and herbs through a cheesecloth and pour the liquid back into the pan. When the liquid is warm but not hot, add one cup of raw, organic honey, and stir until everything is fully blended. Pour into jar or container and store it in the refrigerator.

This should make about one quart of syrup. Feel free to add mint leaves, cinnamon, or some whole cloves for more healing benefits and added taste.

Lemony "Calm Balm" Syrup: In a small pot of water, add ¾ to one cup of lemon balm leaves. Cover them with water and put the cover on the pot. Let this simmer until the liquid is reduced to about half the original content. Use a cheesecloth or strainer to remove the leaves and let the liquid strain into another pot. Return the liquid to the original warm pot, and add some raw, organic honey to taste. Administer one spoonful, usually before bed, as it has a calming effect.

If all this sounds like way too much work, health stores and whole-foods stores sell herbal syrups by the bottle. Pay close attention to ingredients and dosage amounts, and make sure that no allergens are present if giving it to children. Though buying something premade takes a lot of the fun out of making it yourself, it may be more convenient and is always a much better alternative than pharmaceuticals and over-the-counter cough and cold syrups with chemicals and additives.

✦ ✧ ✦ ✧ ✦ ✶ ✶ ✶ SALVES AND BALMS ✦ ✧ ✦ ✧ ✦ ✶ ✶ ✶

Making a lip balm or skin salve may sound like a lot of work, but it really is quite simple. It's also a lot cheaper than buying expensive, name-brand products and wondering what "other" chemicals you're exposing your skin and body to. Many of the ingredients can be grown in your herb garden, indoor and out. Yes, you can buy all-natural salves and balms in nice, pretty tins and jars, but that takes all the fun out of being a kitchen witch and herbal healer, not to mention that these salves

and balms make great gifts to friends and family.

These homemade salves and balms don't contain petroleum and other products that typically serve as binders and preservatives. The only items you need to buy are the small tins and jars to keep the product in after you make it and some good, old beeswax. Beeswax is what provides firmness and thickness and keeps the other ingredients moist and unified. Some choose to add vitamin E oil as an added preservative, but it isn't a must.

The great thing about salves and balms is that anyone can carry them in a purse, pocket, or backpack to stop chapped, dry lips; soothe sore, dry skin; or add some healing power to a cut or scrape. Even children can use them topically without problems, but it's always good to perform an allergy test inside the elbow first. People who travel on planes or stay in air-conditioned hotels suffer from dry skin and lips. Balms are not liquid and can be kept in a purse or carry-on for a quick, moisturizing healing boost.

Confusion often occurs over the difference between salves and balms. The truth is, they are somewhat interchangeable terms for semisolid preparations of fatty oils and waxes with no water or a small amount of water or tincture mixed with herbs/plant parts. They are meant to be applied externally to the skin or mucous membranes, according to the *Miller-Keane Encyclopedia and Dictionary of Medicine, Nursing and Allied Health.* Often called ointments and unguents, these medicinal substances can be made with a base of heat-stable vegetable oils like olive, sunflower, or apricot and beeswax or a vegetable wax such as carnauba or canella. Lard is an older staple of making salves and balms, but animal fats are not used by vegetarian and vegan herbalists. Coconut oil works as a heat-stable oil and is readily accessible while known for being healthy for skin, hair, and lips in its semisolid form.

Balms differ from salves in that many contain shea butter or cocoa butter as extra ingredients. They also contain more volatile oils and are usually more aromatic than salves. Balms can be a little creamier in texture. Salves, on the other hand, are easier to spread on the skin for treating sore muscles and in chest rubs. When making salves, you are dealing with a more liquid form when you introduce the essential oils or flowers, which makes it easier to stir. You then pour it into the jar or container while it's still liquid so the volatile oils don't evaporate away and seal it up, and it will harden enough to spread easily once it has cooled appropriately. A nice chest salve can be made out of olive oil you may already have in your cupboard, mixed with the wax of your choice, and about 5 percent of a favorite essential oil or oil blend. That's it!

Some of the most popular herbal salves include:

Arnica Flowers	Lavender Flowers
Calendula Flowers	Myrrh
Chamomile Flowers	Nettle Leaves
Chickweed	Plantain Leaves
Comfrey	Thyme Leaves
Echinacea Roots	Yarrow Leaves/ Flowers
Ginger Roots	

You can save yourself money in beauty supplies by making your own balms and salves, which is a lot easier to do than you think.

Beeswax comes in white and yellow forms. The yellow is best, as it is not processed and bleached. Some people refuse to use beeswax unless they can guarantee that the product comes from a reputable and ethical producer of bee-based products, so if that is a concern, do your research before buying. You can buy beeswax in pastilles or pellets, which melt down more easily than chunks or blocks. Vegan salves can include an infused oil mixed with candelilla or carnauba wax instead of beeswax, but carnauba can be hard and takes longer to get to the right consistency.

> Beeswax comes in white and yellow forms. The yellow is best, as it is not processed and bleached.

Be sure if making a lip balm that all ingredients are edible. You can even make it in large batches and store some for future use. It's easy to find fun, little containers for salves and balms online or in craft stores. You can also buy an emulsifying wax that comes from natural fat and ester sources and is processed into flakes. This works best for making creams, lotions, and more fluid products with higher oil and water contents.

If you want to avoid the waxy texture altogether, think about making a body butter. You can add in drops of infused or essential oils to cocoa butter, mango butter, or shea butter. Simply melt the oils you choose along with the butter, then add the oils and remove immediately from the heat. Let it cool, fluffing it up with a spoon or spatula to keep it at the easy-to-spread butter texture. Cocoa and shea butters are inexpensive and found in most drugstores or warehouse stores, so you don't have to hunt for them.

Balms, salves, ointments, and butters are all nontoxic as long as you don't introduce a toxic herb or plant. Balms are the hardest in consistency, followed by salves, ointments, and butters. Always try these out on a small patch of skin first to test for allergic reactions. Always use clean fingers or a cotton swab to apply lip balms, so germs and dirt on your fingers are not introduced to the rest of the product. You can do a lot of experimenting with ingredients and textures, and the worst thing that will happen is that you toss out a bad batch. Just remember a few simple tips:

- Use any essential oils you like for lip balms as long as they are edible.

- Use any oils or herbs for salves, butters, and ointments applied to the skin, but watch for allergic reactions, especially if making for children.

- Always sterilize containers before pouring in your salves, balms, etc.

- Use enamel or stainless-steel pans and measuring tools. You can stir with a wooden spoon.

- A harder salve or balm requires more wax. A softer salve or balm requires more oil.

- Test for the right consistency by removing a teaspoon of your salve or balm and refrigerating it until it's hard, then pushing on it with your finger.

- More than one infusion can be mixed into a salve, so get creative.
- Avoid getting water on your finished products to keep mold from growing.
- Never dispose of solid oils or wax in the sink. Wipe pans and tools down with a towel and dispose of beeswax in the trash.
- Salves and balms can last up to six months but even longer when refrigerated. If it looks and smells bad, though, toss it and make a new batch.

Try mixing peppermint and lavender for getting rid of headaches. Rose and chamomile soothe the skin and the spirit. Rosemary added to anything does wonders for healing skin issues such as acne; rashes; and itchy, scaly skin; it also energizes and uplifts. Lemon balm cools and relaxes. Arnica soothes muscle pain and bruised skin. Plantain heals wounds and cuts. Comfrey salves and balms are good for just about everything that ails you. Jojoba oil is a great addition to a lip balm. The only thing to keep in mind is that you will be licking your lips and therefore must make sure that the products you use are edible.

If you are using your own infusions and don't want to cook them, you can put your herbs in a jar, cover them with oil leaving one inch at the top, seal the jar, and leave it in the sunshine for three to four weeks for a sun-kissed herbal mix. Gently shake the infusion a few times a week. Use cheesecloth to later strain the oil out of the jar while pushing down on the herbs with a spatula.

Easy Peasy Lip Salve: Mix five parts warm olive oil to one part beeswax. Once they are warmed enough to easily blend, remove from heat, let cool, and put in a nice, little container. Vitamin E drops can be added for extra skin and lip protection and healing. Once you master the basics

of making salves, you can really mix and match and get creative on your own.

Muscle Ache Salve: Mix three tablespoons of dried calendula flowers with one cup of olive oil and one ounce of beeswax or vegan wax product. Add in twelve to fifteen drops of chamomile or lavender essential oil.

Dry Skin Salve: Mix one cup of coconut oil with dried lavender, rose, and chamomile, and add an ounce of beeswax. Add in twelve to fifteen drops of an uplifting essential oil like peppermint.

Calendula/Marigold Salve: Combine three cups of dried calendula/marigold flowers and one cup of olive oil or another carrier oil. Make sure the oil is organic! Add in a few drops of chamomile essential oil or tea tree oil. After you make the infusion, heat the infused oil in a pot or double boiler and add in two ounces of beeswax (shaved or pastilles) and melt it down, mixing often with a spoon. Pour it through a clean cheesecloth into your storage container and

A member of the sunflower family, arnica can be used for treating bruises and muscle pain.

seal. Let it cool before applying to skin. Keep it in a cool, dark place when not in use. Great for healing bruises, burns, breakouts, rashes, diaper rash, dry skin, eczema, and chapped skin.

Lemony Lips: Combine your carrier oil (almond oil) with beeswax and melt it down to a salve. Add in pure, organic honey, and mix until fully blended. Remove from heat and add seven or eight drops of lemon essential oil. Pour into container and cover.

Lemon Balm Lip Saver: Make an infused oil with lemon balm, then add two tablespoons of coconut oil, half a tablespoon of castor oil, one tablespoon of shea or cocoa butter, and two to three tablespoons of melted beeswax (or candelilla if vegan) in a bowl placed in a few inches of water inside a larger metal pot. Use a low heat to melt down the beeswax and mix thoroughly, then remove from heat. Quickly stir in any essential oils and vitamin E oil. Immediately pour into tubes or tins and cover. Let them sit before use, and check for consistency. If you want it firmer, heat up and melt a little more beeswax to add to the mixture. To turn this recipe into a salve or body butter, just add more shea or cocoa butter to get the fluffy consistency you want.

Comfrey Healing Salve: Combine comfrey with coconut oil and your choice of wax in a pan or double boiler. Heat to melting, then pour into a jar to let cool. Just before it cools, add in a few drops of tea tree or lavender oil, then cover and store.

Simple Body Butter: Use four tablespoons of shea butter

Healing Salve

(Recipe by Katie Wells, *Wellness Mama*)

Infuse 1 teaspoon of echinacea root (optional)
2 tablespoons of dried comfrey leaf
2 tablespoons of dried plantain leaf (the herb, not the banana!)
1 tablespoon of dried calendula flowers (optional)
1 tablespoon of dried yarrow flowers (optional)
1 tablespoon of dried rosemary leaf (optional) in 2 cups of olive or almond oil

Infusion can be done in two ways. You can either combine the herbs and the olive oil in a jar with an airtight lid and leave for three to four weeks, shaking daily, OR heat the herbs and olive oil over low heat in a double boiler for 3 hours until the oil is very green. Strain the herbs out of the oil by pouring it through a cheesecloth. Let all the oil drip out and then squeeze the herbs to get the remaining oil out. Discard the herbs. Heat the infused oil in a double boiler with ¼ cup beeswax pastilles until melted and mixed.

or cocoa butter. Add two teaspoons of carrier oil such as olive oil or vitamin E oil. Add ten drops of your favorite essential oil. Mix by hand or with a mixer until you get a fluffy consistency, then use a spoon or spatula to pour it into your jars or containers. If you need to soften it up, you can add a tiny bit of coconut oil and mix the salve up to get the fluffy texture back. Store in a cool place to keep it from getting too soft or liquidy.

Herbal Healing Lip Balm: Combine one teaspoon of wax or body butter and your choice of herbs or flower parts in a pan or double boiler. Melt it down, then add four teaspoons of infused oil or oil blend. Stir until everything is completely blended and to avoid solidification. Add in three drops of skin-protective essential oil such as chamomile and stir again, then remove from heat. Pour into clean lip balm containers, and let it cool before use. Ideally, you want to let it cool for an hour or two before putting on the cap and storing or using the balm. Hot balm on dry lips hurts! Use your fingertip to test. This recipe can be stored for a year or more, but ideally, you want to make sure you identify the expiration dates of the ingredients themselves and go from that. Variations of the above include using lavender essential oil, hemp oil, vitamin E oil, peppermint oil, or raspberry seed oil for extra lip protection and soothing. This natural balm keeps lips moist and prevents cold sores. You can double these amounts for more product. This should make enough for two small (12 ml) containers.

Marshmallow Root Lip Balm: Combine two tablespoons of marshmallow root-infused oil (use almond or sunflower oil as the carrier oil), 1½ tablespoons of coconut oil, and 1½ tablespoons shredded beeswax or pastilles in a pot or double boiler, and melt them on low heat until completely mixed. Remove from heat and pour into your lip balm tubes or containers to let sit until the right consistency for use.

Pine Resin Salve: Combine ¼ cup of pine resin and half a cup of infused oil or your choice of carrier oil in a pot or double boiler, and let it simmer until the resin melts. Strain out the mixture using cheesecloth or a coffee filter, and put the liquid back into the pot, adding one ounce of grated beeswax or pastilles. Melt until the beeswax is fully mixed in, remove from heat, and pour into glass or metal containers for use. Store in a cool, dark place.

Rich Honey Hand Balm (recipe by Stephanie Pollard): Combine ¼ cup coconut oil, ¼ cup almond oil, ¼ cup olive oil, five tablespoons of beeswax pastilles, and one tablespoon of shea butter in a microwave-safe bowl. Microwave on high in 30-second increments for 2 minutes or until the oils and beeswax have completely melted. Whisk in 1½ tablespoons of raw honey and ten to twenty drops of the essential oil of your choice, and immediately pour into an eight-ounce glass jar or several small tins. Let cool to room temperature before testing. If you would like to adjust the texture, remelt the balm and add either more beeswax or more oil until the desired texture is reached. Yields eight ounces.

Multipurpose Balm: Combine two cups of olive oil with lemon balm infusion and one cup of olive oil with calendula infusion over a low heat, then add ¾ cup beeswax or candelilla wax, stirring until it's melted down. Remove from heat and stir in two to three drops of your favorite essential oil. Immediately pour into containers and cover them. Let them cool before using.

RITUALS, TRADITIONS, AND CELEBRATIONS

Those who follow the ways of Earth need not belong to a particular religion or spiritual system. Every culture contains people who use some form of spell casting and green magic or kitchen witchery. All over the world, people cook and grow their own gardens and engage in making herbal medicines to bring about healing more naturally and lessen their dependence on drugs and chemicals.

Many people have a desire to follow a spiritual path that reflects their beliefs and honors the laws and forces of the natural world. Pagans, witches, and Wiccans have the same need to perform rituals and celebrations associated with life cycles and the deities associated with them as traditional religions do. The spiritual and the religious are not as distant and disconnected as we may think. Both types of traditions serve to elevate the consciousness of the individual and the collective of humanity and instill a reverence and respect for life itself.

SOLITARY OR GROUP?

One of the most important decisions you will make before taking part in any rites or rituals is whether you wish to work alone as a "solitary" witch or practitioner or as part of a coven or circle of like-minded people. If you like to do your own thing, then solitary work might be best, but you also have the chance to take part in larger rituals on certain sacred holidays. These are open to the public sometimes, too, as a way to introduce others to the various nature-based traditions.

If you choose to be a part of a coven or circle, know that it is an intimate and tight-knit entity that will have rules and traditions specific to the group. Ask if you can visit several to see if one is a better fit. Once you become a member, it is a commitment, and you will be expected to own up to that sacred commitment and not let the other members down by only showing up when you feel like it. Covens and circles may only meet on the Sabats and Esbats, described in this section, or they may meet weekly or biweekly. Some may have an initiation for new members, and other groups will be more loosely accepting. Some may have formal, structured meetings and rituals, and others wing it and go with the flow. The more serious and committed

the entire group is, the more they will want to weed out potential troublemakers or slackers who won't pull their magickal weight. Covens and circles at their best are like families and become trusted close friends outside of the practice. If you are sociable, this might be for you.

Once you decide whether you are a solitary practitioner or a group member, then you can begin taking part in the rituals that mark the calendars of the cycle of time and the seasons.

RITUALS AND CYCLES

The cycles of birth, life, and death are to be celebrated and marked with traditions and rituals that honor the associated deities, depending on the tradition you are following. Some will honor the Norse deities, some the Roman, and some the Greek. Life events such as baptisms, funerals, births, marriages, puberty, first menses, and coming of age exist everywhere as they mark the passage of the individual through his or her journey. These are all a part of the wheel of each year that turns and turns, over and over, to make up the lifetime of an individual, but also the collective, whether it be a village, town, neighborhood, club, family unit, or group of friends.

In a section of her *Circle Sanctuary* website called Pagan Rituals, Selena Fox wrote, "Rituals are an important part of spiritual practice for pagans of many paths and place. Through rituals, pagans attune themselves to the rhythms of nature, create community, celebrate life passages, and make magic. Through rituals, pagans deepen their relationships with the Divine in one or more sacred forms. Through rituals, pagan culture flourishes and evolves."

Fox goes on to write that pagan rituals can be quite diverse, ranging from small, quiet rites to big, noisy celebrations with singing, chanting, and drumming. They can last for an hour or for days. Some pagans dress to the nines in their finest garb, and others prefer to go skyclad, or nude. They can take place indoors or outdoors, privately or publicly, and can focus on worship, healing, celebration, thanksgiving, consecration, protection, or community building. Rituals can create a sense of a spiritual collective for a group of like-minded people or be all about partying and having fun like a great wedding reception with a conga line. They can honor sacred spirits and natural forces, individual gods or goddesses, or the whole of existence and Mother Nature's abundant bounty.

The term "ritual" shouldn't scare off anyone who doesn't desire to join or belong to a particular group or even identify as a witch, Wiccan, or pagan or have to wear a dark cloak and robe and speak in Latin. According to Isaac Bonewitz, author of *Real Magic: An Introductory Treatise on the Basic Principles of Yellow Magic*, rituals are quite basic, and all follow the same formula. "Almost every magical-religious ritual known performs the following acts: emotion is aroused, increased, built to a peak. A target is imaged and a goal made clear. The emotional energy is focused, aimed, and fired at this goal. Then there is a follow-through; this encourages any lingering energy to flow away and provides a safe letdown." This is the structure of a ritual no matter who performs it or where it is performed, and this is what separates true ritual from informal celebration or acknowledgment.

> Rituals are an important part of spiritual practice for pagans of many paths and place. Through rituals, pagans attune themselves to the rhythms of nature, create community, celebrate life passages, and make magic.

Whether the ritual is done in a dry, formal manner or with wild abandon, the above formula is the purpose behind it. Rituals are designed to bring us into a state of altered consciousness to achieve the chosen goal whether to bless a baby or a new business venture. They differ from parties or celebrations because of the specific formula or structure that is focused on a goal or manifestation rather than just having a good time and eating cake. Historically, rituals also bonded groups of people, including families, communities, and the village elders, and served an important need for our ancestors—the need to belong and be together for a shared, common goal.

In secret societies like the Freemasons, Rosicrucians, Golden Dawn, and other esoteric schools and organizations, rituals are the tool that binds initiates into the mystery teachings as a way to bring them into an existing tradition or school of thought. Only those involved in the organization or invited by the organization could take part in the rituals and teachings and pass them on to new members. Rituals were formal, sacred, and only for a chosen few. Those who partook felt elevated and important to be singled out from the rest of society, and the bonds between group members were not to be broken or betrayed. Modern pagans and Earth traditionalists may or may not be as formal and secretive with their knowledge and how they pass it on.

Rituals exist for everything. From naming ceremonies for newborn babies and blessings of houses and new business locations to rites-of-passage ceremonies as a child goes off to college or gets a first job, ritual is still a part of our everyday lives. A boy becoming a man, a girl experiencing her first period, a pregnancy, the onset of menopause, the adoption of a child, and other defining life milestones and situations are worthy of honor and acknowledgment. Modern humans rush through these life events as if trying to get to some end point, only to look back and realize that they should have given them more time and attention. Life events are important landmarks on our individual journeys. They are signposts that should be acknowledged and appreciated. Time won't let us ever do them over later.

The cycles of the sun, moon, and seasons and the position of stars and planets in the sky dictate when some rituals take place, although others are based upon life events and milestones that occur at any time. Birthdays and anniversaries are cause for celebration, as are the deaths and funerals of loved ones, as it is all a part of the cycle of life and the wheel of time that passes each year.

✧₀✿✦✶✷ THE WHEEL OF THE YEAR ✧₀✿✦✶✷

Eight specific pagan holidays make up the Wheel of the Year. Also called sabbats (from the Greek word *sabatu*, meaning "to rest"), these days honor the changes of seasons and the ongoing cycles of life that are a part of many Earth-based traditions. Many of them have been adopted by religions and merged with their own traditions but have paganism at their roots. These eight holidays are evenly spaced around the wheel and have Celtic and Germanic origins (even though the word *sabbat* is rooted in Hebrew and Judaism). The word also comes from "sabbath," which means meeting or gathering to practice a rite or ritual. Sabbats are considered pagan high festivals that traditionally honor sun gods, but you can also honor goddesses, too, and create a wholeness and unification of the masculine and the feminine. Festivals and holidays that honor goddesses are called esbats. More on those later.

The holidays are Imbolc/Candlemas, Beltane, Lammas/Lughnasa, Samhain, Yule, Ostara, Litha, and Mabon. The lesser sabbats of Yule, Ostara, Litha, and Mabon fall upon solstices and equinoxes and are also called sun sabbats, and the greater sabbats of Imbolc,

Every April 30 to May 1, the festival of Beltaine, the Celtic May Day, is held. It celebrates unions, fertility, harvest , and sexuality—all parts of the beginning of life. This photo shows the Beltaine celebration in Waterlooville, Hampshire, England.

Beltane, Lughnasa, and Samhain fall on what are called cross-quarter days and are also called moon sabbats. Because the year in pagan traditions is in the shape of a wheel or circle, the year has no fixed starting point, although many prefer to celebrate the pagan new year on either Samhain or Yule. The holidays break down as such:

Samhain/Halloween (October 31 to November 1)—This is the witches' new year that is most often honored and is considered one of the most important and widely celebrated pagan holidays most likely because of its association with Halloween. This is a magical time of the year when the veil between the living and the dead is said to be the thinnest and most traversable by spirits who want to come and visit their loved ones. Celebrate by visiting the gravesites of loved ones or by having a "dumb supper," a feast in which chairs and plates are put out for those who have passed on.

The lighting of the jack o' lantern is a tradition that invites the spirit to follow the lighted path to visit the living. It is a powerful time for new intentions, renewal, and rejuvenation and for communing with the dead for guidance, direction, and support. Just as everyone celebrates New Year's Eve and New Year's Day as a time of transformation for putting to rest old things and starting new things, Samhain is the perfect time to do so while honoring the past with a bonfire. Write down things you wish to leave in the past on small pieces of paper, then take turns throwing them into the flames. A variation of this is writing heartfelt messages to the deceased, then burning them in the flames as a way for the message to enter the aether, so they can receive it. This is a perfect time to hone one's divination skills. Many

a feast is given to celebrate the reunion of the living and the dead and to affirm the birth–life–death cycle.

Yule/Winter Solstice and Equinox (December 20–23)—Yule is when the days are at their shortest, and this holiday celebrates the dark period of rest before the coming of the light. It is a time of death but a necessary point on the Wheel of Life. This pagan tradition is the root of Christmas with its lights and trees representing everlasting life even during the "deadest" time of year for plant growth and the light of longer days ahead. Yule is a time to go within and use the darkness to reflect. It is also a time to honor fire and the sun that gives light as we light fires in the hearth to stay warm. The full moon following Yule is considered the most powerful time of the year for witches and pagans. Yule is the time of Saturnalia and honors Jesus; Mithras, the sun god; Odin; Saturn; and the Holly King. It's a time to give gifts, sing carols, feast, and make merry.

The Holly King represented the death aspect of God and is overcome by the Oak King of rebirth. This is when the sun goes from waxing and powerful to waning and weak as darkness takes over. The twelve days of Christmas we sing about in holiday carols comes from a twelve-day celebration that begins the Yule period on Mother's Night and ends twelve days later on Yule. The lighting of candles and the Yule log represent the light and warmth of the fire that takes things from ashes to ashes, dust to dust in the colder winter months. We use the color red to represent fire and green for growth and rebirth during this time on the wheel.

Imbolc/Candlemas (February 2)— The return of light, greenery, budding flowers, and the spring. The word *imbolc* means "in the belly" in the Gaelic language and represents a time of coming rebirth. The promise of spring is a time for joy and preparation and a perfect time to bless the coming abundance of food and crops. The fertility goddess Brigid is honored on Imbolc, also called Brigid's Day, and festivals are devoted to the maiden and goddess figure. Like a pregnant maiden, this is the time of year for things that are about to be birthed into reality. Rituals involve lighting candles, cleaning out the house, house blessings, purification rites, initiation rites, and intention setting. White, green, and lavender candles are lit to represent the colors of purity and the Divine, physical growth, and spiritual growth. You can make a Brigid doll for your altar or find cute stuffed cows and sheep, which are represented by this time of year. Find cow and sheep trinkets or charms to wear on a bracelet when spell casting or doing rituals.

Ostara/Spring or Vernal Equinox (March 10–22)—It's no surprise that the words "Ostara" and "Easter" sound so similar. Easter celebrates the resurrection of Christ, and Ostara represents the resurrection of life as the days become warmer and longer. Life buds and blooms all around, and the hare and eggs of Ostara symbolize fertility. This is the time when light and darkness are in complete balance. Ostara was named after the Teutonic goddess of spring and new life,

Eostre, which is no doubt where the word "Easter" originated from.

We also honor the god Dionysus and the Green Man, or Pan, who symbolizes fertile growth. Easter bunnies, eggs, and Easter baskets are all pagan symbols of fertility and abundance, used to gather flowers such as violets, peonies, tulips, and daffodils, which are also symbols of fertile life in all its vast and colorful glory. The blossoming of flowers and plants represents the success of the masculine to pollenate the feminine for new growth. The colors are pinks, yellows, and greens to mimic the lovely spring flowers that abound.

> Easter celebrates the resurrection of Christ, and Ostara represents the resurrection of life as the days become warmer and longer.

Beltane/Mayday (May 1)—The festival of fire celebrates the halfway point between spring and summer and the full bloom of colorful flowers and plants. This is the last of the three holidays devoted to fertility. Thanks to warmer and longer days, summer is in the air, and everyone is grateful for the beauty of their surroundings. On the eve of May 1, the celebrations begin with food and drink, song and dance. It's a time to play and become childlike again. On May 1, people dance around the Maypole wearing flower crowns to symbolize fertility and fecundity. This is another magical time when the veil between the living and the dead is thinner, and it is a potent time for spell casting and magic.

Beltaine unites the Lord and Lady in love and is the time to join two halves to create a whole. Ribbons and wreaths decorate doorways. Pink, lavender, blue, yellow, and white ribbons, decorations, and flowers are everywhere. Picking fresh flowers in the morning to place indoors brings nature into the home along with beautiful, floating candles that represent the colors of the season. This is the time most handfastings occur. We honor the May queen, Flora, and the May king, Jack, with green, and love and romance are in the air. Place a red and white candle on your altar to represent the passion of love and the purity of a good heart. Make a batch of Irresistible Love Tea with dried red berries, hibiscus, and cardamon to take advantage of the passion in the air.

Litha/Summer Solstice (June 19–23)—The longest day of the year, sometimes called Midsummer, is celebrated as a time when we are at our most productive. Handfastings and festivals abound, and people feel blessed with a full crop that will be harvested soon. It's the height of the sun's power and life-giving warmth. Herbs gathered on this day are magically powerful, and some say that this is when elves and fairies come out to play. This is time to honor Mother Earth and the sun/sky king with bonfires, vigils, dancing, singing, and being with the people we care about.

This is a time of high passion with reds, golds, and yellows representing the heart and the proliferation of maize and the sun. Sunflowers symbolize Midsummer days and nights, as do red and yellow decorations on the mantle braided with green ivy. Candles of gold and red are burned to honor the high time of summer on the wheel.

Lammas/Lughnasa/Lugnasadh (August 1)—The time of preharvesting and preparation for the fall months ahead, this marks the midway point between the pagan summer and autumn. New harvests of grains, breads, fruits, and vegetables are celebrated, and thanks is given for the bounty of food to get through the winter. Lughnasa is dedicated to the grain god Lugh, who married Mother Earth. This is a popular time for country fairs and festivals.

Harvesting is both physical and spiritual, making Lammas an especially powerful time for inner and outer inspection and reflection. The sun god is honored and thanked for all the bounties of spring and summer. Bread is baked, and cakes are made to share and give thanks. The colors of Lammas are those we most associate with modern Thanksgiving—reds, golds, browns, yellows, greens, and black. Earth tones and the colors of fire and the sun mix and mingle in our decorations and the candles we burn to celebrate the coming harvest ahead. This is the time to prepare foods by canning, picking and drying herbs, and taking stock of pantries.

> Harvesting is both physical and spiritual, making Lammas an especially powerful time for inner and outer inspection and reflection.

Mabon/Autumn Equinox (September 21–24)—Officially autumn and harvest time, also known as Michaelmas. The fruits of one's labor are celebrated, and preparations are made for winter. What we sow earlier, we reap now in Mabon to honor this sky god. This is the time to rest and complete all harvesting activities before darker days come. Although we often celebrate Thanksgiving in November, this is the pagan time of thanksgiving and feasting.

This is the second harvest festival, and this is when we commune with the bounty that nature has given us. Festivals are filled with wonderful produce grown earlier in the year, and corn and cornbread are a popular way to symbolize

a successful sowing in many cultures where corn and maize are a staple food. The last of homegrown gardens and herbs are picked and either put into meals or stored for later use. Fall festival colors are reds, yellows, browns, greens, blues, and oranges. Candles and decorations mirror the colors of the turning of the leaves, and the cornucopia adorns the dining tables of many homes to signify the overflow of the harvest and the abundance of the season.

✳✳✳ CROSS-QUARTER CEREMONIES ✳✳✳

Smaller holidays, called cross-quarter ceremonies, divide the sabbats. On these days, offerings of food, drink, and trinkets are given to the gods and goddesses being honored. The "quarter" ceremonies are Samhain, Imbolc, Beltane, and Lammas. The cross-quarters are:

• Yule—Winter Solstice
• Ostara—Spring Equinox
• Litha—Summer Solstice
• Mabon—Fall Equinox

All pagan holidays change depending on the country they are practiced in or the hemisphere they are located on. Obviously, countries in the southern hemisphere have their own markers on the Wheel of Life, and their cycle of seasons falls opposite those in the northern hemisphere. The oldest belief systems on Earth recognize the seasons and cycle of life and the patterns that emerge from those seasons whether in the form of food, shelter, surroundings, or positioning of the stars and the sun and moon. The celebrations and rites reflect this recognition whether they have Celtic, Roman, Native American, or Nordic origins.

In a more general sense, each season marks its own important points along the wheel. The seasons are all represented by their own influences upon the internal and external worlds and the living and the dead. Just as the Wheel of Life passes through the eight holidays, it moves from season to season in a never-ending cycle of birth, life, death, and new birth.

Winter—Reflection and hibernation; a time to look inward, as the days are short, and the nights are cold and long. We may look back on the year that passed and take the lessons it has to offer, beginning to clear out old patterns and blocks that might hamper our coming year. The seeds we plant in the winter will be the harvest we reap in the coming months, so we turn to the spirits for guidance and direction to best plan that harvest.

Spring—New beginnings, new growth, and renewal; the dead plants take on new life as flowers bud. The land, and our goals and dreams, are in fertile soil now, ready to burst forth as we come out from the cold darkness into the light again.

Summer—Long days, warm nights, and the pleasure of the sun on our skin again. Summer is a time to enjoy the world around us and the extra time to be productive and experience more of life. Everything is in full bloom, and the glorious sunshine reminds us that it's our time to shine now, too.

Autumn—We continue to reap the harvest we have planted earlier and enjoy the fruits of our hard work, but we know we must begin thinking about the coming cold months again. We look around and assess our situation and what we need to change in the winter that did not come to full fruition this time. It's a time to be both outer focused on the bounty around us and inner focused on how to better serve our needs next time the wheel turns.

It is easy to see the influence of these older pagan days of celebration on today's most widely known holidays. Just as our ancestors understood the importance of honoring the old with the new, our modern traditions are still rooted in the past when nature was something to be respected and protected. We no longer in a collective sense seem to respect or protect our planet as we should, sparking a modern resurgence of Earth-based traditions devoted to bringing the old ways into these new days as a way to restore balance and harmony.

Holidays can be celebrated in conjunction with their historic origins, along with today's modern dates, or both. No hard and fast rules honor the symbolism each holiday represents. The eight sabbats of pagan traditions can be strictly adhered to or loosely interpreted as time and location permits. The intention of the sabbats is to mark the passages of

The seasons have always been celebrated by humans, and each acts as a marker in time so we know what needs to be done, how warmly to dress, and when the time is right for both sowing and reaping. Pagan holidays serve to mark these important changes of the year.

the seasons and attune ourselves to nature's changes as she moves through the Wheel of Life. Many pagans begin sabbat celebrations at sundown and continue until sundown of the end date, but if you work or are traveling to be with others, no gods or goddesses will strike you down for starting at noon or ending in the morning.

If you are working with energies, then perhaps it behooves you to be stricter and more disciplined with exact times of the day and night, positions of the sun and moon, and other musts for the proper pagan rituals and ceremonies, but the balance, harmony, and respect for nature that is at the heart of these sabbats is the "thought that really counts."

✧ ✧✧ ✧ ✧ ✦ ✦ ✦ ESBATS ✧ ✧✧ ✧ ✧ ✦ ✦ ✦

Another Wheel of the Year consists of thirteen lunar cycles. These cycles, called esbats, occur in a solar year. Their focus is on the moon and moon dieties and are celebrated during all moon phases. The movements of the moon were the first true "calendar" our primitive ancestors followed as they marked its various phases and positions in the sky. Lunar deities were just as important as solar gods and goddesses, and in matriarchal cultures, they deserved reverence and celebration as representative of the feminine Divine and her energies and influences on nature and humans.

Some cultures had male moon gods, too, and the waxing period of the moon was considered masculine energy as compared to the waning moon's feminine energy. The full moon and new moon were the most powerful times of the lunar year, as they represented the fullness of power and the newness of possibility. Cultures the world over have given the thirteen lunar cycles and their full moons names that reflect their heritage.

Our solar year consists of 365 days, but the thirteen full lunar cycles measure 374 days. Certain traditions and cultures divided the lunar cycle into months of twenty-eight days or more, and later cultures tweaked and altered those months to fit their own calendar systems. The word "month" means a unit of time corresponding approximately to one full cycle of the moon's phases, which takes place about every thirty days (four weeks on average).

Those who honor Earth traditions know the importance of the moon and the sun and that one is not superior to the other. Both make up the whole of time and the passage of the Wheel of the Year. Moon worship and celebrating beneath the light of a full moon are ancient rituals and traditions that honor and celebrate the triple goddesses of maiden, mother, and crone, which represent the moon's main phases and align with the age-old cycle of birth, death, and rebirth. The birth of all life is a feminine force, and the moon was given a feminine nature that represents virgin, mother, and old woman. This trinity was the first one, long before Christianity adopted the Holy Trinity of Father, Son, and Holy Spirit.

The waxing phase of the moon stood for the virgin/maiden. Fresh, adventurous, and sexual, ripe with beauty and femininity. The full moon is the nurturing mother, the protective and powerful female force that is strong and giving of life. The old woman, or crone, was represented by the waning phase, when the moon was losing its bright light but certainly not its wisdom, experience, and understanding. In many cultures of modern times, the crone is shunned and thrown away. Old people are treated like dirt, useless and bothersome, but those of Earth traditions know of the true power of the crone and her place beside the youthful maiden and the ripe mother. The crone is the elderly grandmother who has seen it all, done it all, and knows it all.

The word "esbat" may be related to the Greek word *estrus*, which means "of the month" and signifies the female menstrual cycle. It may also come from the Old French word *s'esbattre*, which means "to frolic or amuse oneself, diversion." Certainly, esbat celebrations are times to frolick, but they are not goofy distractions. Esbats are done to honor the moon and the feminine nature, whether alone or with a coven, a group of witches who practice together. These celebrations can be simple ceremonies that occur in someone's home or joyful, outdoor parties under the light of the full moon with food, drink, and merriment. Janet and Stewart Ferrar claim that esbats are times for love, healing work, and psychic training in their book *The Witches' Way: Principles, Rituals, and Beliefs of Modern Witchcraft*.

New moon esbats are times to go inward and reflect on the darkness, the hidden worlds and realms of both the universe itself and our spirit world within. Full moon esbats are times to express fullness and ripeness of life in all its forms. Group or coven activities might involve making food and ales together, doing a ritual or ceremony under the moonlight, then spending time talking and dancing by the moonlight. An individual might do the same but spend more time in a silent communion with the moon and the goddess energy. Types of rituals and celebrations vary, and no right way exists to honor the moon as long as you are indeed honoring the moon. No violence or bloodshed is permitted, as these are ridiculous concepts placed upon most pagan rituals by the media, traditional religions, and those who do not understand what they've never experienced.

Depending on the time of year and the particular month, a different goddess might be honored. Springtime is a great time to honor the huntress, the maiden aspect of Diana, or the Greek huntress and moon goddess Artemis, the twin sister of Apollo. The full moon is a time for celebrating the lush ripeness of womanhood in the form of Venus or Aphrodite. Colder winter months honor Hecate or goddesses of the Lower World and death. Death to those who honor nature is as much a part of life as birth, as the cycle cannot be complete without it. Death also means transformation, turning inward, and endings that will soon turn into new beginnings. Some covens prefer to honor just one moon aspect or goddess, while others celebrate them all along with the solar sabbats to make a complete, unified Wheel of the Year.

✶✶✶ DRAWING DOWN THE MOON ✶✶✶

Esbats, especially those of the Wiccan tradition, are all about the moon. The full moon is the most magical time to honor the goddess in all her full, bright glory; magic performed under the full moon is said to possess three times the power in homage to the triple goddess. The full moon is when the plans that come to fruition are celebrated with generous thanksgiving to the goddess. Each phase brings with it its own opportunity to amplify the positive associations and banish the negative.

One of the most powerful rituals is called "drawing down the moon." In this special ritual, you cast a circle and bless it, creating a sacred space within. You can go skyclad (nude) or wear a colorful or symbolic robe. You can do this indoors if the weather is not cooperating, making sure to create a sacred circle with candles or smudge the inner circle with smoke to ward off negative energies. Light a silver candle to represent moon energy. Stand before your altar or, if outside, under the moonlight with your arms spread wide. Tilt your face to the moon and close your eyes as you say:

Moon goddess who lights up the
    night,
Constant, yet changing. The great
    Divine feminine.
I ask for your guidance and wisdom,
    your direction and knowledge,

The ultimate way to be close to nature is to go skyclad. Nudity is something up to the individual, but some rituals prefer participation skyclad.

That your influence and power may
    always watch over me. I ask
    that your healing light always
    shine down upon me, even on
    the darkest of nights, and that
    your moonglow and energy fills
    my body, mind, and spirit. So
    mote it be.
Moon goddess, who governs the
    tides and the bloodflow of
    menses,
Keeper of secrets and intuitions,
Fill me with your essence, your
    power, and your everlasting
    wisdom now.
So mote it be.

Complete the ceremony by silently standing for a few moments, feeling the infusion of the moonlight and energy moving into and through your body. Then, if indoors, open your eyes and blow out the silver candle. If outdoors, open your eyes and lower your arms. You may then leave the circle safely. Add a bottle of moon water to your altar, or sprinkle it around the circle, for extra moon energy. Use the bottled water for spell casting or to water a special plant that honors the moon like night-blooming jasmine.

Charles G. Leland writes in *Aradia, Gospel of the Witches* of a way to call down the powers of the goddess Diana in a long invocation. Part of it reads, "When I shall have departed from this world, whenever ye have need of anything, once in the month, and when the moon is full, or in a forest all together join to adore the potent spirit of your queen, My mother, great Diana." Calling upon Diana can be as easy as repeating these words or paraphrasing them into a more personal invocation, asking her for guidance and direction in this life and freedom and peace in the afterlife.

Drawing down the moon can be done anytime, anywhere, and is about inviting the moon and goddess to unify with you. You want to raise your arms in a welcoming manner, and as far as the actual call, you can use one already written that you might find in a book or online or, better yet, write something intimate yourself that truly resonates. No wrong things to say exist as long as you call the moon down with respect, reverence, awe, and gratitude.

Many pagans, witches, and Wiccans end this ritual, and others, with "An it harm none, so shall it be" or some variation, much like Christians say "Amen" at the end of each prayer. This allows the ritual and the energies drawn upon to be positive and beneficial, and the "so shall it be" is a way to set intention out into the universe to be made manifest. You can also say, "And so it is."

✦✦✦✦✦✦ ✶✶✶ CAKES AND ALES ✦✦✦✦✦✦ ✶✶✶

The feast or ceremony of cakes and ales is another ritual that is common at esbats whether in a coven or solitary. It is performed around the time of the full moon and involves breaking bread and sharing a drink in a cup or chalice. It has commonalities with the Christian act of communion and receiving bread or a wafer as the body of Christ and wine as the blood of Christ. In *Aradia or the Gospel of the Witches*, Charles Leland writes, "The supper of Witches, the cakes of meal, salt, and honey, in the form of crescent moons, are known to every classical scholar. The moon or horn-shaped cakes are still common … and though they are known all over the world, I believe they owe their fashion to tradition."

Our ancestors shared bread and wine together because these two things were sacred. They were staples of the diets of nomads and tribes and had more importance than just feeding people. Cakes can be loaves of bread, pastries, cookies, or anything else the coven or solitary practitioner desires, but the symbolism is still the same. It's about sharing the body of the Mother Goddess in the form of bread or cakes and the blood from her womb in the form of wine.

The Mother Goddess celebrates fertility, menstruation cycles, and life itself.

The bread and wine are often put on an altar before the celebrants. It is blessed by a priest or priestess and then offered as a gift to everyone participating. The bread is passed first in a clockwise fashion around the circle, followed by the wine, also clockwise. Each person takes a small bite and a small sip. You might pass on a quick blessing to the person you hand the bread and wine to, or you can just say "Blessed be," a warm and loving greeting between pagans, witches, and Wiccans. When everyone has partaken, the goddess is given thanks, and the circle is blessed and broken. A prayer might be something like this:

Blessed be the Goddess who gives herself to us in the bountiful harvest.
Blessed be the Goddess who shares with us her bread as a symbol of her body.
Blessed be the Goddess who loves, nurtures, and sustains us
By all that is sacred, so mote it be.

This can be modified for the passing of the wine with the words "Blessed be the Goddess for the blood of her being, which gives us life, and life to all things new." Again, no rules exist on what to say during the passing of the cakes and ales or bread and wine. You can even say something simple like:

Blessed be the Goddess who feeds our bodies, our minds, and our spirits with this bread and this wine. We come from the womb of the Goddess, and to that womb we shall one day return. Blessed be the Goddess for her gifts of food and drink here today.

RITES OF PASSAGE

Life is filled with defining moments and rites of passage that deserve to be honored in special rituals and celebrations.

Every religious tradition and culture on Earth has its own ways of marking events that make up the stories of our lives.

✳✳✳ NAMING A BABY ✳✳✳

The coming of a new child into the world is mirrored in the birth part of the cycle of life and is something to be celebrated. The name of a child carries spiritual weight and should be carefully chosen with the highest intentions for the child. Names are sacred and identify us to others for the rest of our lives. The act of naming a new human being is deserving of a sacred ritual much like baptism or holy communion in Christianity. Modern humans pick names that sound fun and goofy or look good on a mug or T-shirt and have forgotten the symbolism and power involved. It seems that we live in a world all too anxious to outdo each other with dumb, meaningless, or ridiculous names that make the head-

lines without any thought to the children who have to go to school and interact with others with those names.

Once you have chosen the right name for your baby, a baby-naming ritual can look something like this: An officiator gathers the group in a sacred circle around the parents and baby, then blesses the circle. The circle members join hands. The officiator gives a blessing for the newborn, then blesses the parents to be the best they can be when raising the child. Each parent gives their vows to the baby to love, support, cherish, and honor the child. The officiator asks everyone in the circle to promise to love, support, and protect the new baby. The parents whisper the baby's name into his/her ear, then announce it to the circle. Celebrants cheer the new baby and parents. The circle is blessed and broken, and the reception begins.

This is just one variation of a basic rite-of-passage ritual and can be adjusted to the desires of the parents.

✿˚✿✿˚✿✱✱✱ HANDFASTING ✿˚✿✿˚✿✱✱✱

Pagan traditions have long called their marriages handfasting, but today, many couples are choosing handfasting over the usual wedding ceremonies in churches because of the simple focus on beauty and the sacredness of joining two souls together in a natural setting. When two hearts and souls choose to unite, a handfasting ceremony binds them together literally and figuratively. Handfasting is a pagan custom that began in western Europe, and the verb "to handfast" means to formally promise or make a contract with another; the origin of the word itself comes from the Old Norse word *handfesta*, which means "to

strike a bargain by joining hands." Hand-fasting marriages can last forever or for a shorter duration and did not carry with them the "until death do we part" stigma. It is basically a contract to unite two people for as long as they agree the contract should continue.

Any minister or priest/priestess of an Earth-based tradition can legally perform a handfasting (so long as they are licensed to do so in their specific state). These ceremonies are usually outdoors amid trees and flowers, but they don't have to be. The bride and groom invite guests just as in a traditional wedding ceremony, who may be invited to stand around the couple in a sacred circle of love and support. In some countries like the Ukraine, handfasting is considered a civil ceremony much like couples going to the courthouse for a quick marriage in the United States. The bride and groom stand facing one another and recite vows they have written themselves to express their intention of the bonding. They state that they are marrying one another of their own free will and recite their vows in front of their loved ones and the deities they believe in just like a traditional marriage ceremony.

The "handfasting" comes in during the recital of vows, when the minister/priest/priestess wraps the couple's hands together at the wrists with a sacred cloth. Often, the cloth is draped with one cord for each vow made. The officiator may invoke the four directions of Earth and the elements of fire, air, water, earth, and spirit. They may, if the

Handfasting is often used in Wiccan and pagan ceremonies. A couple will bind their hands together during the wedding ceremony as a symbol of their connection and their devotion to one another, or a group of people will join hands to express unity.

couple has requested it, refer to the Divine Spirit, God, a particular god or goddess, or the universe when asking for the bonding of the two and blessings for their happy union. Interestingly, the use of handfasting cloth or ribbons is a more recent addition to the old pagan custom, having become popular in neopagan weddings of the modern twentieth century.

After the couple have their hands bound, the officiator will ask questions such as:

- Do you vow to honor and respect one another?

- Do you vow to never break the bond made here today?

- Do you vow to share the good times and the bad times, the joys and the pains?

As you can see, these are similar to the questions asked in traditional marriage ceremonies. No wrong ways exist to do a handfasting, but the symbol of the bound hands is a must throughout. The actual ceremony can last as short or as long as the couple wants it depending on the invocations they've requested and the vows they've written.

After the vows are made and the officiator's questions are answered with "I do," the cloth is removed, and rings are exchanged. The couple kiss and turn to meet their friends and loved ones in the circle as one. The circle is blessed and broken, and the reception begins with food, drink, and celebration, maybe even a conga line or the hokey pokey. Some things never change.

✿ ✿ ✿ ✖ ✖ ✖ DEATH AND FUNERALS ✿ ✿ ✿ ✖ ✖ ✖

Death is sacred. Death is part of the Wheel of Life and the cycle of birth, life, death, and rebirth. In the pagan and Earth-based traditions, death is nothing to be afraid of and a critical time for ritual and honoring the links between the seen and unseen realms. Death is not the end but the beginning of a different kind of existence and a necessary part of the turning wheel. Death rituals and traditions are as varied as cultures, regions, and belief systems are, but all recognize the gift of transformation and change that death symbolizes. Death rites and rituals allow the dead to be honored, but they also enforce for the living the importance of gathering together to celebrate those who pass on whether human or animal. Yes, the death of beloved pets is something to be celebrated, honored, and remembered.

Wiccan death rituals might involve calling upon the elemental forces of nature—earth, water, air, fire—to come into the sacred space and symbolize the way we return to the elements upon death of the body. The fifth element of spirit marks the eternality of our spirit self, which lives on in the ether. Witches may invoke the god and goddess or other deities to accompany the dead into the afterlife, and Native and indigenous traditions might hold sacred dancing and chanting to honor the dead as they return to Earth.

A pagan funeral rite will ask that all who attend become a part of the ritual, standing in the circle, chanting, dancing, singing, or moving about to raise the energy necessary to send the beloved deceased into the next realm of experience. The mood may be somber, or it may be joyful and celebratory, with feasts of cakes and ales afterward. Often, a coven or group will tell the attendees funny jokes or stories about the deceased, much like modern funerals, and allow others to speak about their own stories and experiences. Candles might be lit and held as a song or spell for protection is offered up to the deceased. Those who attend will be blessed by the priest or priestess leading the ceremony and then everyone will sit around the circle and share experiences about death, laugh, talk, or just reflect.

✦ ✧ ✧ ✦ ✦ ✧ ✦ ✱ ✶ OTHER RITES OF PASSAGE ✦ ✧ ✧ ✦ ✦ ✧ ✦ ✱ ✶

When a child enters adolescence, puberty, and first menstruation, it is a powerful time to celebrate their transformation into adulthood. This is a time of the death of childhood ways and thoughts and the rebirth of more mature individuals who are coming into society. All cultures and traditions have rites of passage for this time of change. In some cultures, the celebrations and rites for boys are held for males only and girls for females only with elders and fathers leading the rituals to pass on their knowledge, experience, and insights to the child coming of age.

Moving into middle age and the senior years marks the passage of time and the maturing of the individual. Boys become men, who then become fathers and grandfathers. Girls become maidens, then wise ones, crones who guide and inspire. The passages of time are always marked with reverence. In Earth traditions, unlike modern society, getting older is not something to be feared or avoided but something to honor, celebrate, and welcome. It is part of the cycle, part of the Wheel of Life.

Divorce is also marked. Couples who divorce need all the support they can get, so marking this as another transitional passage of the life cycle allows each person to give thanks for the love they had and go on to the next stages of their lives feeling empowered and understood. No shaming or judging is involved. Everything changes and nothing stays the same in life, in nature, and in our human interactions.

Going off to college, getting a first job or a big promotion, graduating high school or college, opening your first business, coming out as gay or lesbian, overcoming an illness or disease such as beating cancer or completing physical therapy after an accident, getting a new pet, letting go of a deceased pet, buying or building your first home and moving in … our lives are filled with milestones and markers that are meant to be acknowledged and celebrated.

DAYS OF THE WEEK

The days of the week have their own significance and correspondences. Each carries its own magic and energy that can be used during rituals and spell casting. We take the days of the week for granted, focusing mainly on getting through the work weekdays to the weekend, when we get to relax or get out and do fun things. Each day is symbolic and honored in Earth traditions and pagan belief systems, a time not to be rushed through, ignored, or discounted.

According to *llewellyn.com*, "Every day of the week, Sunday through Saturday, is a magical day. Each of the seven days of the week has its own magical correspondences such as deity association, colors, crystals, and herbs. Each individual day also carries its own bewitching specialties." Honoring each day allows you more opportunities to practice practical magic in a way that keeps you in tune with the forces of nature all the time rather than just waiting for sabbats and esbats to engage and commune with the deities. Focusing on the daily correspondences allows you to understand how working with each day adds to the impact of, and personalizes, your own practice, and since many of us work during the week, we can use all the good energy and assistance we can get!

Monday—Monday is the day of the moon and the day of moon goddesses such as Diana, Artemis, Luna, and Selene. Monday's colors are the moon's colors of white and silver and sometimes blue to signify a blue moon. This is a time of women's intuition, female mysteries, emotions, prophecy, and beauty. Mondays are the best days for turning inward for insight, wisdom, and strength. Mondays can be the best times for practicing divination and scrying or delving into dreams and their symbols and archetypes. If you wish to spell cast, focus on spells for love, peace, fertility, and inner renewal. Monday is a day of beginnings, after a restful Sunday, and because of its association with the moon and the tides, it is a time for water mag-

The days of the week have their own significance and correspondences. Each carries its own magic and energy that can be used during rituals and spell casting.

ick and washing and cleansing crystals, gems, and magickal altar tools. Chamomile and mint teas offer restful sleep and calm the nerves. The moon in the night sky is meant to be gazed upon, and the night-blooming flowers of gardenias, white roses, jasmine, and bluebells are to be gathered by moonlight. Wear silver and white, including sterling silver jewelry with moonstones or pearls to represent the moon.

Tuesday—Tuesday honors the masculine gods of war, Mars and Ares. The colors are red and black, and the corresponding planet is Mars. This is a day of victory, success, strength, courage, protection, conviction, determination, and rebellion. Unlike the mysterious Monday, it is bold and confrontational, even warlike. This is a day for doing the spells that didn't work before or involving more ambitions and potent desires. This is a day for love and lust spells and warding off hexes and curses. This is the day to win a fight or court battle or become more skillful in business endeavors. This is a day for passion and intensity in love, work, and play. Wear red, black, or orange, colors associated with fire. Wear or carry bloodstone or garnet. Cut snapdragons, red roses, and holly for more bravery and protection. Light fiery-colored candles, and use earthy, lusty essential oils in the bath for a sensual escape.

Wednesday—Midweek, hump day, is the day to put purple and orange on display. This is the wild and fun day to celebrate the arts and be crafty and creative. Wednesday corresponds with Mercury, so it is a great day for communicating. It's also a good time to test your luck and make changes, and games of fortune and gambling should work in your favor. Wednesday honors the Norse gods Woden/ Odin, Hermes, and, of course, Mercury. This is a good day to travel or learn something new and a great day for divination and seeing into the future. It's also a trickster day, so beware of playful, mischievous energies. Wear agate and lavender to honor this day and increase its positive influences. The goddess Athena, patron of the arts, is honored on Wednesdays and can help inspire a new project or concept. Plants associated with Wednesday include ferns, aspen trees, and lily of the valley.

Thursday—This is the day honoring the god Thor—"Thor's Day"—and it also honors the beneficent Jupiter and Juno. The associated color is blue all the way around, and the planet is the mighty Jupiter. This is a day of abundance, prosperity, expansion, wealth, and healing. Thursday brings luck and power, and spells for fortune, good health, wealth, and general long-term happiness are best done on this day. However, do not sign contracts or make new deals on Thursdays. Court cases and justice issues are resolved on Thursdays, so cast spells accordingly. Also, be sure to bless family, friends, and your home on the day of protection and authority. Wear shades of blue, especially royal blue, to honor Jupiter. Carry a blue stone such

as turquoise or lapis lazuli with you for more protection and good energy. Honeysuckle should be included in spells and herbal mixes, and the leaves of the mighty oak tree are particularly sacred, as they honor Thor. Add some dried leaves to charms for added power.

Friday—This is the day honoring the Norse goddess Freya but also Venus, Eros, and Aphrodite. Friday is the end of the work week and a time for love, friendship, courtship, fertility, pregnancy, birth, and romantic interludes. The colors are pink, red, and aqua, and the planet is, of course, Venus. Do all your love, sex, and attraction magic on Fridays. This is a day to spend close to Mother Nature, picking plants and flowers for herbal remedies and spell casting. It's a day for pleasure, inside and out, and a time for herbal baths, mirror glamour magic, and creating love potions and concoctions. Carry a rose quartz with you all day for loving vibes for yourself and everyone you come into contact with. Pink roses are a special delight, as is burning a pink candle as you relax in an herbal bath or sip chamomile tea. The god Eros brings sexual passion on Friday, so spend time with your lover enjoying each other. Feed each other ripe strawberries, chocolates, and other aphrodisiacs, preferably by the light of a full moon.

Saturday—This is the day to honor the planet and god Saturn and the goddess Hecate. Though it is the first day of the fun weekend, it is also a day of endings, banishings, protection, cleans-

> The god Eros brings sexual passion on Friday…. Feed each other ripe strawberries, chocolates, and other aphrodisiacs, preferably by the light of a full moon.

ings, and finding clarity after a long week. The colors are black and purple, and the spells that work best on Saturdays involve endings, banishings, bindings, and letting go of the old. This is also a day of communicating with those who have died and with spirits of ancestors. Saturday is about patience, wisdom, and severing toxic bonds. It's a time to recover from grief and mourning and overcome the challenges of addictions and behavioral blocks. Saturn governs karmic law and time and is traditionally the last day of the week. Wear black and deep shades of purple for protection, courage, and strength. Burn black candles to cast out negative energies and burn purple candles for wisdom and insight. This is a spiritual day for looking inward. It's also a cleansing time, so perhaps clean your house and your altar and use obsidian, hematite, or jet and some amethyst in a spell to honor Hecate and ask her for guidance.

Sunday—Sundays are all about the sun and the colors gold and yellow to honor the sun deities of Brigid, Helios, and Apollo. This is a day for success, prosperity, good health, fame, fortune, and luck. The day of rest for those who practice more traditional religions is a day of celebrating personal potential and possibility and the golden, warm influence of the sun on our skin. This is a day to sit outside and welcome the sunrise with a ritual in honor of the goddess Brigid. Celebrate the light and the beautiful flowers and plants that thrive on sunlight. Plant or pick sunflowers, wear gold and yellow clothing and jewelry, or plant some marigolds in little pots to bring the sun indoors. Oranges and lemons, solar fruits, are a great addition to breakfast or squeezed into tea. Everything about Sunday can be built around gratitude for the sun and its life-giving gifts. This is the day for casting spells for big things, seeking new inspiration, and for setting the intentions for the coming week. The bigger the better on Sundays!

✴✴✴ MONTHLY CORRESPONDENCES ✴✴✴

Moon magic and moon energy is directly tied into the months, but so is solar/sun energy. Carving out twelve months of a year was not only functional for planning things like planting, harvesting, looking for prey, changes in the weather, and gathering herbs, but it was also a way to plan magic and spell casting for those who were concerned about the best times to ask for love, money, or good health.

January (Roman *Januarius*) honors Janus, the god of gates and doors and of beginnings and endings. A gate or door symbolizes the entry into something and, in this case, a new year full of possibilities. The month of January is when the festival of Janus is celebrated and is always thirty-one days long thanks to Julius Caesar's decision in 46 B.C.E. to add on the extra day. Janus represented all types of beginnings, including births, engagements, new plantings, and new harvests, and we have given this same symbolic importance to our New Year's resolutions every January 1. This list of things we hope to undertake throughout the new year is like a gateway or doorway to a life different from the one we left behind in December. In terms of moon magic, the full moon that takes place in January is a time for shedding and cleansing the energies of the prior year.

February (Roman *Februarius*) is the shortest month of the year with twenty-eight days (twenty-nine on a leap year). This month represents purification and a time for inner work since it was usually too cold and rainy for planting to take place. Though it is a short month, it is also a time when winter moves into the promise of spring and is therefore a time to plan and set goals.

March (Roman *Martius*) honors Mars, the god of war, and it always has thirty-one days. Though it can be cold and stormy, the first hints of the coming spring appear. The original Roman calendar placed March as the start of the year and a time for war. Many religious scholars have suggested that March was the actual month of the birth of Christ based upon the association with Pisces and fish symbolism among other clues in the Bible that correspond more to

March than December. March marks the end of the first quarter of the year and is a time to get ready for warmer days ahead. We literally and figuratively "march forward."

April (Roman *Aprilis*) may come from the Latin word *aperire*, which means "to open," as in opening the way to spring's blossoming glory. April honors the Greek goddess of love and beauty, Aphrodite (Venus in Roman mythology), and is a time for "April showers that bring May flowers." April is the time of the "growing moon" and therefore a time for spells that allow for growth and expansion, gathering what we've done, and beginning new things with what we've learned.

May (Roman *Maius*) honors springtime, growth, and all the blooming life that was "watered" in April. The name signifies increase, and this is an abundant time of the year when flowers abound in all their colorful glory. Maia was the Greek goddess who was the mother of Hermes/Mercury and the wife of Vulcan. Maia means "the great one," and the name signifies her sacred role in the cycle of the year. May is a time for play and romance, getting outside and "smelling the roses." Mayday festivals and picnics, warmer weather and more sunshine, flowers in the hair, and dancing by the light of the moon were all things that honored the spring deities of all traditions.

June (Roman *Juno*) honors Juno, the goddess of marriage and wife of the mighty Jupiter in Roman mythology. She was considered the "queen of heaven" and "queen of the gods" and signified ripeness and bounty. In June, the sun is back, the days are long again, and the animals of the woods and fields are plentiful. Grass is green and fruits grow from trees, so it's a month when people moved outdoors more. June is a popular month

March is named after the Roman god of war, Mars.

for marriage, and today, we celebrate graduation from schools and colleges in June before students get out for the joyful freedom of summer break. It can be a dry month with little rain, but it's a month that celebrates the sun and the nourishment it gives to all life on the planet.

July (Roman *Julius*), a warm and sunny month, was named in 44 B.C.E. for the emperor Julius Caesar by the Roman Senate and is considered the "meadow month" when cattle returned to the meadows to feed from the lush grasses. It marks just past half the calendar year but is still all about being outdoors and enjoying time to play under the sun. July is often thought of as midsummer and a time for working spells with the sun as well as the moon for fullness, expansion, power, success, and integration of all the things we've accomplished in the past six months into what our goals are for the rest of the year.

August (Roman *Augustus*) is the second month in a row to be named for a Roman emperor—in this case, Octavius Augustus. This is the month when we begin to notice a change in the sun, signifying the coming harvest months. The days are getting a little shorter but are still warm enough for outdoor pleasantries and growth, yet we are ever aware of the point when we must soon reap what we've sown. Greenery is lush and ripe for the harvest, yet not quite ready to be picked. This is a great time for working with the energies of the Green Corn Moon, which asks us to lay to rest old resentments and grievances and let go of any excess baggage, emotional and physical, that we are hanging on to. It's a month for releasing spells and asking the deities to open our hearts to letting go.

September (*septem* in Latin, meaning "seven") is the ninth month of the Gregorian calendar, though in Roman times, it was the seventh. This is harvest time and the beginning of autumn. Leaves change, and we pick what we've planted. We reap what we've sown and benefit from the labors of the past year. Spells cast in September might be more powerful if done under the fullness of the Harvest Moon. Ask for help with completing things, taking care of things left undone, fixing what is broken, and making sure we've tied up loose ends. We want to begin the harvest season and go into the colder winter months with a clean slate and little baggage to weigh us down.

October (*octo* in Latin, meaning "eight"), again, would have been the eighth month of the Roman year, but now, it is the tenth. This is the time of the Blood Moon and Halloween, during which the veil between the living and the dead is at its thinnest. This month celebrates the bountiful harvest and the gifts of our hard work. We enjoy what we have made and grown, even as we begin to plan for the months ahead when we need to store away some of that abundance. We celebrate the colorful fall leaves, knowing they will soon give way to bare trees. The flow of life and death and the give and take of nature is never more potent than it is during the month of October.

November (*novem* in Latin, meaning "nine"), our eleventh month, is our time of thanksgiving as we enjoy the harvest's bounty before things get serious. Winter is on its way, and we must not only be thankful for what we have but plan for what we will need. This month, we spend more time indoors and with family, as the days are shorter and the weather colder. It is a time to reassess and take stock of our physical, emotional, and spiritual lives and cast spells for insight, wisdom, and direction.

December (*decem* in Latin, meaning "ten") is our final month of the year and the gateway to the shortest day of the year around Yule. December is the start of winter and a time for staying indoors and turning inward before a new year dawns. The winter solstice marks the shortest day of the year, so it's all about the coming of the light again from there on. With the excitement of the coming Yule, or Christmastime, and the knowledge that we are winding down a whole year, December is both a time for powerful endings and amazing possibilities for new beginnings. People turn inward but also spend time with family and friends celebrating, lighting up the darkness for the holidays, eating, exchanging gifts, and sitting around the Yule log. For spell casting, it's all about coming to the end of things and preparing for new things. It's a time of deep introspection and looking into our darkness so we, too, can find the return of the light.

✧ ° ✧✧ ° ° ✦ ✦ ✦ ECLIPSES ✧ ° ✧ ✦ ✦ ✦

How terrified our ancestors must have been the first time they saw an eclipse! Whether a solar or lunar eclipse, until it happened a few times without the entire world ending, the antics of the night sky must have sparked concern, even dread, until humans realized that just as the phases of the moon come and go in cycles, so, too, do eclipses.

The eclipse of the Sun by the Moon's shadow is an awesome visual event here on Earth if you happen to be in the best place to see it. It is easy to view it as a symbol of the end of old ways and a rebirth of new ways.

A solar eclipse occurs during the time of a new moon, when the moon passes between the sun and Earth. During a new moon, the sun and moon are located in the same zodiacal sign on the sky. This causes the sun to be fully or partially obscured by the moon. When the moon is large enough in the sky, a full eclipse occurs, and the sun is obscured but for a reddish ring around the moon. Though it only lasts a few minutes, we see either a partial or a full eclipse depending on where we are on the planet.

A lunar eclipse is when the moon passes just behind Earth and becomes obscured in its shadow. Lunar eclipses only occur when the sun, moon, and Earth are closely, or exactly, aligned and only on the night of a full moon. Often called a Blood Moon because of the reddish color the moon takes on when no sunlight is able to reach it, a lunar eclipse is visible from most places, and a total lunar eclipse lasts for a couple of hours. Total lunar eclipses occur somewhere on Earth every eighteen months.

Working with eclipse energy amplifies the spells we cast by imbuing them with extra solar or lunar influence. Eclipses represent the life cycle of birth, death, and rebirth displayed in the sky for all to see. Remember making moon water? You can also make eclipse water, charged by the moon and the sun, to use in spell casting for the months that follow. Find a mason jar or glass jar, fill it with filtered or purified water, and set the water outside before the eclipse begins. Let the water remain for the entire duration of the eclipse. Set your intention or spell work during the charging of the water. Collect the eclipse water and cover the jar to place on your altar. You can also water plants and herbs with the charged eclipse water. Add a few drops to your normal drinking water for an extra energetic boost; use a few drops in herbal infusions, remedies, and baths; or give some to your pets when they are not feeling well.

✦ ✦ ✦ ✦ ✦ ELEMENTS AND DIRECTIONS ✦ ✦ ✦ ✦ ✦

Practitioners of magic and nature traditions often refer to the five elements and the four quarters or directions. Calling the quarters is a powerful ritual performed by many groups and traditions that evokes the energies of the elements and the four cardinal directions. These energies combine with the energy of the practitioner or group to amplify the intention. The elements are earth, fire, water, and air, but in spiritual practice, a fifth exists—spirit/ether. A direction corresponds with four of the main elements:

- North pairs with earth.
- South pairs with fire.
- East pairs with air.
- West pairs with water.

When you "call the quarters," you turn in a "deosil," or clockwise circular motion (as opposed to "widdershins," or counterclockwise), and honor each element and direction. You can begin in the west, which honors dead ancestors, or in the east, where the sun rises; no hard and set rule exists except that you must continue around the circle deosil. Each tradition will have its own way of calling the quarters. If you practice in solitary, you can get creative as you honor the elements and their directions. With each turn to each direction, you can speak a spell to honor the deities, draw the forces into your circle, or just meditate on what each quarter represents to you. Always dismiss or release any spirits, dieties, or energies called during this ritual when you end it. You might be working with elementals—entities associated with each element like fairies, sprites, elves, or angelic beings or the higher beings that supervise over them, the watchtowers. They need to be dismissed from attendance just like children at the end of math class.

Each element and direction has a correspondence to a part of us, who we are. Earth represents the physical form, the body. Fire is the soul. Air is the intellect. Water is the emotional nature. Spirit is, obviously, the spirit part of you. You can call the quarters to work on any of these areas you feel might be imbalanced and ask your guides for help bringing all of the parts of you into harmony again. The elements themselves are the root of all matter in existence, as suggested by the Greek philosopher Empedocles, who named and identified them.

The four quarters of Earth are sacred and should be treated as such. Hierarchies of elementals and watchers can be called upon. In her book *The Encyclopedia of Witches and Witchcraft*, author Rosemary Ellen Guiley writes that "the elements are associated with the cardinal points of the magic circle and with a hierarchy of spirits—lower-level beings called elementals, who in turn are governed by higher beings, devas, also called the Lords of the Watchtowers, the Mighty Ones, and the Guardians."

Elementals are not gods or goddesses, but they can be invoked during spells and rituals. To invoke an elemental or watchtower, you would call the quarters saying something like, "We call upon the elementals of the air ...," "I call upon the Lord of the Watchtowers of the East, I summon you, Lords of air ...," or "We call upon the Spirit Guards of the Watchtowers of the East...." A ritual to the east could sound like this: "We call upon the Lords of the East, the spirits and guides of the Watchtowers of the East. We honor the breath of the Mother, the breath of life. We ask that you work with the forces of air to assist in our intention. We ask that you bring us guidance through the air and into our minds as thoughts and inspirations. So mote it be." You can then call upon the rest of the quarters in similar fashion, asking for what you need from each: groundedness and a strong center from the north/earth; passion and vitality from the south/fire; intuition and emotional balance from the west/water.

North is represented by anything associated with Earth, the planet we live upon, and the earth itself: rocks, soil, dirt, clay, sand ... the foundations we stand upon. Earth is fertile, stable, and associated with the goddess. Solid and firm but nurturing, earth is the sacred mother who gives birth to us all and to the cycles of birth, life, and death. The colors green and brown are most prevalent in spell and ritual work to represent earthiness and greenery along with the pentagram, the solid and foundational symbol of paganism and witchcraft. When calling the quarters, you can place an earthenware bowl filled with crystals or salt in the north part of the circle. The north/earth governs money, success, business, prosperity, security, protection, responsibility, loyalty, and physical health. Other associations include caves, wells, the womb, the season of winter, shelter, buildings, farms, gardens, practical things, and working with your hands. Earth is about family and friends. The associated deities are Pan, Gaia, and the Horned God. Do magic to the north for divination powers, binding spells, money and prosperity spells, finding lost items and treasures, and working with plants, herbs, and clay or dirt.

South is fire, electricity, lightning, charges, and electrical forces of nature. Think of the colors red and orange, and light a red candle in the southern corner of the circle to represent the passion of the inner fire within each of us as well as the fiery creation of Earth from earthquakes and volcanic activity. Fire both creates and destroys, gives life, and takes

> **Elementals are not gods or goddesses, but they can be invoked during spells and rituals.**

life away. It purifies, cleanses, and banishes. It is masculine energy and the only element that cannot exist without feeding on something else to exist. Fire is intense, and it inspires and takes us higher. It is the direction and element of leadership, power, and force. Call upon the fire elementals for love and passion spells and to assist in spells for success in any endeavor. Fire burns away what is not necessary, so use it to clean out clutter from your life. Fire is represented by the dagger, sword, athame, or knife. It is associated with high noon, the height of summer, the prime of youth and vitality, and the flames of passion and desire. Fire honors the gods Horus, Vulcan, Re, Apollo, Lugh, and Prometheus and the goddesses Brigid, Pele, Vesta, and Hestia.

East is the direction of air and the sky, represented by birds, clouds, feathers, and incense that floats through the air. The colors yellow and light blue speak of the sun and the blue skies; invoking elementals of the east will assist in matters involving the intellect and mind. Air is associated with the breath of life and the power of the mind to solve problems and carry away obstacles. Air is the way of the wind and the season of spring. It governs travel, movement, thoughts, actions, ideas, imagination, discovery, and places where people meet to learn or travel. Air is also the place of mountaintops, windy fields and plains, the sky, and expansiveness. The associated deities are Thoth, Hermes, and Mercury and the goddesses Aradia, Nuit, and Urania. Air governs analysis, rational thinking, debating, and problem solving. This is also the world of the psyche and psychic abilities, especially telepathic communications. Try honoring the element air by doing spell casting at dawn in the springtime with yellow and white flowers or using feathers. The energy of

air is masculine, and the tools are wands, swords, and sticks. Air magic is great for prophesizing and divination. Use herbs and candles that have strong scents that carry on the breeze. Put some feathers in the eastern part of your circle.

West is the place where water reigns. The color blue represents intuition, and the chalice and cup are the tools of choice in rituals, as they are receptive like water. This is the direction of emotions and inner knowing, or intuition. Water is feminine energy and related to the goddess and the moon that governs the tides. Water governs the subconscious mind and the gods Ea, Osiris, Neptune, and Poseidon. The goddesses of water and the west are Isis, Tiamat, Mari, and Aphrodite. Spell casting by the ocean, lakes, rivers, and ponds is amplified, especially during the autumn months. Honor the twilight hour when the sun sets in the west by making brews, doing your ritual or herbal bathing, mixing herbal infusions, or tossing objects in the water. It is also a good time for mirror and water scrying, lucid dreams, and doing love and money magick. Look to the west and raise your cup, goblet, or bowl to receive blessings. Place a bowl or chalice of water in the west part of your circle.

The fifth element of spirit or ether can be the center of the circle where the practitioner stands, perhaps wearing white or holding a white candle to represent the Divine connection, the inner self, the unity of body and spirit, and dreams, mystical knowledge, and visions. Aether is immaterial and universal, represented by the union of the Lady and the Horned God that creates new life. Stand in the center of your being and feel the aether move in you and through you, permeating all things.

Working with the elements and directions adds a whole new layer of depth to spell casting and rituals. Calling in the powers, forces, and spirits of these archetypal symbols and entities can balance any unharmonious energies and patterns of behavior that keep you from manifesting your desires and achieving your goals. Like animal and spirit guides and familiars, guides are waiting to come to your aid from all four corners of Earth and from the ground, the sea, and the sky.

Going outdoors in nature is a wonderful way to reconnect with the elements in their most natural settings. Being around the roaring waves of the ocean, feeling the sand beneath your feet, grounding yourself in the moment, and allowing the sun's warmth to caress your skin as a breeze blows through your hair—the presence of the elements are always ready and available.

If you've wondered why the pentacle and pentagram are so important to witches, Wiccans, and pagans, it's because the shape of the star represents the four elements or cardinal directions topped by the spirit/aether as the fifth point of the star. It also looks, not coincidentally, like the shape of a human.

✳✳✳ CHANTING, DRUMMING, DANCING✳✳✳

Rituals and group practice often involve using sound and movement to put participants in an altered state of mind. This is a practice as old as time and found in Native and indigenous cultures all over the world. Drums, shakers, rattles, songs, chants, movements,

The five-pointed star, or pentacle, is a symbol of the four elements of Nature and the fifth element of spirit/aether. The pentacle is an important symbol among Wiccans and pagans.

dances, stomping, banging on things—these all serve to create a setting conducive to ritual work or journeying beyond the confines of the five senses. Children are scolded for banging on containers and pots and pans, but even they recognize the power of percussion and sound, especially when it's rhythmic. Watch children dance around in circles. It may look boring and repetitive, but the child is putting himself or herself into a state of rapturous joy that we adults have forgotten exists.

What is it about repetition? When we repeat words or phrases over and over, move our bodies in the same way again and again, or listen to rhythmic, repetitive music, we go into a trance or an altered state of consciousness when we allow our minds to be taken over by the sounds and movements. Ritual chanting, dancing, and drumming are all tools or methods by which the participant moves beyond the confines of the five senses and enters a deeper state of union and connectedness with the inner and outer worlds. Shaking rattles, hand clapping, stomping, and making deep, guttural sounds are a part of the rituals of various traditions all over the world. Lest you think this was just our primitive descendants banging about on drums and acting like cavemen and cavewomen, think of today's marching band drum lines and the hypnotic and exciting effects the various drums have on the body. Modern meditation and yoga practices suggest using a sacred word or phrase called a mantra to assist in getting into the proper frame of mind, and who can deny that modern music is driven by a repetitive bass line accompanying the drums or guitar riffs that repeat over and over to create a powerful hook that stays in the mind?

Religious or spiritual chants, dances, drumming, rattling, or other types of music create a fertile environment for prayer, meditation, intention work, spell casting, and magic because they raise the psychic power and energy of those participating. The added benefit of sage and incense or scented candles encourages the analytical, critical mind to step back and let the experiential, imaginative mind come front and center. In this correct state of mind, we are not only transported to places beyond the confines of our known reality, we are made more receptive to the signs, symbols, lessons, and insights we might receive there. Even marching in lockstep or unison has the effect of lulling the mind and body. Any kind of repetitive motion or sound works, but when the motions, movements, words, and phrases have meaning and symbolism, the potency of the intention work is much stronger.

Drumming was a sacred ritual to ancient cultures and Earth traditions. It brought the community together to en-

Drums are used in many cultures during sacred rituals. Americans are likely familiar with their use in indigenous ceremonies, but they are also played everywhere from South America to Siberia.

gage in healing and common intentions. Shamans in Siberia, South America, and Central America use rhythmic drumming and the shaking of rattles to achieve an altered state of consciousness that allows them to travel on a journey between the Lower World, Middle World, and Upper World for divination, healing, access to spirit and animal guides, and insight. African tribes and Native American tribes alike use drums and rattles in their rituals and celebrations along with dancing and singing or repeating chants as they move in rhythmic patterns around a roaring fire.

The combination of the shaking rattles or drums and voices singing or chanting is a way to raise power and set it in force into the Cosmos outward and to our dream world inward. Those engaged in these activities become more connected to the planet, the deities, and the forces of nature they seek to work with. Even today, Native Americans dance, chant, and drum at powwows, and tribal peoples all over the world continue to drum and chant to connect with Mother Nature. Drum circles have popped up everywhere as people become more familiar with their spiritual and physical benefits.

Scientific research conducted by Dr. Barry Bittman in 2001 found that just one hour of group drumming boosts the immune system and increases NK (natural killer) cell activity. It also reduces stress and improves mood. In an article titled "The Healing Power of Drumming" for the March 28, 2015, Energy Life Sciences Institute blog, musical therapist Aerin Alexander wrote, "I have experienced the healing power of rhythm and drumming in helping patients to relax or become more energized as needed; in supporting premature infants to stabilize their heart rate and breathing rate; and in promoting parent-infant bonding, drumming for stress release...." Other studies showed that drumming boosts immunity and creative thinking. Perhaps it lulls the analytical left brain to allow for right-brain thinking and creativity to shine through.

Michael Harner wrote in *The Way of the Shaman* that the repetitive sound of drumming is fundamental to a shaman entering a state of consciousness where they can do their healing and spiritual work of journeying. "With good reason, Siberian and other shamans sometimes refer to their drums as the 'horse' or 'canoe' that transports them into the Lower World or Upper World. The steady, monotonous beat of the drum acts like a carrier wave, first to help the shaman enter the SCC (shamanic state of consciousness), and then to sustain him on his journey."

Dance serves a dual purpose of bringing us back to our physical bodies while also showing us how to transcend our bodies. When we whirl or dance in circles, as Native Americans and the Whirling Dervishes of Turkish tradition do, we put ourselves into a trance state using our bodies as the mechanism. The white-clad Whirling Dervishes of Sufism and the Mevlevi Order in Turkish traditions have for over seven hundred years twirled in a ritual dance to bring about a trance state and communion with God. During the whirling, the Dervish holds its right hand up to the sky to receive God's goodness, and its left hand is turned down toward Earth to represent conveying God's gifts to those who witness the ritual. It is a powerful, beautiful, sacred tradition.

A stigma is attached to Earth-based healing and traditions—that these are "women's work" and feminine things not worthy of men—yet, that could not be further from the truth. Earth doesn't discern or discriminate based on gender. The forces of nature don't care if you are male or female. The sun and moon will go on doing what they were made to do despite the sexual organs you were born with. The power of Earth healing and Earth magic is that it is both masculine and feminine. It is the wholeness of the two parts, the unification of the Divine male and female, in all its aspects. Our interpretations of forces and objects as being more related to one gender over another is a human trait. Nature doesn't care. It is what it is. However, much of the destruction and disrespect of the natural world comes from our inability to unite the two sides and understand that the things we deem masculine are just as important as those we deem feminine—AS important—not MORE important.

Gods and goddesses make up the myths of the world. Matriarchal societies once existed and had their time along the cycle of the larger Wheel of Existence just as patriarchal societies do. The imbalances of today's world cry out for harmony and a restoration of balance between the two. Respect for that balance is at the core of Earth-based medicine, healing, belief systems, and a general love of nature itself, yet we have become distanced and detached from our natural roots thanks to the proliferation of industry and technology.

Those who cry for a return to the Divine feminine do so because warring, politics, and destruction of the environment are disregarding Mother Nature. It isn't about feminism as much as getting back the equilibrium between the two forces of masculine and feminine energies. We need them both, but when one is over-dominant and extreme, we all suffer. The planet suffers. Nature suffers.

The return of millions of people to Earth-based forms of healing and spirituality is not a surprise. It was always there for many practitioners, and, for many more, it has become a place to find inner and outer healing and a reconnection to nature. The emptiness is felt at a soul level. The disconnect and isolation, despite the Internet, social networking, texting, and cell phones, is deeper and more profound than ever. The exodus to natural ways of living and being is nothing more than coming home again.

Glossary

Altar—A table or flat-topped area used in religious rituals, especially when offerings are included. A place for sacred, consecrated objects during a ritual or spell.

Aphrodisiac—A food, drink, drug, or any other stimulating thing that incites sexual desire and lust. Aphrodisiacs range from music to wine to specific foods and spices to bodily scents such as pheromone-based perfumes and lotions.

Apothecary—A person or place that sells herbal remedies and natural medicines. A person who formulates and mixes ingredients for such remedies. An older term now replaced by "pharmacy" and "pharmacist."

Archetype—A recurrent symbol in art, literature, and myth that is based upon an original mold or symbol. An original sample or prototype that is copied or duplicated.

Athame—A double-blade ritual knife with a black handle used in Wicca and witchcraft to direct energy and draw symbolic patterns. It represents the element of air or fire, and the male/God energy and is used by the High Priest in a coven during ceremonial rituals.

Bach Flower Remedies—Dilutions of flower materials with water, created by British homeopath Edward Bach in the 1930s. Bach believed the dew on flower petals could retain the healing properties of each plant.

Beltane—An ancient Celtic pagan holiday celebrated on May 1, or May Day. One of the eight Wiccan sabbats celebrated as part of the Wheel of the Year. It occurs at the halfway point between the spring equinox and the summer solstice.

Bitters—A bitter, sour, or sweet-sour tasting mix of alcohol and herbs and/or plant parts used for medicinal purposes or as part of a mixed recreational alcoholic beverage.

Book of Shadows—A special book used for Wiccan, pagan, or witchcraft practices containing invocations, rituals, instructions, spells, herbal remedies, and other important items. Each individual or coven will have its own Book of Shadows unique to them, like a magical journal or diary.

Brew—A drink made by boiling, soaking, or fermenting ingredients. In witchcraft, a brew can be any liquid infusion or concoction that includes the

226

GLOSSARY

fermentation process, such as beer, ale, and mead.

Calling the Quarters—A traditionally Wiccan ritual designed to invoke the assistance of the spirits that govern the four elements of air, water, earth, and fire, and their corresponding directions. Used when casting the sacred circle for protection during spells and rituals.

Carrier Oil—A base oil, usually vegetable, used in the dilution process of making essential oils. The carrier oil serves to protect the skin from any potentially toxic or allergy-causing ingredients.

Cauldron—A large cast iron or metal cooking pot with a handle and lid, often placed directly over a fire. Cauldrons are often associated with witches mixing up potions and brews and are found on altars in smaller sizes to burn incense or mix batches of herbs during spells and rituals.

Chakras—Seven key points of the body that serve as energy meridians or vortices through which "chi" (Qi or prana) or life energy flows, each with its own correspondences to different bodily organs and glands. These points, when balanced, create physical, emotional, spiritual, and mental well-being.

Chalice—A large, footed cup or goblet, often gold or silver, used to drink wine or an herbal mixture, usually placed on an altar for spells and rituals. The chalice represents female energy and receptivity and is a part of many rituals involving the high priestess in Wiccan traditions.

Charm—To control by magic, or an object intended to control a person or situation, usually positively, as in enchanting or delighting them. Charms can be spells or objects themselves, or they can be the act of using spells and objects to influence someone or something.

Composting—The recycling of organic matter or waste products that creates nutrient-rich soil via the process of decomposition. Composting piles can include the introduction of worms to speed up the decomposing. Can be done in a backyard pile or a large bin.

Concoction—A mixture of various ingredients in a liquid base, often used for medicinal purposes or spell casting.

Consecrate—A rite or ritual designed to make something sacred or cleanse something before use in magical practices. In witchcraft, candles, crystals, gems, and other altar items are consecrated before they are put to use in spells and rituals.

Correspondences—A close similarity, complimentary influence, or association between things. Wicca and witchcraft use the power of corresponding colors, directions, elements, properties, and other aspects of their tools to amplify spells and increase their power.

Coven—A group or gathering of twelve Wiccans or witches who meet regularly to practice spells and ritual work. Covens often only allow new members via initiation and are a close-knit group of people with the same goals and beliefs.

Crystal—A solid material whose atoms, ions, or molecules are arranged in a highly ordered structure on the microscopic level and are said to have extensive healing powers and properties. Many witches and pagans use crystals to amplify spells and ritual work, and they wear them to benefit from their specific properties and correspondences. Quartz and rose quartz are on the altar of most witches and are popular healing aids with the general public, too.

Decoction—The liquid result of plant parts concentrated via the process of boiling or healing. Decoctions are the breakdowns of plant parts to their liquid essence, used in medicinals and spells.

Deity—A divine entity such as a god or goddess found in polytheistic religions and pagan traditions. In monotheistic religions, the deity is the Godhead, supreme being, or creator.

Deosil—The Gaelic term for moving to the right, or clockwise in a circle.

Divination—The act and process of knowing the future or prophesizing using an occult or spiritual ritual or method. Divination methods include reading Tarot cards, astrology, numerology, scrying, tea leaf reading, and many others. Often a part of a pagan tradition for spell and ritual work.

Dowsing—The use of a forked stick or bent hangar that serves as a pointer to locate underground water sources. The dowser holds two handles and lets the pointer move downward when influenced by the presence of water below the ground.

Drawing Down the Moon—An important Wiccan ritual in which the chosen High Priestess goes into a trance state and channels the feminine divine or Triple Goddess, usually done during a full moon phase. The Goddess then speaks wisdom through the High Priestess.

Eclipse—An astronomical event during which one object temporarily obscures another by passing into the shadow of another object. A solar eclipse occurs when part of the Earth is engulfed by the shadow of the moon, obscuring the sun in part or whole. A lunar eclipse occurs when the moon passes behind the Earth and into its shadow, and it only occurs on the night of a full moon.

Elementals—Mythical beings that correspond with the four elements. These can by dryads, nymphs, gnomes, mermaids, and other creatures and entities associated with fire, water, earth, and air. They are sometimes called upon in rituals and spells for assistance and insight.

Elements—The four elements of Earth in both pagan and Ayurvedic traditions refer to earth, air, fire, and water. There is a fifth element of aether/spirit used in pagan traditions. The elements are considered the fundamental building blocks of existence and are called upon in rituals and spells.

Elixir—A potion or liquid made for either magical or medicinal purposes. Elixirs can include many herbal ingredients and often include alcohol as a base or stabilizer.

Equinox—The moment when the plane of the Earth's equator passes through the midpoint of the sun, occurring twice each year in spring (vernal) and fall (autumnal). The equinoxes are major pagan and Wiccan celebration times and holidays as part of the Wheel of the Year.

Esbat—A Wiccan time for coven meetings other than sabbats, usually reserved for feasts, healings, and trainings of coven members. Esbats are usually held on nights of a full moon.

Essential Oils—Oil compounds extracted from herbs and plants and used for medicinal and healing purposes. The often-aromatic oils are collected via the process of distillation or other mechanical methods such as cold pressing.

Familiar—Animal guides and supernatural entities that assist witches with their magical practices. The concept comes from European folklore and belief of "familiar spirits" that usually took an animal form. In the case of pop culture witches, that form is often a black cat.

Feast of Cakes and Ales—A Wiccan and pagan ritual to thank the deities for their blessings by offerings of homemade cakes or cookies shaped like crescent moons, and alcoholic ale or non-alcoholic cider, juice, or water.

Fetish—An inanimate object that is worshipped for its supposed magical properties or ability to embody a spirit. Small carvings of animals or deities are considered fetishes, as are decorated stones, feathers, poppets, voodoo dolls, and animal fur.

Folk Magic—A broad term that encompasses folksy belief systems and traditions, including voodoo, Druidism, back country witchery, conjuring, and healing practices of the people. Folk magic is often considered the practices of rural communities and has its roots in ancient paganism. The term also applies to modern kitchen witchery and everyday practical magic.

Glamours (also Glamors)—Spells intended to charm, fascinate, or attract using alluring influences and enchantment. Glamours often involve the spell caster themselves embodying the attractive, desired quality by using a physical object such as a piece of clothing, makeup, or fetish object they wish to project, as in "glamouring" a pretty scarf or favorite tie to be worn to an interview to influence the outcome.

Golden Rule—A basic rule or principle for success. Also, a religious or spiritual principle of being aware of how our actions and behaviors affect others and doing to others as we would wish to be done to ourselves. This rule is found in every major religious tradition and in pagan traditions, too.

Grimoire—A textbook of magic spells and practices that includes instructions for creating amulets, talismans, and sigils, and using them to cast spells and summon entities and spirits, including angels and demons. Often interchangeable with Book of Shadows.

Handfasting—A Wiccan and neopagan tradition of marriage in which a couple's wrists are bound with ribbon or cord during the reading of the ceremony and vows to symbolize the divine union. Handfasting is becoming popular among secular society as a new way of marking the union between two people.

High Priest—The chief male priest in a pagan or Wiccan ritual, coven, or ceremony. He represents the God in human form.

High Priestess—The chief female priestess in a pagan or Wiccan ritual, coven, or ceremony. She represents the Goddess in human form.

Imbolc/Candlemas—A traditionally Gaelic celebration, and one of the sabbats on the Wheel of the Year, celebrating February 1 as the beginning of spring. It is observed as the halfway point between the winter solstice and the spring equinox and is marked with feasts, divination, and spring cleaning.

Incantation—A chant or spoken spell or ritual to invoke a spirit or entity to assist in spell casting and magic.

Incense—Aromatic condensed plant materials that release smoke when burned. Used in aromatherapy, religious and spiritual rituals, meditation, and general relaxation, and it also works as an insect repellent.

Infusion—A liquid drink or medicinal remedy using the extracts of soaked leaves and plant parts in a base liquid, then separated from the plant parts. Infusions can be "cooked" over a fire, or kept in sunlight, or just soaked overnight before being drained and utilized.

Initiation—A ritual to introduce a new member to an existing group, such as a coven or secret society. A rite of passage into a group or section of society. The initiate is often imparted with wisdom teachings not available to anyone outside of the group.

Invocation—A ritual or spell that serves to invite a deity or supernatural entity to assist or impart knowledge and understanding.

Journeying—The act of traveling through alternate worlds used by shamans. Drumming, chanting, and dancing serve to create an altered state of consciousness. The shaman then journeys to a lower, middle, or upper world to access guides, healing, and knowledge.

Kitchen Witchery—Folk magic involving the use of kitchen tools, herbs, cooking, plants, cleaning, and gardening. The kitchen witch lives a magical lifestyle that includes the daily acts of cooking and cleaning as times for magical practice. Also called "cottage witchery" and "practical magic."

Law of Attraction—A metaphysical law stating that thoughts have the power to manifest in physical reality, and that as one thinks, so one shall be. Positive thoughts bring positive results, and negative thoughts bring negative results. An important part of effective spell casting.

Law of Threefold Effect (Rule of Three)— A metaphysical law honored in Wiccan and pagan traditions that states what we put out in the world comes back to us threefold. Put out good,

good returns three times over. Put out bad, bad returns three times over. Also called the Law of Threefold Return.

Litha/Midsummer—The Wiccan and pagan celebration of the summer solstice, sometime between June 19 and 25, marked by feasts, celebrations, bonfires, singing, dancing, and parties on the preceding evening and the day of the solstice. One of the sabbats on the Wheel of the Year.

Lughnasa/Lammas—A Gaelic festival marking the beginning of harvest time, celebrated on August 1 as part of the sabbats of the Wiccan Wheel of the Year. Celebrations include fairs, fasting, offering of first fruits, harvest festivals, athletic contests.

Mabon—The second of three pagan harvest festivals/sabbats celebrating the Autumnal equinox on September 21–22. Festivals mark the abundant harvest, gratitude, blessings, and the completion of projects. It also marks the point when day and night are of equal length.

Magic/Magick—The use of charms, spells, and rituals to achieve a certain outcome or desire, often using supernatural forces or having power of natural forces. Magic includes rites and incantations and can be for good (white), bad (black), or neutral (grey) purposes. Magick denotes ceremonial rituals and practices in particular.

Matriarchal—Relating to a form of social organization with a woman at the head of power.

Moon Magic—Rituals, practices, and spells associated with the various moon phases. moon magic is oriented toward Goddess worship and the celebration of the divine feminine energies.

Moon Water—Blessed water made by leaving it beneath the full moon's light overnight. Can be used in infusions and elixirs, potions, spells, rituals, bathing, or washing.

Neopagan—Any spiritual tradition that seeks to revive the ancient polytheistic traditions of Europe and the Middle East, which have a close connection with ritual magic and modern witchcraft.

Ostara—The sabbat celebration of the spring equinox in honor of the Anglo-Saxon goddess of the dawn and the Horned God, Pan. The origin of the Christian observance of Easter, which comes from the German spring goddess, Eostre. A time to celebrate fertility, love, blooming nature, and the return of greenery.

Pagan—Beliefs and traditions that predate Christianity and involve the worship and celebration of nature and the natural world, and the deities that represent nature and its many forces; polytheism, as in the belief in many deities.

Pantheon—A group or collection of the deities relevant to a particular religion.

Patriarchal—Relating to a form of social organization with a man at the head of power.

Pentagram/Pentacle—The pentagram is the premier symbol in paganism, Wicca, and witchcraft. It symbolizes the human body and the five elements of air, water, earth, fire, and aether/spirit. The pentacle is a pentagram with a circle around it.

Philter—A potion or drink used to arouse love or lust in the person who drinks it.

Piezoelectricity—An electrical charge that accumulates in certain solids when mechanical stress or intense heat is applied, including crystals. It is believed this is what gives crystals their healing properties.

Potion—A magic-infused drink using herbs and plant materials to bring about love, lust, wealth, healing, or success. Most potions are directed toward achieving the love or desire of a particular person or of acquiring money. Potions can also be lotions or bath liquids.

Psilocybin—Mushrooms that produce a psychedelic effect. There are over 200 species of so-called "magic mushrooms."

Raising the Cone of Power—A Wiccan ritual during which a coven uses collective energy to raise a cone of power that is then directed toward a particular goal. Solitary witches can also raise the cone of power, but it is far more potent and effective when done in a group setting.

Rede (Wiccan)—A long statement that serves as the moral and ethical foundation for neopagan religions, including Wicca, that ends with the famous lines, "An ye harm none, do what ye will." There are several forms of the Rede, and the origin is a bit murky, but the general form used is the full Rede.

Ritual—An established and repeated form of ceremony performed by a religious group or person. Rituals can include dances, incantations, chanting, music, movement, and spoken words, as well as particular clothing such as robes or hoods.

Rootwork—Voodoo and conjuring practices involving the use of plant roots for spells, rituals, and medicinal purposes.

Sabbat—One of the eight major Wiccan seasonal festivals along the cycle of the Wheel of the Year. Sabbats mark the chief solar events of solstices and equinoxes and the midpoints between each. Sabbats are commonly held throughout pagan traditions, although names and methods of celebrations may vary from region to region.

Samhain—The major end of harvest third festival in the Wheel of the Year. This sabbat is celebrated on the traditional Halloween of October 31 through November 1 and includes fire festivals, feasting, divination, and preparing for the long winter months ahead. It is also a time to honor the thin veil between the living and the dead and honor deceased loved ones with offerings of cakes and leaves or altars of remembrance.

Scrying—A divination method of telling the future by gazing into an object such as a crystal ball, a bowl of water, a candle flame, or a mirror. Scrying utilizes an altered state of consciousness to glean insight, prophecy, and future visions.

Shaman—A sacred and revered person who can access other realms of reality via a trance state brought about by drumming, chanting, and journeying to heal and help others or to divine the future. Shamans are traditionally from indigenous cultures of North and South America and the Siberian region.

Sigil—A symbol with magical powers and properties that is drawn, carved, or painted onto something. Sigils can be tattoos, or painted rocks, or drawings on canvas or parchment paper and are chosen by the individual as their sacred personal seal.

Sky Clad—Performing spells and rituals in the nude. Some covens choose to go sky clad, while others do not. Being sky clad allows less restrictions and blocks between the body and the channeled energy of the Goddess.

Smudging—The burning of plant materials to cleanse a person, place, or object with sacred smoke during a ritual or spell. Smudging purifies the environment depending on which herbs or plants are used.

Solitary—A Wiccan or witch who chooses to practice alone and not be a member of a coven.

Solstice—The two times each year when the sun reaches its highest or lowest point in the sky at noon, marked by the longest (summer) or shortest (winter) days of the year. The solstices are major sabbats celebrations for Wiccans and pagans.

Spell—The use of words and phrases to influence, change, or alter someone or something via magical powers. Spells bring about a state of enchantment via spoken or written power words and the belief of the spell caster.

Tinctures—An extract of plant or animal materials dissolved in a base of alcohol or ethanol for medicinal purposes. Tinctures are taken in small doses that are usually measured with a dropper.

Voudon—Scholarly term for voodoo, the polytheistic folk magic/religious tradition of African and Caribbean nations. The word means "force" or "mystery."

Waning—The phases of the moon when the visible light is smaller and lesser leading to the new moon, and the time for spells and rituals involving letting go and releasing.

Waxing—The phases of the moon where the visible light is increasingly bigger, leading to the full moon, and a time to cast spells for abundance, increase, health, success and love.

Wheel of the Year—The annual cycle of eight seasonal festivals celebrated and honored by modern pagans,

Wiccans, and witches that mark the solar events (solstices and equinoxes) and the midpoints between them. Many traditions refer to the four main events as "quarter days" and the four midpoints as "cross quarter days." These are times of great celebration and symbolic importance.

Wicca—A modern pagan nature-based witchcraft tradition developed in England in the early twentieth century and introduced to the public by Gerald Gardner in 1954. It is now a popular and growing tradition in the United States and England.

Widdershins—To walk or move to the left, counterclockwise in a circle.

Witch/Witchcraft—A person who practices a nature-based magical tradition involving spells, rituals, and beliefs focusing on influencing and controlling natural forces. Witches may believe in a God, a Goddess, both, or a pantheon of deities, but always the focus is on the natural world and its forces. Witches can also be healers and diviners.

Witches Bottle—A decorative bottle filled with herbs, trinkets, and other items kept for on-the-go spell casting or overnight spells. Witches bottles can be specific to the goal in mind, with items effective for love, healing, money, health or success. Boxes, charm bags, and pouches are alternatives to bottles.

Yule—The festive season/sabbat traditionally known as Christmas in Christian traditions, marking the Winter Solstice around December 23 and the shortest day of the year. Yule celebrations can last through the New Year and include festivals devoted to the return of the light, decorating trees with lights, giving gifts and offerings, and feasts and meals with family and friends.

Zodiac—The zodiac is the area of the sky extending from 8" north or south, measured in celestial latitude, of the ecliptic, which is the path of the sun across the celestial sphere over the course of one year. All of the paths of the moon, Earth, and visible planets are within the zodiac belt. In astrology, we think of the zodiac as the constellation patterns that mark the twelve signs of the horoscope.

Further Reading

Abram, Christy Lynn. "How to Clear, Activate, and Store Your Crystals." MindBody-Green.com. https://www.mindbodygreen.com/0-14887/how-to-clear-activate-and-store-your-crystals.html (accessed July 9, 2019).

Adler, Margot. *Drawing Down the Moon: Witches, Druids, Goddess-Worshippers and Other Pagans in America.* London: Penguin Books, 2006.

Alchemy Works. "Growing a Witch's Garden." Alchemy-Works.com. https://www.alchemy-works.com/witchs_garden.html (accessed February 18, 2019).

Alternative Daily. "The Healing Power of Frankincense and Myrrh." AlternativeDaily.com. Httpsz;//www.alternativedaily.com/healing-powers-frankincense-myrhh/ (accessed October 15, 2019).

Andrews, Ted. *Animal Speak: The Spiritual and Magical Powers of Creatures Great and Small.* New York: Llewellyn Publications, 2002.

Ardrian, Sheela. "All About Skyclad." WitchesAndPagans.com. https://witchesandpagans.com/paganism-101/introductions-to-paganisem/250-all-about-skyclad-ow14.html (accessed November 29, 2019).

Avalon, Annwyn. *Water Witchcraft: Magic and Lore from the Celtic Traditions.* Newburyport, MA: Weiser Books, 2019.

"Ayahuasca: A Strong Cup of Tea." *New York Times*, June 15, 2014. https://www.nytimes.com/2014/06/15/fashion/ayahuasca-a-strong-cup-of-tea.htm.

Baser, K. H. C., and G. Buchbauer. *Handbook of Essential Oils: Science, Technology and Applications.* New York: CRC Press, 2010.

Berger, Helen. *A Community of Witches: Contemporary Neo-Paganism and Witchcraft in the United States.* Columbia, SC: University of South Carolina Press, 1999.

BH & G Garden Editors. "How to Make Compost." *Better Homes and Gardens* January 22, 2020. https://www.bhg.com/gardening/yard/compost/how-to-compost/.

Biblical Archeology."Why Did the Magi Bring Gold, Frankincense, and Myrrh?" BiblicalArcheology.org, December 21, 2018. https://www.biblicalarcheology.org/daily/people-cultures-in-the-bible/jesus-historical-hesus/why-did-the-magi-bring-gold-frankincense-and-myrrh/.

Blackthorn, Amy. *Blackthorn's Botanical Magic: The Green Witch's Guide to Essential Oils for Spellcraft, Ritual and Healing.* Newburyport, MA: Weiser Books, 2019.

Bollinger, Ty. "Medicinal Mushroom Benefits: Five Stunning Reasons to Consume Them Regularly." FoodRevolution.org, July 11, 2018. https://foodrevolution.org/blog/medicinal-mushrooms-benefits/.

Budapest, Zsuzanna. *The Holy Book of Women's Mysteries: Feminist Witchcraft, Goddess Rituals, Spellcasting, and other Womanly Arts.* Wingbow Press, 1989.

Buckland, Raymond. *The Witch Book: The Encyclopedia of Witchcraft, Wicca, and Neo-Paganism.* Detroit, MI: Visible Ink Press, 2002.

Cabot, Laurie. *The Power of the Witch: The Earth, the Moon, and the Magical Path to Enlightenment.* New York: Delta Books, 1990.

Carr, Juliet Abigail. "Infused Honey: Syrup Elixirs for Winter Colds." OldWaysHerbal.com, January 7, 2014. https://oldwaysherbal.com/2014/01/07/infused-honey-syrup-elixirs-for-winter-colds/.

Celtic Connection. "Crystals and Gemstones A–Z." Wicca.com. https://wicca.com/celtic/tones/stones-e.htm (accessed March 14, 2019).

———. "An Introduction to Using Divination Tools." Wicca.com. https://wicca.com/divination/introduction (accessed September 18, 2019).

———. "Introduction to Animal Guides." Wicca.com. https://wicca.com/celtic/wyld kat/anmlintro.htm (accessed March 29, 2019).

Chamberlain, Lisa. *Wiccan Moon Magic: A Wiccan's Guide and Grimoire for Working Magic with Lunar Energies.* Chamberlain Productions, 2016.

Coker, Crystal. "25 Popular Holidays With Surprisingly Pagan Origins." List25.com, July 21, 2017. https://list25.com/25-popular-holidays-with-surprisingly-pagan-origins/.

Corley, Craig. *Magic Words: A Dictionary.* San Francisco: Weiser Books, 2008.

Crowley, Vivianne. *The Old Religion in the New Age.* London: The Aquarian Press, 1989.

Cultural Awareness. "How Cultures Honor the Dead." CulturalAwareness.com. https://www.culturalawareness.com/how-cultures-honor-the-departed (accessed September 11, 2019).

Culture Trip. "A Brief History of the Whirling Dervish." TheCultureTrip.com. https://theculturetrip.com/europe/turkey/articles/a-brief-history-of-the-whirling-dervish/ (accessed April 4, 2019).

Cunningham, Scott. *Cunninham's Encyclopedia of Magical Herbs.* New York: Llewellyn, 2012.

———. *Wicca: A Guide for the Solitary Practitioner.* Woodbury, MN: Llewellyn Publications, 2010.

Difference Between. "Difference between Amulets and Talismans." Difference Between.net. http:// www.differencebetween.net/religion-miscellaneous/differ ence-between-amultes-and-talismans/ (accessed July 25, 2019).

———. "Difference between Maceration and Percolation." DifferenceBetween.com. https://www.differencebetween.com/difference-between-macera tion-and-vs-per colation/ (accessed October 25, 2019).

Dr. Axe. "Earthing: 5 Ways It Can Help You Fight Disease." TheScienceOfEating.com, September 4, 2017. http://thescienceofeating.com/2017/09/04/earthing-5-ways-can-help-fight-disease/.

Drew, A. J. *Aradia; or, the Gospel of the Witches by Charles G. Leland: A Modern Introduction and Commentary.* Franklin Lakes, NJ: New Page Books, 2003.

Dugan, Ellen. "Magic, Seven Days a Week." Llewellyn.com, November 8, 2004. https://www.llewellyn.com/journal/article/710.

Exemplore. "Animal Guide Meanings: Traits and Characteristics." Exemplore.com https://exemplore.com/spirit-animals/Finding-your-spirit-guideanimal.totem (accessed July 12, 2019).

———. "Beginner's Guide to Candle Magic." Exemplore.com. https://www.exemplore.com/wicca-witchcraft/withcraft-beginners-guide-to-candle-magic.

Farrar, Janet, and Stewart Farrar. *A Witches Bible.* New York: Magickal Childe, 1988.

———. *The Witches Way: Principles, Rituals, and Beliefs of Modern Witchcraft.* York: Phoenix Publishing, 1984.

Fermenting for Foodies. "Homemade Herbal Elixirs." FermentingForFoodies.com. https://www.fermentingforfoodies.com/homemade-herbal-elixirs/ (accessed August 4, 2019).

Fleckenstein, Alexa. "Healing Herbs to Use in a Bath." *Prevention Magazine*, November 5, 2014. https://www.prevention.com/health-conditions/a20472817/healing-herbs-to-use-in-a-bath/.

Fox, Selena. "Pagan Rituals." CircleSanctuary.org. https://www.circlesanctuary.org/index.php/circle-magazine/sample-articles/pagan-rituals/ (accessed October 3, 2019).

Frontier Co-Op. "How to Make Herbal Salves." FrontierCoop.com. https://www.frontiercoop.com/community/how-to/how-to-make-herbal-salves (accessed May 30, 2019).

Gaia. "The Benefits of Chanting: Reclaim the Powers of Creation." Gaia.com, June 15, 2016. https://www.gaia.com/articles/benefits-of-chanting/.

———. "Psilocybin and Depression: Psychedelics Can Reset Brain Function." Gaia.com. https://www.gaia.com/article/psycedelics-for-depression/ (accessed February 27, 2019).

Gardner, Gerald. *Witchcraft Today.* London: Rider Books, 1954.

Goetzman, Amy. "Foraging for Medicinal Roots, Berries, and Herbs." *Star Tribune*, Sepember 18, 2014.

Green, Patrice. "The Nine Sacred Herbs of the Saxons." HerbsTalk.org, May 25, 2016. http://www.herbstalk.org/blog/the-nine-sacred-herbs-of-the-saxons/.

Grimassi, Raven. *Encyclopedia of Wicca and Witchcraft.* St. Paul, MN: Llewellyn, 2000.

Group, Edward. "10 Homemade Organic Pesticides." GlobalHealingCenter.com, April 10, 2017. https://www.globalhealingcenter.com/natural-health/organic-pesticides/.

Gruben, Michelle. "Magickal Timing: Choosing the Right Day of the Week for Your Spell." GroveAndGrotto.com, June 23, 2015. https://www.groveandgrotto.com/blogs/articles/35309377-magical-timing-choosing-the-right-day-of-the-week-for-your-spell.

Haas, Saumya Arya. "What is Voodoo? Understanding a Misunderstood Religion." *Huffington Post*, May 25, 2011.

Harner, Michael. *The Way of the Shaman.* New York: Bantam Books, 1980.

Hart, Avery. "Big Power in a Little Symbol: How to Create Sigils." TheTraveling Witch.com, December 21, 2016. https://thetravelingwitch.com/blog/2016/12/21/creating-sigils.

Hawthorn, Leah. "How to Start a Butterfly Garden in Your Backyard." TheSCA.org. https://www.thesca.org/butterflygarden (accessed January 10, 2020).

Herbal Academy. "How to Make a Healing Salve." TheHerbalAcademy.com, January 9, 2014. https://theherbalacademy.com/how-to-make-a-healing-salve/.

————. "How to Make Herbal Homemade Wines and Meads." TheHerbalAcademy .com. https://www.theherbalacademy.com/herbal-homemade-windes-and-meads/ (accessed February 28, 2019).

History on the Net. "Crazy Potions and Nasty Nostrums: Six Bizarre Medieval Medicines." HistoryOnTheNet.com. https://www.historyonthenet.com/vrazy-potions-and-nasty-nostrums-six-bizarre-medieval-medicines (accessed November 20, 2019).

How To Culinary Herb Garden. "10 Tips for a Successful Indoor Herb Garden." HowTo CulinaryHerbGarden.com. https://howtoculinaryherbgarden.com/indoor-herb-garden/ (accessed June 14, 2019).

Hubs, Mark. "Scientific Evidence That Crystal Healing Works." RemedyGrove.com, March 29, 2018. https://remedygrove.com.bodywork/the-incredible-science-of-crystals/.

Hunter, Candace. "How to Make an Herbal Syrup: Easy Herbal Home Medicine." *The Practical Herbalist,* October 17, 2008.

Hutton, Ronald. *The Triumph of the Moon: A History of Modern Pagan Witchcraft.* Oxford, England: Oxford University Press, 1999.

Isokauppila, Tero. "Medicinal Mushrooms: The Top 5 You Should Know How to Use." BetterNutrition.com, November 6, 2017. https://www.betternutrition.com/features-dept/5-medicinal-mushrooms.

Jackowski, Karol. *Sister Karol's Book of Spells, Blessings and Folk Magic.* Newburyport, MA: Weiser Books, 2019.

Jennings, Kerri-Ann. "Why Shiitake Mushrooms are Good for You." Healthline.com. https://www.healthline.com/nutrition/shiitake-mushrooms#section5/ (accessed September 31, 2019).

Jones, Marie D. *Destiny vs. Choice: The Scientific and Spiritual Evidence of Fate and Free Will.* Pompton Plains, NJ: New Page Books, 2011.

————. *The Power of Archetypes: How to Use Universal Symbols to Understand Your Behavior and Reprogram Your Subconscious.* Wayne, NJ: New Page Books, 2017.

Jones, Marie D., and Larry Flaxman. *The Deju Vu Enigma: A Journey through the Anomalies of Mind, Memory, and Time.* Pompton Plains, NJ: New Page Books, 2010.

————. *Demons, the Devil and Fallen Angels.* Detroit, MI: Visible Ink Press, 2018.

————. *The Trinity Secret: The Power of Three and the Code of Creation.* Pompton Plains, NJ: New Page Books, 2011.

Joybilee Farm. "Better Than Bath Salts: Create Healing Herbal Baths from Your Garden." https://joybileefarm.com/healing-herbal-baths/ (accessed May 7, 2019).

Justis, Angela. "How to Make an Herbal Syrup." TheHerbalAcademy.com, October 5, 2016. https:theherbalacademy.com/herbal-syrup.

Kerr, Breena. "Must Be the Season of the Witch." CNN.com, October 31, 2018. https://www.cnn.com/2018/10/31/opinions/halloween-witches-were-women-fighting-power-kerr/index.html.

Kingsbury, Kathryn. "How to Make Herbal Wine." MotherEarthLiving.com, June/July 2005. https://motherearthliving.com/cookingmethods.

LaLiberte, Kathy. "Attracting Butterflies, Hummingbirds, and Other Pollinators." Gardeners.com. https://www.gardeners.com/how-to/attracting-butterflies-humming birds/7265.html (accessed March 29, 2019).

Learn Religions. "Do Pagans Practice Nude?" LearnReligions.com. https://www.learn religions.com/do-pagans-practice-nude-2561851 (accessed January 3, 2020).

———. "The Four Classical Elements." LearnReligions.com. https://www.learnreligions.com/four-classical-elements-2562825 (accessed May 30, 2019).

———. "Hold an Esbat Rite—Celebrate the Full Moon." LearnReligions.com. https://learnreliouns.com/esbat-rite-celebrate-the-full-moon-2562864 (accessed May 22, 2019).

———. "How to Make a Book of Shadows." LearnReligions.com. https://www.learnreligions.com/make-a-book-of-shadows (accessed December 4, 2019).

Lopez, Danielle. "How to Find Your Animal Guide." Exemplore.com, December 13, 2016. https://exemplore.com/spirit-animals/finding-your-spirit-guide/animeal-totem.

Madden, Kristin, and others. *Exploring the Pagan Path: Wisdom from the Elders.* Franklin Lakes, NJ: New Page Books, 2005.

Mama Rosemary. "Bath Magic! An Instructive for 5 DIY Herbal Baths." MamaRosemary.com, December 4, 2013. https://www.mamarosemary.com.

McCoy, Edain. "What Witches Do: The Esbats." Llewellyn.com, August 7, 2008. https://www.llewellyn.com/journal-article/1722.

Mooney, Delia. "Everything You Need to Know about Bitters." TastingTable.com, June 20, 2017. https://www.tastingtable.com/drinks/national/what-are-bitters-cocktails.

Murphy-Hiscock, Ann. *The Green Witch: Your Complete Guide to the Natural Magic of Herbs, Flowers, Essential Oils, and More.* New York: Adams Media, 2017.

Naturally Simple. "Everyday Elixirs." NaturallySimple.org, January 30, 3023. https://www.naturallysimple.org/living/2013/01/30/everyday-elixirs/.

"The New Power Trip: Inside the World of Ayahuasca," *Marie Claire,* January 2014.

O'Connor, Bess. "Clear Your Energy and Lift Your Spirits With the Sacred Art of Smudging." Chopra.com, March 27, 2015. https://chopra.com/articles/clear-your-energy-and-lift-your-spirits-with-the-sacred-art-of-smudging.

One Willow Apothecaries. "How to Make Herbal Love Potions: Infused Honeys, Elixirs, and Aphrodisiac Recipes." OneWillowApothecaries.com, February 14, 2013. https://onewillowapothecaries.com/how-to-make-herbal-love-potions-infused-honeys-elixirs-aphrodisiac-recipes/.

Original Botanica. "10 Common Herbs and Roots Used in Spell Work." OriginalBotanica.com, November 1, 2016. https://www.originalbotanica.com/blog/20-common-herbs-and-roots-used-in-spell-work/.

———. "How to Make and Craft Mojo Bags." OriginalBotanica.com, May 15, 2017. https://www.originalbotanica.com/blog/mojo-bags-conjure-toby-gris-gris/ (accessed March 25, 2019).

Palermo, Elizabeth. "Crystal Healing: Stone-Cold Facts about Gemstone Treatments." LiveScience.com, June 23, 2017. https://www.livescience.com/40347-crystal-healing.html/.

Patterson, Susan. "5 Essential Oils to Heal Your Sick Pet." OffTheGridNews.com. https://www.offthegridnews.com/alternative-health/5-essential-oils-to-heal-your-sick-pet/ (accessed January 22, 2020.)

———. "5 Healing Weeds Your Doctor Probably Mows Over." OffTheGridNews.cp,/ https://www.offthegridnews.com/alternative-health/5-healing-weeds-your-doctor-probably-mows-over/ (accessed January 22, 2020).

Petruzzello, Melissa. "9 Mind Altering Plants." Britannica.com. https://www.britannica.com/list/9-mind-altering-plants (accessed June 1, 2019).

Pike, Sarah M. *New Age and Neopagan Religions in America.* New York: Columbia University Press, 2004.

Polizzi, Nick. "10 Medicinal Herbs That Might Live in Your Backyard." GreenMed Info.com. https://greenmedinfo.com/blog/a0-medicinal-herbs-that-might-live-your-backyard/ (accessed March 5, 2019).

Price, Annie. "Ayahuasca: Understand the Dangers and Possible Side Effects." *CHHC,* January 17, 2018.

PsychicGuru. "A Beginner's Guide to Reading Tea Leaves." PsychicGuru.org. https://www.psychicgurus.org/how-to-read-tea-leaves/ (accessed October 22, 2019).

Psychics Today. "The 12 Most Common Types of Divination." PsychicsToday.com. https://www.psychicstoday.com/types-oif-divination/ (accessed May 22, 2019).

Rabinovitch, Shelley T., and James R. Lewis. *The Encyclopedia of Modern Witchcraft and Neo-Paganism.* New York: Citadel Press, 2004.

Rana, Sarika. "5 Natural Pesticides You Could Use to Grow Your Own Kitchen Garden." FoodNDTV.com. https://food.ndtv.com/food-drinks/5-natural-pesticides-you-could-usse-to-grow-your-own-kitchen-garden (accessed July 4, 2018).

Ratsch, Christian. *The Encyclopedia of Psychoactive Plants: Ethnopharmacology and Its Applications.* New York: Park Street Press, 2004.

Rettner, Rachael. "Healing Herb? Marijuana Could Treat These 5 Conditions." Live-Science.com, August 12. 2016. https://www.livescience.com/55750-medical-marijuana-conditions-treat.html.

Rhoades, Heather. "Growing Herbs at Home: Making an Herb Garden in Your Yard." GardeningKnowHow.com. https://www.gardeningknowhow.com/edible/herbs/hgen/plant-herb-garden.htm (accessed May 24, 2019).

Savvy Gardening. "7 Best Herbs for Container Gardening." SavvyGardening.com. https://savvygardening.com/best-herbs-for-container-gardening/ (accessed May 14, 2019).

Scott, Elizabeth. "Understanding and Using the Law of Attraction in Your Life." Very-WellMind.com, December 23, 2017. https://www.verywellmind.com/understanding-and-using-the-law-of-attraction-3144808/.

Schultes, Richard Evans. *Plants of the Gods: Their Sacred, Healing, and Hallucinogenic Powers.* Rochester, VT: Healing Arts Press, 2001.

Sellar, Wanda. *The Directory of Essential Oils.* Essex, England: The C.W. Daniel Company: 2001.

Sheloya. "Five Basic Witchcraft Potions for Beginners." WithUniversity.com, November 16, 2014. http://witchuniversity.com/2014/five-basic-witchcraft-potions-for-beginners/.

Smart Witch. "Herbalism in Magic." TheSmartWitch.com. http://www.thesmartwitch.com (accessed June 7, 2019).

Spiritual Spells. "Herb Magick: Leaves from the Spiritual Spells Book of Shadows." SpiritualSpells.com. http://spiritualspells.com/herbs-book.html (accessed January 5, 2020).

Starhawk. *The Spiral Dance: A Rebirth of the Ancient Religion of the Great Goddess.* New York: Harper & Row, 1979.

Szalay, Jessie. "Inflammation: Causes, Symptoms, and Anti-Inflammatory Diet." LiveScience.com, October 19, 2018. https://www.livescience.com/52344-inflammation.html.

Tea Perspective. "How to Read Tea Leaves: The Art of Tasseography. Tea Perspective." TeaPerspective.com. https://www.teaperspective.com/how-to-read-tea-leaves-tasseography/ (accessed January 22, 2020).

Thomason, Timothy C. *The Role of Altered States of Consciousness in Native American Healing.* Flagstaff, AZ: Northern Arizona University, n.d.

Thoricatha, Wesley. "What Are the Medicinal and Spiritual Benefits of Psilocybin Mushrooms?" PsychedelicTimes.com, June 23, 2016. https://psychadelictimes.com/2016/06/23/what-are-the-medicinal-and-spiritual-benefits-of-psilocybin-mushrooms/.

Tucker, Acadia. "Building Compost for Healthier Soil." *Stone Pier Press,* February 27, 2016. https://stonepeerpress.org/gardneingnews/howtocompost.

Valiente, Doreen. *Witchcraft for Tomorrow.* London: Robert Hale, 1978.

Vanderlinden, Colleen. "Composting 101: How to Make Compost." TheSpruce.com, January 11. 2018. https://www.thespruce.com/how-to-easily-make-a-compost.

Wade, Davis. "Hallucinogenic Plants and Their Use in Traditional Societies—An Overview." CulturalSurvival.org. December 1985. https://www.culturalsurvival.org/publications/cultural-survival-quarterly/hallucingenic-plants-and-their-use-traditional-societies (accessed August 8, 2019).

Wellness Mama. "How to Make an Herbal Tincture from Dried Herbs." WellnessMama.com. https://wellnessmama.com/8168/herbal-tinctures/ (accessed July 30, 2019).

Wells, Katie. "Homemade Healing Salve." WellnessMama.com. https://wellnessmama.com/3520/homemade-healing-salve/ (accessed June 1, 2019).

White, Ethan Doyle. *Wicca: History, Belief, and Community in Modern Pagan Witchcraft.* Chicago, IL: Sussex Academic Press, 2016.

White Magic Love Spells. "Basics of Sigil Magic: What is a Sigil?" White-Magic-Love-Spells.info. https://www.white-magic-love-spells.info/sigil_magic.html (accessed August 6, 2019.

Wicca Living. "Wiccan Esbats: The Magic of the Full Moon." WiccaLiving.com. https://wiccaliving.com/wiccan-esbats-full-moon/ (April 26, 2019).

Wigington, Patti. "9 Ways to Make Magic with Your Garden." LearnReligions.com, March 11, 2018. https://www.learnreligions.com/making-magic-with-your-garden-2561666.

———. "Introduction to Candle Magic." LearnReligions.com, July 14, 2019. https://www.learnreligions.com/introduction-to-candle-magic-2561684.

———. "Moon Phases and Magical Workings." LearnReligions.com. January 1, 2019. https://www.learnreligions.com/moon-phases-and-magical-workings-2562405.

Witches Lore. "The Five Elements." WitchesLore.com. https://witcheslore.com/bookofshadows/witches-workshop/the-five-elements/4683/ (accessed November 30, 2019).

World Pantheism. "A Religion of Nature, Earth, Gaia." Pantheism.net. https://www.pantheism.net/earth/ (accessed November 3, 2019).

Wright, Mackenzie Sage. "How to Cast Spells Using the Magical Timing of Moon Phases." Exemplore.com. Htpps://www.exemplore.com/wicca-witchcraft/How-to-cast-spells-magical-timing-with-moon-phases (accessed November 19, 2019).

———. "Learning Witchcraft: Magical Potions, Brews, and Other Concoctions." Exemplore.com, October 11, 2017. https://exemplore.com/wicca-withccraft/Learning-Witchcraft-Magical-Potions-Brews-and-Other-Concoctions.

————. "Types of Witches: How to Be a Kitchen Witch." Exemplore.com, August 10, 2017. https://exemplore.com/wicca-witchcraft/Types-of-witches-what-is-a-kitchen-witch-and-how-to-be-one/.

————. "A Witchcraft Primer: Magic and Spellcasting Basics." Exemplore.com, August 10, 2017. https://exemplore.com/wicca-witchcraft/A-Witchcraft-Primer-Magic-and-Spellcasting-Basics.

Yronwode, Cathrine. *Hoodoo Herb and Root Magic: A Materia Magica of African-American Conjure,* 4th edition. Lucky Mojo Publishing, 2002.

Zell-Ravenheart, Oberon, and Morning Glory Zell-Ravenheart. *Creating Circles and Ceremonies: Rituals for All Seasons and All Reasons.* Franklin Lakes, NJ: New Page Books, 2006.

Zodiac Birthstones. "Birthstones by Zodiac Sign." Zodiac-Birthstones.com. http://www.zodiac-birthstones.com/ (accessed December 11, 2019).

Website Resources

Bach Flower Remedies. https://www.bachflower.com

Better Homes and Gardens. https://www.bhg.com/gardening/yard/

The Celtic Connection. https://wicca.com/

Circle Sanctuary. https://www.circlesanctuary.org

Crystal Links. https://www.crystalinks.com

Divination. https://www.paranormal-encyclopedia.com/d/divination/types.html

DIY Natural. https://www.diynatural.com

Exemplore.com. https://exemplore.com/

Global Healing Center. https://www.globalhealingcenter.com/

GreenMed Info. https://greenmedinfo.com/

Grove and Grotto. https://www.groveandgrotto.com/blogs/

Herb Lore. https://herblore.com/overviews/tinctures

The Herbal Academy. https://www.theherbalacademy.com/

Katie Wells, Wellness Mama. https://wellnessmama.com/

Learn Religions. https://learnreligions.com/

Learning Herbs. https://learningherbs.com/

Mountain Rose Herbs. https://blog.mountainroseherbs.com/how-to-make-herbal-syrups

Mother Earth Living. https://motherearthliving.com/

One Willow Apothecaries. https://onewillowapothecaries.com/how-to-make-herbal-love-potions-infused-honeys-elixirs-aphrodisiac-recipes/

Pagan Federation. https://www.paganfederation.org/festivals.php

The Smart Witch. http://www.thesmartwitch.com

ThoughtCo. https://www.thoughtco./folk-magic-95826

The Traveling Witch. https://www.thetravelingwitch.com

Verywell.com. https://www.verywellhealth.com/

Wicca Living. https://wiccaliving.com/

Wicca Spirituality. https://www.wicca-spirituality.com/

Witches and Pagans. https://witchesandpagans.com/

Witches Lore. https://witcheslore.com/

Witchipedia.com. http://www.witchipedia.com/

Index

Note: (ill.) indicates photos and illustrations.